EAST ASIAN STRATEGIC REVIEW 2021

The National Institute for Defense Studies, Japan

AST ASIAN STRATEGIC REVIEW

Edited by:
The National Institute for Defense Studies
5-1 Ichigaya Honmura-cho, Shinjuku-ku, Tokyo 162-8808, Japan
URL: www.nids.mod.go.jp

Published by:
Interbooks Co., Ltd.
Kudan-Crest Bldg 6F, 5-10 Kudan-Kita 1-chome,
Chiyoda-ku, Tokyo 102-0073, Japan
Phone: +81-3-5212-4652
URL: https://www.interbooks.co.jp
books@interbooks.co.jp

ISBN 978-4-924914-68-1

The National Institute for Defense Studies
East Asian Strategic Review 2021

 Printed in Japan

Preface

The *East Asian Strategic Review (EASR)* was established in 1996 by the National Institute for Defense Studies (NIDS), Japan's sole national think-tank in the area of security affairs. The aim at that time was to support the then Defense Agency's efforts to foster mutual understanding and to build trust with neighbors and regional countries in the post-Cold War era. Without the critical but constructive comments and encouragement received from readers and experts, this annual report would have not grown into the flagship publication of NIDS and marked the 25th year of publication this year.

Over these 25 years, the strategic geography of "East Asia" has expanded, and Japan's security challenges have become more complex and diverse. However, we have kept our editorial policy the same; the contents are scholarly analyses of individual researchers and the views expressed do not necessarily represent the official position of the Government of Japan or the Ministry of Defense. In recent years, *EASR*'s standing as an academic work has become more explicit as is evidenced from specifying contributors and their responsible parts as well as providing citations at the end of each chapter.

The year 2020 dawned with the outbreak of the novel coronavirus disease (COVID-19) that the world has yet to contain successfully. What are the security environment implications of this pandemic, which changed our life? Grappling squarely with this question, Chapter 1 discusses "pluralization" in international politics even under the divisive pressure of U.S.-China competition. Focusing on the roles of non-U.S. and Chinese major powers as well as small and medium-sized countries in the Pacific and Europe, it presents the struggle for agency and autonomy of those countries. Chapters 2 to 6 are country and region-based analyses of major developments during January to December 2020, including each country/region's responses to U.S.-China competition as well as the impact of COVID-19 on domestic politics and foreign policy. This edition of *EASR* examines the increasingly assertive diplomatic and military positions of the Xi

Jinping government, South Korea's search for reconciliation with the increasingly coercive North Korea, ASEAN member states' responses to the pandemic and the South China Sea dispute, the Putin administration's constitutional amendments, and the U.S. policy toward China and outlook for the Biden administration. Chapter 7 presents relevant policy reviews, including Japan Self-Defense Forces' response to COVID-19 as well as the Japan-U.S. Security Treaty that marked its 60th anniversary.

This edition was authored by: Ishihara Yusuke and Tanaka Ryosuke (Chapter 1); Iida Masafumi (Chapter 2); Watanabe Takeshi (Chapter 3); Matsuura Yoshihide and Tomikawa Hideo (Chapter 4); Hasegawa Takeyuki and Sakaguchi Yoshiaki (Chapter 5); Kikuchi Shigeo (Chapter 6); and Tsukamoto Katsuya (Chapter 7). It was edited by Sukegawa Yasushi, Masuda Masayuki, Kurita Masahiro, Oshite Junichi, Tanaka Ryosuke, Asami Asaki, Aizawa Riho, and Oguma Shinya.

As the debate continues about what our post-COVID-19 world might look like, it is our hope that *EASR* will cultivate knowledge and awareness of the East Asian strategic environment and promote an intellectual discourse among the public, which will eventually serve as the building block of the emerging security architecture.

Izuyama Marie

Editor-in-chief

Director, Security Studies Department

April 2021

Contents

Acronyms and Abbreviations

A2/AD	anti-access/area denial
ABMS	Advanced Battle Management System
ACM	Alliance Coordination Mechanism
ACPHEED	ASEAN Center for Public Health Emergencies and Emerging Diseases
ACSA	Acquisition and Cross-Servicing Agreement
ADB	Asian Development Bank
ADD	[ROK] Agency for Defense Development
ADF	Australian Defence Force
ADMM-Plus	ASEAN Defence Ministers' Meeting Plus
AFB	Air Force Base
AFC	[U.S.] Army Futures Command
AFP	Australian Federal Police
AFP-GHQ	Armed Forces of the Philippines – General Headquarters
AI	artificial intelligence
AIIB	Asian Infrastructure Investment Bank
AIS	automatic identification system
AIT	[U.S.] American Institute in Taiwan
ARF	ASEAN Regional Forum
ASBM	anti-ship ballistic missile
ASDF	[Japan] Air Self-Defense Force
ASEAN	Association of Southeast Asian Nations
ASIO	Australian Security Intelligence Organisation
ATACMS	Army Tactical Missile System
AUSMIN	Australia-U.S. Ministerial Consultations
AWACS	Airborne Warning and Control System

BAKAMLA	[Indonesia] Badan Keamanan Laut Republik Indonesia (Indonesian Maritime Security Agency)
BAPPENAS	[Indonesia] Badan Perencanaan Pembangunan Nasional (Ministry of National Development Planning)
BIS	[U.S.] Bureau of Industry and Security
BRI	Belt and Road Initiative
BTF	[U.S.] Bomber Task Force
CAI	Comprehensive Agreement on Investment
CBP	Continuous Bomber Presence
CCG	China Coast Guard
CCP	Chinese Communist Party
CDC	[U.S.] Centers for Disease Control and Prevention
CECC	[U.S.] Congressional-Executive Commission on China
CEE	Central and Eastern Europe
CFC	Combined Forces Command
CIS	Commonwealth of Independent States
CISA	[U.S.] Cybersecurity and Infrastructure Security Agency
CIUS	Confucius Institute U.S. Center
CJADC2	Combined Joint All-Domain Command and Control
CLCS	Commission on the Limits of the Continental Shelf
CMC	[China] Central Military Commission
CNQP	[Vietnam] Cong Nghiep Quoc Phong (General Department of Defense Industry)
COC	Code of Conduct
CONUS	Continental U.S.
COVID-19	novel coronavirus disease
CSDP	Common Security and Defence Policy
CSG	carrier strike group
CSTO	Collective Security Treaty Organization

DFE	dynamic force employment
DMO	Distributed Maritime Operations
DOC	Declaration on the Conduct
DOD	[U.S.] Department of Defense
DPRK	Democratic People's Republic of Korea
DTT	Defense Trilateral Talks
E2DE	escalate to de-escalate
EABO	Expeditionary Advanced Base Operations
EAR	Export Administration Regulations
EAS	East Asia Summit
EASR	*East Asian Strategic Review*
EEZ	exclusive economic zone
EMS	electromagnetic spectrum
ESDP	European Security and Defence Policy
EU	European Union
EUGS	EU Global Strategy
FBI	[U.S.] Federal Bureau of Investigation
FCC	[U.S.] Futures and Concepts Center
FDI	foreign direct investment
FOIP	Free and Open Indo-Pacific
FONOP	freedom of navigation operation
FSB	[Russia] Federal'naia sluzhba bezopasnosti (Federal Security Service)
FTA	Free Trade Agreement
GDP	gross domestic product
GSDF	[Japan] Ground Self-Defense Force
GSOMIA	General Security of Military Information Agreement
HA/DR	humanitarian assistance and disaster relief
HIMARS	High Mobility Artillery Rocket System

HR/VP	High Representative of the Union for Foreign Affairs and Security Policy/ Vice President of the European Commission
HVP	hyper velocity projectile
IMF	International Monetary Fund
INF	Intermediate-range Nuclear Forces
IRF	Interim Readiness Frigate
ISR	intelligence, surveillance, and reconnaissance
IUU	illegal, unreported, and unregulated
JADC2	Joint All-Domain Command and Control
JADO	Joint All-Domain Operations
JSTARS	Joint Surveillance Target Attack Radar System
JWC	Joint Warfighting Concept
KAMD	Korea Air and Missile Defense
KCNA	[DPRK] Korean Central News Agency
KPA	[DPRK] Korean People's Army
LCS	littoral combat ship
LMC	Lancang-Mekong Cooperation
LMS	littoral mission ship
LNG	liquefied natural gas
LOCE	Littoral Operations in a Contested Environment
LRASM	long-range anti-ship missile
L-SAM	long-range surface-to-air missile
LST	landing ship tank
MD	Minister of Defense
MDC2	Multi-Domain Command and Control
MDL	Military Demarcation Line
MDO	Multi-Domain Operations
MDOC-F	[U.S.] Multidomain Operations Center – Forward

MDT	Mutual Defense Treaty
MDTF	[U.S.] Multi-Domain Task Force
MEF	minimum essential forces
MERS	Middle East respiratory syndrome
MOD	[Japan] Ministry of Defense
MPA	maritime patrol aircraft
MRL	multiple rocket launcher
MRO	maintenance, repair and overhaul
MSDF	[Japan] Maritime Self-Defense Force
MSI	Maritime Security Initiative
MSSARS	multipurpose submarine search-and-rescue ship
NAS	Naval Air Squadron
NATO	North Atlantic Treaty Organization
NBC	nuclear, biological, and chemical
NCSC	[U.S.] National Counterintelligence and Security Center
NDPG	[Japan] National Defense Program Guidelines
NDS	[U.S.] National Defense Strategy
New START	New Strategic Arms Reduction Treaty
NHK-1	Nike Hercules Korea-1
NIDS	[Japan] National Institute for Defense Studies
NLL	Northern Limit Line
NPC	[China] National People's Congress
NPT	Treaty on the Non-Proliferation of Nuclear Weapons
NSC	National Security Council
NSM	Naval Strike Missile
NSS	[Japan] National Security Secretariat
OAS	Organization of American States
ODNI	[U.S.] Office of the Director of National Intelligence

OPCON	Operational Control
OSCE	Organization for Security and Co-operation in Europe
PC	Project Convergence
PCR	polymerase chain reaction
PESCO	Permanent Structured Cooperation
PIF	Pacific Islands Forum
PLA	[China] People's Liberation Army
PPE	personal protective equipment
PRC	People's Republic of China
PSBB	[Indonesia] Pembatasan Sosial Berskala Besar (large-scale social restrictions)
QMV	Qualified Majority Voting
RAFPMP	[Philippines] Revised AFP Modernization Program
RAMSI	Regional Assistance Mission to Solomon Islands
RIMPAC	Rim of the Pacific Exercise
RINO	Republican in name only
RMAF	Royal Malaysian Air Force
RMN	Royal Malaysian Navy
ROK	Republic of Korea
SAR	[China] Special Administrative Region
SAREX	Search and Rescue Exercise
SARS	severe acute respiratory syndrome
SCM	Security Consultative Meeting
SCO	Shanghai Cooperation Organization
SDF	[Japan] Self-Defense Forces
SIGMA	Ship Integrated Geometrical Modularity Approach
SLBM	submarine-launched ballistic missile
SM-3	Standard Missile-3
SMA	Special Measures Agreement

SRBM	short-range ballistic missile
SSA	Space Situational Awareness
SVR	[Russia] Sluzhba Vneshney Razvedki (Foreign Intelligence Service)
THAAD	Terminal High Altitude Area Defense
TPP	Trans-Pacific Partnership
TSD	Trilateral Strategic Dialogue
TTIP	Transatlantic Trade and Investment Partnership
UAV	unmanned aerial vehicle
UN	United Nations
UNC	United Nations Command
UNCLOS	United Nations Convention on the Law of the Sea
UNESCO	United Nations Educational, Scientific and Cultural Organization
USFK	United States Forces Korea
VFA	Visiting Forces Agreement
WFP	World Food Programme
WHO	World Health Organization
WPK	[DPRK] Workers' Party of Korea
XPSB	[China] Xinjiang Public Security Bureau
XUAR	[China] Xinjiang Uygur Autonomous Region
17+1	17 Central and Eastern European countries plus China

Chapter 1

World Politics amid Great Power Competition

The Pacific and European Experiences during COVID-19 Crisis

ISHIHARA Yusuke (Lead author, Sections 1 and 2)
TANAKA Ryosuke (Section 3)

Japan-France-Australia-U.S. naval exercise La Pérouse conducted in 2019 (Photo courtesy of the French Navy)

Summary

The pandemic caused by the novel coronavirus disease (COVID-19) in 2020 has further stimulated the existing debate on the transition of the international order. This chapter focuses not on the United States and China and their great power relations that tend to dominate discussions on this topic; the emphasis is rather on developments in other major powers and small and medium-sized countries. Scholars have differing views on the options available to non-U.S. and Chinese countries and the role they will play in the future international order.

Section 1 of this chapter presents and analyzes two leading views about the role of non-U.S. and Chinese countries. On the one hand, many scholars argue that the world is being divided into a U.S.-China bipolar order, and that countries other than these two great powers ultimately have little choice but to make their positions clear, either to cooperate with the United States against China or to value their relations with China and distance themselves from the United States. On the other hand, many scholars also point out that the world is becoming multipolar or "pluralistic," and that non-U.S. and Chinese countries have options that are increasingly diverse and promote self-initiative. This section contends that a trend toward "pluralization" in international politics continues to be observed, even amid the divisive pressures of U.S.-China competition in recent years, and that this trend is driven by the determination of many countries to defend and promote their autonomy.

Sections 2 and 3 explain efforts undertaken by countries other than the United States and China toward "pluralization" and their struggle for agency and autonomy. The analyses focus on the international affairs situations of the Pacific region, including Australia, as well as Europe centered on the European Union (EU). Australia in the Pacific region has been affected by the competition between the United States and China but continues to develop its own regionalism and promote regional cooperation on the COVID-19 response. Meanwhile, European countries are searching for "strategic autonomy," and in doing so, seek to manage their relations with the great powers of the United States and China that entail increasingly complex issues. For discussions on Sino-U.S. relations and COVID-19-related developments in countries and regions other than the Pacific and Europe, please refer to the analyses in Chapter 2 onwards.

1. Division or Pluralization?

(1) The Transformation of World Politics and the COVID-19 Crisis

The COVID-19 crisis that escalated in 2020 is further intensifying the existing debate over the transition of postwar international order.[1] In this context, many scholars have noted the trend of waning U.S. leadership. Richard Haass, president of the Council on Foreign Relations, notes that the rise of authoritarian states including China is challenging the power and leadership of the United States on which the traditional "liberal world order" has been sustained, asserting, "[e]ven the best-managed order comes to an end."[2] Haass adds that COVID-19 will further "accelerate" existing trends, including "waning American leadership." C. Raja Mohan, former member of the National Security Advisory Board of India and current Director of the Institute of South Asian Studies at National University of Singapore, also points out the diminishing U.S. leadership, giving greater focus to the economic aspects. According to Mohan, there had already been a movement in the United States and elsewhere since the beginning of the 21st century to question the "Washington Consensus" (policies favoring economic liberalization and globalization promoted by international institutions established after World War II), and the COVID-19 crisis is accelerating such long-term trends and putting unprecedented "stress" on the traditional "borderless world."[3]

Of course, this is by no means the first time that the "crisis" of the international order or a "waning" of U.S. leadership has been pointed out in the last 75 years since the end of World War II. In the 1970s, for example, the "United States-led order" that had been maintained following World War II was under duress, and a sweeping transformation of this order was a subject of lively debate.[4] In the immediate aftermath of the war, the United States accounted for 40% of the world economy, and its overwhelming national strength supported the growth of Western economies and security arrangements. By the end of the 1970s, however, the U.S. share of the world's gross domestic product (GDP) declined to about 25%, while Japan and Germany, which recovered and rose from the devastation of the war, accounted for about 10% each.[5] In the security field, the Soviet Union continued to build up a wide range of armaments in the 1970s, including nuclear weapons and naval power. As a result, "It cannot necessarily be said that the United States is superior in all areas of weaponry, including strategic nuclear weapons, theater nuclear weapons, and naval and air force capabilities" (*Defense of Japan 1979*).[6] Against this backdrop, the 1970s remains an important subject of study for understanding the period of the shake-up in the United States-led order. Yet, the ongoing transition of the international order in the 21st century is clearly distinctive from the past experiences, including the ones in the 1970s, particularly in the following two regards.

First, the main competitors for the United States have significantly different national strengths and international economic standings now compared to back then. In the 1970s, the United States faced the economic rise of its allies, such as European countries and Japan, while at the same time facing the apparent buildup of Soviet military capabilities. In 2020, China is the leading competitor for the United States in both the economic and security fields.[7] According to the World Bank, the U.S. and Chinese shares of the global nominal GDP were overwhelmingly disparate at the start of the century in 2001, at about 32% and 4%, respectively. In 2019, they were at about 24% and 16%, respectively, with China's share increasing to 70% of the U.S. share.[8] In contrast, the Soviet share is assessed to have peaked out at around 50% of the U.S. share (although even that is a high estimate) when the economy was at its highest in the mid-1970s. The Soviet economy since saw a downward trend.[9]

The second difference is the U.S. approach toward multilateralism. The United States' disinterest in existing multilateral institutions was particularly salient during the Trump administration. Since its inauguration in 2017, the Trump administration made it clear that it was skeptical of existing multilateralism, withdrawing from the Trans-Pacific Partnership Agreement and the Iran nuclear deal without regard for the concerns of its allies. Furthermore, the administration continued to decline to support the filling of vacancies on the World Trade Organization's Appellate Body for dispute settlement. The

Trump administration likewise disregarded many other existing institutions, deciding to withdraw from the United Nations (UN) Human Rights Council and the UN Educational, Scientific and Cultural Organization. On top of this, it presented no alternative vision for multilateral cooperation. In contrast, the U.S. administrations of the 1970s continued to play an important role in building new multilateral cooperation, at least in the areas of currency, trade, and cooperation among developed countries.

The COVID-19 pandemic in 2020 and related international developments did not so much as create but reaffirm the continuation of the above two trends. First, the trend toward a narrowing of the gap in economic power between the United States and China has not been reversed since the outbreak of COVID-19.[10] Indeed, China's economy declined by 6.8% year-on-year in the first quarter of 2020 partly due to the pandemic. Yet, the Chinese economy returned to positive growth of 3.2% year-on-year in the second quarter of 2020 when the spread of the disease was halted, and grew 4.9% and 6.5% in the third and fourth quarters, resulting in positive growth of 2.3% for the full year. On the other hand, the United States, which had the world's largest number of COVID-19 cases at the time of this writing, suffered steepest quarter-on-quarter economic declines on record, -1.3% in the first quarter and -9.0% in the second quarter.[11] The U.S. economy showed signs of a rapid recovery in the third quarter at 7.4% (-2.9% year-on-year), but the country is seeing a resurgence in COVID-19 cases and the prospects for continued recovery in the fourth quarter are uncertain at the time of this writing. According to the International Monetary Fund (IMF) outlook for 2020, China achieved positive growth of 1.9% for the full year of 2020 and is projected to achieve 8.2% positive growth in 2021. On the other hand, the United States is expected to post negative growth of -4.3% for the full year of 2020 and positive growth of 3.1% in 2021, both significantly lower than the growth rates of the Chinese economy.[12] If these estimates are correct, the pandemic could narrow the disparity in economic leverage between the United States and China, at least at a faster pace than in the past few years.

Second, COVID-19 has reaffirmed the Trump administration's lukewarm attitude toward multilateralism. Ever since the pandemic spread globally, the Trump administration criticized the World Health Organization (WHO) for coming under the influence of China. It announced the United States would halt payment of contributions to the organization in April 2020 and withdraw from the organization in May, indicating the possibility of establishing new international institutions but never disclosed anything concrete.[13] The United States is certainly not the only country that expressed dissatisfaction with the role played by WHO in the pandemic and the organization's mechanisms. As members of WHO, however, many of these countries have made ongoing efforts to reform WHO and carry out an inquiry into the international response to COVID-19 as much as possible, marking a divergence from the U.S. policy.

Along with confirming these trends, the outbreak of the pandemic has moved the United States and China in the direction of further great power competition. As is known, the U.S.-China relationship has become more competitive over recent years to the extent that it is called the "New Cold War" or "Cold War 2.0." This is compounded by the COVID-19 crisis that has created a new point of contention between the two great powers. The Trump administration claimed that China mishandled the initial response in Wuhan and the sharing of information with the rest of the world, which in turn made the global pandemic considerably more serious, and declared that China must be held "accountable."[14] China responded that it has not been confirmed as the origin of the outbreak and condemned the administration for "shifting the blame" for the U.S. mishandling of the disease to another country.[15] In addition, the U.S.-China standoff over COVID-19 intensified over Taiwan's participation in the World Health Assembly as an observer. The Trump administration supported giving observer status at the World Health Assembly to Taiwan, one of the successful examples of combating COVID-19. The dispute with China, which objected to Taiwan's participation, unfolded at the World Health Assembly in May 2020 and in the international negotiations for its resumed session in November.

(2) A Pluralist World?

The transformation of U.S.-China relations and the outbreak of COVID-19 have further intensified the debate on the transition of the international order. A variety of views on this issue have been put forward by experts, among which the following two are particularly representative. One of them is the bipolarity discourse.[16] Although there are various definitions of what exactly is meant by bipolarity, many experts who discuss the future international order envision that the increased competition between the United States and China will divide the world into blocs or spheres of influence with the two countries at their core.[17] They anticipate many countries in the world will be forced to choose sides between one or the other as the rivalry between the two countries intensifies. This may be more accurately described as a "divided" world image, i.e., a world divided into two. Yan Xuetong of Tsinghua University notes that Sino-U.S. competition is creating "pressure [on other countries] of taking sides with either the United States or China."[18] Yuen Foong Khong of the National University of Singapore notes, even if small and medium-sized countries like Southeast Asian nations do not confront a decisive choice between the United States and China, their cumulative day-to-day policy choices will elucidate which of the two camps they will ultimately align with.[19] This question of "choosing" China or the United States has long been a subject of intense debate in East Asia. In recent years, it has also entered the discourse on Sino-U.S. competition in more geographically distant regions, including Europe.[20]

On the other hand, a number of arguments also emphasize the tendency toward multipolarization of international politics rather than the risk of "division." The classical image of a multipolar world is one where multiple states enter into military cooperation or alliances to maintain balance, aiming to prevent a dominant state or coalition of states from emerging.[21] Accordingly, any change in the distribution of military power results in an overhaul of alliance partners. Moreover, when discussing the future international order, many advocates of "multipolarity" are using the term "multipolar" not necessarily to argue that many more countries than the United States and China would compete and balance militarily against each other and thereby constitute a multipolar structure per se. For example, former Singaporean diplomat Bilahari Kausikan proposes "asymmetric, dynamic multipolarity" based on a multilateral perspective on power.[22] "Asymmetric" implies candid acknowledgement that both the United States and China have comprehensive national strengths, including military might superior to those of other countries, and that their bilateral relationship forms the central axis of international politics. "Dynamic multipolarity" means non-U.S. and Chinese countries have a broader range of choices and roles than simply collaborating with the United States against China, or cooperating with China to distance themselves from the United States. As Nakanishi Hiroshi of Kyoto University suggests, "pluralization" is a more accurate description of the tendency of the instruments of international politics to be diverse and not limited to military capabilities.[23] Hosoya Yuichi of Keio University points out that non-U.S. and Chinese countries, such as Japan and European countries, may play a more important role in the post-COVID-19 world. The power envisaged here is, again, a pluralistic one that encompasses not only military capabilities but also the ability to earn the respect of other countries and promote multilateral cooperation.[24]

As mentioned above, unlike the scholars and practitioners who project the "divided" world image, those who conceive of the world image as "pluralist" discuss prospects for the future international order with more importance given to the roles and agency of the players other than the great powers of the United States and China. The "pluralist" world image offers a variety of arguments, and it is impossible to list them all. The following are three representative examples of the concepts being developed related to the options of non-U.S. and Chinese countries.[25] First, according to Bruce Jentleson of Duke University, one of the concepts is the "pluralization" of diplomacy. This refers to the policy of avoiding overdependence on a single great power as much as possible by building multilateral relationships with other countries, thereby limiting the influence of the great power. A second notion is that maintaining strategic "ambiguity" is becoming a convenient choice for many countries. By refraining from clarifying their positions, countries are more likely to avoid or delay a situation where they are forced to make a clear choice between the great powers of the United States and China. The third is the most classic example of the "pluralist" world image, the idea of many countries other than the great powers protecting multilateralism. Non-U.S. and Chinese countries work together to protect and strengthen multilateral cooperation and principles, which provides a basis for promoting international cooperation in areas where the national interests of the United States and China coincide. It is also thought to enable protection of multilateral frameworks even as U.S.-China confrontation continues. "Pluralist" thinkers believe that many countries are protecting their autonomy by utilizing either of these three choices or their combination, and consequently, the world will not simply be divided into a U.S.-China bipolar structure.

Observations of the international politics surrounding COVID-19 suggest that countries other than the United States and China are playing a creative role in more instances, as noted by those who emphasize the "pluralist" world image. The World Health Assembly in May 2020 adopted a resolution that articulated an intention to review the international response and cooperation on the COVID-19 crisis. China initially adopted the position that an inquiry should not be conducted while the pandemic was continuing. Nonetheless, as negotiations on the draft resolution were carried out under the EU's leading role, China ultimately joined, and the resolution was submitted and adopted by over 130 co-sponsoring countries.[26] Steps are gradually being taken to implement the resolution, and an inquiry is under way with the appointment of former prime minister of New Zealand Helen Clark and former president of Liberia Ellen Johnson Sirleaf as co-chairs of the inquiry panel. Clark described the panel's mandate as "mission impossible" and acknowledged that there are limits on the extent to which an adequate inquiry can be conducted. Knowing the challenges of an inquiry, many countries that co-sponsored the resolution are still focusing on reforming WHO and sharing facts and lessons surrounding the pandemic as much as possible.[27] This approach is markedly different from that of the Trump administration that had notified its withdrawal from WHO. Furthermore, the COVAX Facility has been established for the development of COVID-19 vaccines with the participation of developed and developing countries, including Japan, European countries, and Australia. Under the COVAX Facility, mechanisms are being developed to encourage companies to expand their vaccine development and manufacturing capabilities and to ensure equitable access to vaccines for all countries, including developing countries that lack sufficient funds.[28] This initiative has been noted as a good example of a growing win-win network based on broad multilateral cooperation—an alternative to the power politics approach that uses homegrown vaccines as diplomatic leverage.

Of course, such observations of "pluralist" international politics do not imply that the U.S.-China confrontation is no longer intensifying, or that countries are no longer struggling to find their place between the two great powers. Building on the observation by Soeya Yoshihide of Keio University, international politics at the end of 2020 appears to be in a "hybrid" situation comprised of both "divisive" pressures and "pluralist" phenomena.[29] Various factors may explain why a clearly divided world has not yet emerged despite the intensifying U.S.-China competition. What they hint at is that many countries other than the two great powers are intent on acting autonomously as their own national interests, values, and principles guide their foreign policy. Based on this awareness of the issues, we leave it to Chapter 2 onwards to examine the affairs of the countries and regions dealt with annually in the *East Asian Strategic Review*. This chapter, instead, analyzes two other important regions, the South Pacific and Europe. Section 2 discusses developments in the South Pacific with a focus on Australia, while Section 3 discusses the international activities of Europe. The discussions shed light on the challenges facing non-U.S. and Chinese countries and how they search for autonomy as the international order reaches a turning point.

2. Australia-China Competition and the South Pacific

(1) Pluralist Order in the South Pacific
The South Pacific is dotted with nations large and small that can be classified into

three broad categories. The first is the South Pacific island countries, which have a relatively limited land area and small population but a vast exclusive economic zone (EEZ). Most of the countries do not have military forces, with the exceptions of Fiji, which has a military force of about 3,500 personnel, and Tonga, which has a military force of about 500 personnel.[30] The second category is France and the United States, which have territorial and defense commitments in the South Pacific but whose mainland is located outside the region. France possesses French Polynesia, New Caledonia, and Wallis and Futuna. It stations about 3,000 troops, seven vessels, including Floréal-class patrol frigates, and nine fixed-wing aircraft, including the Falcon patrol aircraft, for monitoring and surveillance of the French territories. In addition, it regularly hosts the international disaster relief exercise Croix du Sud.[31] In recent years, the country has annually published the *France and Security in the Indo-Pacific* report, and French presence in the region is regaining attention.[32] The United States possesses the Hawaiian Islands at the northern apex of Polynesia, along with American Samoa, and maintains agreements to assume responsibility for the defense of the Federated States of Micronesia, the Marshall Islands, and Palau.[33] Secretary of Defense Mark Esper visited Palau in August 2020 and Secretary of the Navy Kenneth Braithwaite in October. The Palauan government made a proposal to build some military facilities and realize their joint use, and this is now under consideration.[34] The third category is the developed countries of New Zealand and Australia, the major regional powers in Oceania. New Zealand is currently in the process of introducing four P-8 Poseidon patrol aircraft and continues to provide capacity building assistance for the maritime surveillance of island countries. According to the *Strategic Defence Policy Statement 2018*, New Zealand places the same level of priority on maritime stability in the South Pacific as it does on defending its territory.[35] Australia is the largest military and economic player in Oceania, having the 13th largest GDP in the world and maintaining a defense budget of approximately 3 trillion yen and a defense force of about 60,000 personnel.[36] In this section, security in Oceania is analyzed with focus given to the Australian perspective. As necessary, it refers to Papua New Guinea, a member of the Pacific

Islands Forum (PIF), although the country is an exception that does not fit into any of the three broad categories above.

The formation and development of the Australian state has always been closely linked with the security of the South Pacific. In 1901, several colonies on the Australian continent united to form the foundation of the current continental federation. This was triggered by the increasing presence of non-British imperial powers in the South Pacific, which in turn led to importance being placed on the unification and self-governance of colonies to ensure the security of the Australian continent.[37] The country has traditionally disfavored the military presence of external powers in the South Pacific, and these security perceptions have been consistently found even after the end of the Cold War. This is demonstrated, for example, in *Defence 2000*, a historic document that significantly influenced the basic framework of Australia's defense policy in the first 15 years of the 21st century. This white paper lists the determinants of the force structure of the Australian Defence Force (ADF), which include not only direct defense of the Australian continent but also ensuring "stability in the nearer region" centered around the South Pacific.[38] One of the reasons cited is to prevent external powers from maintaining a military presence in Australia's neighborhood.

Indeed, Australia has continued to play a leading military role in the South Pacific region in an ongoing effort to forestall the possibility of full-scale intervention by external powers. For example, when a stabilization and peace-building operation was launched in then East Timor in 1999, ADF led the UN peacekeeping force and became the largest force provider, deploying some 5,500 troops.[39] Australia's involvement in Timor-Leste's independence and stability was a sticky foreign policy situation in the context of its relations with the northern giant, Indonesia. The fact that Australia managed this issue and engaged in large-scale military involvement confirmed the country's determination to play a leading role in the "immediate neighbourhood."[40] Furthermore, Australia led a task force consisting of troops contributed by Australia, New Zealand, Papua New Guinea, Fiji, and Tonga for the stabilization operation, the Regional Assistance Mission to Solomon Islands (RAMSI). RAMSI began in 2003 at the request of the government of the Solomon Islands, which continued to experience political instability at the time.[41] The second pillar of Australia's military involvement, in addition to these stabilization operations, is to assist South Pacific countries in managing their territorial waters and EEZs. After the UN Convention on the Law of the Sea (UNCLOS) was adopted in 1982, it became a critical regional issue that South Pacific island countries with small populations and economies effectively manage their vast territorial waters and EEZs. Australia has provided support to these countries and implemented the ADF-led Pacific Patrol Boat Program to maintain order under UNCLOS in the South Pacific.[42] The program provides South Pacific countries with patrol boats, stations personnel in the region, and offers ongoing support for patrol boat operation training and maintenance and management. Since the first patrol boat was provided to Papua New Guinea in 1987, the program has extended capacity building assistance to many countries. With the initially provided Pacific-class patrol boats due to reach the end of their service life, the program has recently begun providing new Guardian-class patrol boats. According to the *Defence White Paper 2009*, it is important that Australia play a "leading" role not only from a "humanitarian perspective," but also from a "strategic perspective" in preventing external powers from increasing their influence over the immediate neighbourhood.[43]

Australia recognizes that over-emphasizing its leading role in the South Pacific may cause island countries to see it as intrusive assistance and create resentment. A range of policies have been put in place to manage such sentiments and ensure Australia's engagement is welcomed. Among them, building regionalism through the PIF has been regarded as offering a vital opportunity. In 2000, the PIF issued the Biketawa Declaration, which affirmed region-wide support for stability in South Pacific countries. This provided a regional basis for legitimizing Australia's subsequent stabilization operations and played a particularly important role in RAMSI in the Solomon Islands discussed above. At the time, the Solomon Islands maintained diplomatic relations with Taiwan, and securing a mandate for stabilization operations via the UN was considered unviable.[44] Therefore, forces were provided by member countries under a regional mandate of the PIF, and regionalism in the South Pacific played a concrete role serving as a source of legitimacy for security operations. Alongside security, regionalism also has a role in the areas of economic cooperation among South Pacific countries. A series of regional agreements have been implemented to deepen economic relations between the island countries and Australia and New Zealand. In this way, the South Pacific has developed a pluralist order in which Australia, New Zealand, and island countries, rather than the great powers outside the South Pacific, utilize multilateralism to promote regional stability and prosperity.

In the last few years, however, Australia has become apprehensive about China's growing economic presence that could cast a long shadow over this Australia-led pluralist regional order in the South Pacific. Since 2014, China has become the largest trading partner for South Pacific island countries along with Australia, and according to a study by the Lowy Institute for International Policy, China surpassed Japan to become the third largest donor of aid to South Pacific island countries for the five-year period from 2014 to 2018.[45] China also appears to be gradually translating its growing economic presence into political influence. In 2019, both the Solomon Islands and Kiribati agreed to switch diplomatic relations from Taiwan to China.[46] In recent years, Australian media and think tanks have warned that China's growing economic presence may gradually lead to a growing military presence. In 2018, there were reports that negotiations were in progress for China to build a military facility in Vanuatu, about 2,000 kilometers from the Australian continent. When the government of Australia confirmed with the government of Vanuatu, then Australian prime minister Malcolm Turnbull denied the fact.[47] Although the reported facility has not materialized so far, the Australian government's quick denial of the reports and the lively discussion that ensued in the Australian policy community confirmed the high level of interest in these issues. Also in 2018, the governments of Australia and Papua New Guinea agreed to expand a base facility for joint use by the Australian navy on Manus Island, which belongs to Papua New Guinea. As one Australian expert explained, the intention was to preempt China's growing influence in the South Pacific and was "preventative."[48] Construction at Lombrum Naval Base on Manus Island has already begun, where Australia is set to carry out a project to help build up Papua New Guinea's maritime management capacity.

Despite Australia's gradually increasing alarm over China's growing presence in the South Pacific, the basis for Australia's leading role has remained firm and steadfast, at least to date, from the following three perspectives. First, Australia maintains a commanding presence in the development assistance sector.[49] A comparison of 2018 aid commitments shows that Australia's was $920 million, while China's was only about a quarter of that at $240 million. In 2018, Prime Minister Scott Morrison unveiled a series of programs called "Pacific Step-up" and announced Australia will increase its development assistance funding. The aid disparity between Australia and China may thus widen even further.[50]

Second, there is still a stark difference in the scale and quality of Australian and Chinese engagement in the security field. Since 2010, China has sent the hospital ship *Peace Ark* to various parts of the world to provide medical assistance and conduct friendship visits. In recent years, it has also been conducting activities in the South Pacific to strengthen relations with island countries.[51] In comparison, ADF's involvement is wide-ranging. In addition to the maritime capacity building assistance and peace operations already mentioned, it continues to demonstrate its presence as a first responder in the areas of medical assistance and disaster relief. When Cyclone Harold struck the South Pacific in April 2020, causing severe damage in Fiji and Vanuatu in particular, Australian and New Zealand forces each transported more than 200 tons of relief supplies.[52] This assistance reaffirmed that the two countries, which are geographically close to the South Pacific island countries and maintain high-quality military forces, have an important presence in disaster assistance. So far, it cannot be confirmed that Chinese forces have led disaster relief efforts as first responders in the South Pacific.

Third, Australia coordinates with other players more closely than China in the South Pacific region. Australia, France, New Zealand, and the United States have formed the Quadrilateral Defence Coordination Group to cooperate and coordinate maritime surveillance in the South Pacific and support fisheries monitoring by the PIF.[53] New Zealand, in particular, provided more aid than China in 2018. It also launched a program of enhanced engagement called "Pacific Reset" and has expressed opposition to "militarization" of the South Pacific.[54] New Zealand has launched the Pacific Maritime Safety Programme since 2011 and has strengthened its capacity building assistance efforts for island countries in the areas of legislative development and search and rescue. Both the Australian and New Zealand governments have agreed to pursue closer coordination between Australia's "Pacific Step-up" policy and New Zealand's "Pacific Reset."[55] In addition, France has further expanded its coordination with Australia, New Zealand, and island countries in the area of multilateral cooperation in the South Pacific, successfully admitting New Caledonia and French Polynesia to the PIF in 2016 and including the representative of the former in the PIF leaders' retreat for the first time in 2018. Furthermore, negotiations for an agreement to strengthen economic ties between the French territories and Australia are currently under consideration.[56] As is evident, the quality and breadth of Australia-New Zealand cooperation and Australia-France cooperation in the South Pacific region far exceeds that of cooperation between these countries and China. In light of the above, it can be assessed that although China's economic presence has expanded in recent years, the pluralist order and Australia's leading position in the South Pacific remain intact.

Some note that COVID-19 is further fueling Australia-China competition for aid to South Pacific island countries. China provided medical supplies, such as masks and protective gear, as well as medical treatment information from an early stage, and also contributed $1.9 million to establish the China-Pacific Island Countries Anti-COVID-19 Cooperation Fund. This fund reportedly can be used not only for direct responses to COVID-19 but also to promote trade and investment relations between China and South Pacific island countries.[57] Similarly, Australia has decided to "focus" its international assistance on South Pacific island countries. In cooperation with WHO and the World Food Programme, the Royal Australian Air Force C-17 aircraft is transporting supplies and experts to help ensure that medical services and food supplies in island countries are not disrupted

A Royal Australian Air Force C-17 aircraft arriving in Port Vila, Vanuatu with disaster relief supplies (Australian Department of Defence/Australian Defence Force)

even after flight routes are reduced. Australia is also providing information and technical training through the Indo-Pacific Centre for Health Security of the Department of Foreign Affairs and Trade.[58] While both Australia and China have stepped up to assist in the COVID-19 response in the South Pacific, Australia's efforts may be considered superior to China's in the following two ways. One is the use of regionalism. The PIF Foreign Ministers' Meeting held online in April 2020 decided to invoke the 2000 Biketawa Declaration that had been used to legitimize peace operations. The meeting viewed responding to COVID-19 as posing a "real and extreme danger" to regional security and stressed the importance of member states working in solidarity as part of the "Pacific Islands extended family." Secondly, Australia has made a greater financial commitment. In addition to its regular budget, Australia established a new fund of more than A$300 million, exceeding China's, to help prevent and respond to the pandemic in the Pacific for realizing the policies discussed above.[59]

In recent years, the United States has continued to express high expectations for Australia, which still maintains a leading position in the South Pacific. Under a policy called the "Pacific Pledge" of the Indo-Pacific Strategy, the Trump administration committed more than $300 million in its budget to Pacific island countries for boosting development assistance, support for domestic governance, including election management, and capacity building assistance for coast guard agencies.[60] In addition, the United States has announced its intention to cooperate with Australia in the construction of the naval base on Manus Island mentioned above, and is providing technical, material, and financial assistance to the

South Pacific region in coordination with Australia for the region's COVID-19 response. For example, Japan-U.S.-Australia cooperation is being pursued for an undersea cable project in Palau's periphery, where the U.S. forces is considering strengthening its deployment.[61] However, the South Pacific policies of the United States and Australia differ clearly in their position on the following two points. First, the U.S. and Australian policies differ on China-Taiwan competition over diplomatic relations with South Pacific countries. In October 2019, the Trump administration launched a formal U.S.-Taiwan dialogue on the South Pacific, and Sandra Oudkirk, deputy assistant secretary of state for Australia, New Zealand, and the Pacific Islands, stated during her visit to Taiwan, "we firmly support Taiwan's relationships with Pacific Island nations."[62] Furthermore, when W. Patrick Murphy, acting assistant secretary of state for the Bureau of East Asian and Pacific Affairs, visited Australia in May 2019 and stated that he encourages South Pacific countries to maintain diplomatic relations with Taiwan, Australian prime minister Morrison stated soon afterward that it was for the South Pacific countries themselves to decide and emphasized Australia's stance of not intervening in this issue.[63] Second, differences in the U.S. and Australian positions on multilateralism are also becoming more manifest. As already mentioned in Section 1, the Trump administration halted contributions to WHO and announced its intention to withdraw from the organization. Australia has maintained a critical stance toward the administration's decisions while choosing its words carefully. As Australian minister for foreign affairs Marise Payne noted, Australia is working closely with WHO's regional office in providing international assistance for combating COVID-19, mainly to the South Pacific, and the country has praised the role of WHO. Considering the above two points, the (sometimes circulated) discourse that Australia is countering China as a proxy of the United States in the South Pacific is misleadingly simplistic. As this section has examined, Australia's primary reason for remaining wary of the presence of external great powers in the South Pacific is its own perception of national security based on history and is not support of the United States. From this perspective, Canberra seeks to protect the Australia-led pluralist order in the

South Pacific by pursuing its own measures against China's growing presence, while being careful not to be inadvertently influenced by U.S. policy toward China.

(2) Deterioration of Australia-China Relations

As was outlined in (1), Australia has been wary of China that is expanding its presence in the periphery region in recent years. Underlying this wariness is widespread distrust of China that extends beyond the South Pacific. In particular, the factor that most exacerbated Australia's perception of China in 2020 was the bilateral conflict over the response to COVID-19. The direct trigger of the issue was Foreign Minister Payne's comments regarding the COVID-19 response.[64] In an interview with an Australian media outlet in April 2020, Foreign Minister Payne urged for "transparency" in the initial response to the virus that originated in Wuhan and that an "independent" and international review was needed. The Chinese ambassador to Australia refuted immediately that China had not been confirmed as the origin of the virus and that the review should wait until the response to the pandemic was under control.[65] The ambassador also noted that the comments of the Australian government could give the Chinese public an unfavorable impression of Australia, suggesting that under such circumstances, Chinese people may not wish to buy Australian products or study or travel in Australia. On the grounds that the remarks by the Chinese senior official could be construed as blatant economic "blackmail," they aroused widespread controversy among the Australian media and policy community.[66]

And, as if to give credence to the statements of the ambassador, the Chinese government continued to put forward measures intermittently to review its economic relationship with Australia. In summary, first, the Chinese government announced in May 2020 that it would impose high tariffs on Australian barley.[67] With China being the largest importing country of Australian barley, concerns heightened in Australia that the country would be shut out of the Chinese market, which could lead to significant business losses. In addition, in June 2020, the Chinese government warned its people that traveling to Australia to sightsee or study could put them at risk of racial discrimination.[68] Travel between Australia and China has become severely restricted due to the pandemic's outbreak, and it remains unclear what effect the Chinese government's warnings will have in practice. At the very least, both tourism and study in Australia rely heavily on Chinese visitors, and this has raised concerns over economic losses in the two industries. Specifically, for the full year of 2018, China was the top country from which people visited Australia and generated an estimated A$12 billion in economic impact.[69] This amount far exceeds that of the second top country the United States (about A$4 billion), making Australia's high level of dependence on China most apparent.[70] Similarly, of the approximately 750,000 international students in Australia in 2019, Chinese students were the largest group by country, accounting for 28% of the total, significantly ahead that of the second top country India at 15%.[71] The Chinese government's warnings that could deter tourists and students from coming could have serious implications for the Australian economy. In November 2020, it was reported that Chinese authorities halted imports of Australian copper, coal, barley, wine, sugar, lobster, and logs.[72] Australian trade minister Simon Birmingham noted that the suspension of imports does not apply to all of the reported supplies and that imports were being delayed due to changes in administration regulations.[73] Conversely, these statements confirmed that imports of some items and products would be suspended or delayed. As Australian exports to China undergo a review in a variety of sectors, the Morrison government has called for intergovernmental ministerial talks, which the Chinese government has not agreed to so far. In this context, the Australian government has urged its export industries to diversify their export markets, and its education arm is working to review its over-reliance on international students for income.

The Morrison government has not lost its willingness to hold dialogue with China. Nevertheless, stabilizing Australia-China relations will no longer be an easy task.[74] Even if the countries succeed to some extent in defusing the conflicts over the COVID-19 response and trade relations, many other issues remain between Australia and China that involve sensitive matters which are politically difficult to deal with. In particular, the management of the Australia-China relationship in recent years has been made more challenging by fundamental disagreements over political values. First, there has been ongoing debate and criticism in Australia of what is often characterized as Chinese infiltration into Australian politics and society. In 2017, senator Sam Dastyari of the largest opposition Labor Party resigned after a scandal over his links to Chinese supporters. Australia then strengthened its legal infrastructure to combat foreign government interference in 2018. In recent years, investigations and controversies under the law have spilled over even into Australian local politics. In June 2020, the office of Shaoquett Moselmane, member of the New South Wales Legislative Council, was raided by the Australian Federal Police (AFP) and the Australian Security Intelligence Organisation (ASIO).[75] According to the announcement by Moselmane, he was not the target of the investigation and Chinese-Australian John Zhang, one of his office staff, was the suspect. According to Australian media reports, Zhang had publicly stated the need to have more pro-China politicians in Australia and is suspected of being under the influence of the United Front Work Department of the Chinese Communist Party (CCP). In connection with this case, it has also been reported that a Chinese consul to Australia and Chinese diplomats have been targeted for investigation.[76] In response, the Consulate General of China in Sydney reprinted, on its website, an article from the English edition of *Global Times*, effectively condemning the Australian government's investigation by citing that it was "barbaric acts" against Chinese "journalists."[77] Furthermore, in November 2020, it was learned Di Sanh Duong, an Australian of Chinese and Vietnamese descent, became a target of investigation by AFP and ASIO and was arrested and charged.[78] This was the first instance that foreign interference laws enacted in 2018 were applied. Duong's arrest was meant to prevent illegal activities from taking place, according to AFP. However, the specifics have yet to be made public.[79] According to the Australian media, Duong is a member of the Liberal Party who was a candidate in the Victorian state parliamentary election and had recently been engaged in political activities.

Second, in recent years Australia has become increasingly critical of the human rights situation in China. In particular, the Australian media has published a series of reports regarding the situation in Hong Kong and the Xinjiang Uyghur Autonomous Region since 2019. The Morrison government has expressed deep concern over Hong Kong's National Security Law, saying that it infringes on various rights, including human rights, and on the high degree of autonomy guaranteed under the Sino-British Joint Declaration, and has openly criticized the Chinese government for its arbitrary detention of Uyghurs in Xinjiang.[80] In addition, the treatment of Australians in China has developed into a political issue. In August 2020, the Australian government announced that Cheng Lei, an Australian anchor on the Chinese state-run television network CGTN, was detained by Chinese authorities.[81] In September 2020, two Australian journalists in China sought protection from the Australian consulate in China and returned to Australia. According to reports, local police in China approached and questioned them about Cheng, and it is known that Australian diplomats in China advised the two to return to Australia.[82] Regarding this case, Foreign Minister Payne stated that freedom of the press should be protected and that it was disappointing there would not be Australian journalists present in China.

Australia presents the interpretation that the overall deterioration of its relations with China was a secondary effect of the intensifying great power competition between the United States and China. In his August and November 2020 speeches, Prime Minister Morrison noted that all of Australia's policy choices tend to be understood through "the lens of the strategic competition between China and the United States," and as a result, it "needlessly deteriorates" Australia-China relations.[83] In consideration of these issues, the Morrison government has made it clear that it does not agree with all of the Trump administration's policies on China, and has emphasized to China that Australia is not a pawn of the United States and is an "independent sovereign state." In fact, at the press conference of the Australia-U.S. Ministerial Consultations (AUSMIN) held in July 2020, Foreign Minister Payne indicated that Australia and the United States do not agree on all aspects of their policies on China, and clarified Australia's stance of maintaining a certain distance from the U.S.-China great power competition.[84] Despite these efforts, Australia has not succeeded in changing China's perception. From the "14 grievances (provisional name)," a document about Australia-China relations which the Chinese embassy in Canberra reportedly distributed to the Australian media in November 2020, it can be inferred that, as China sees it, Australia did America's "bidding" in criticizing China's COVID-19 response.[85] There are no signs that the deterioration of Australia-China relations will come to a halt as of the end of 2020. In light of the above, it can be assessed that so far, Australia's efforts to reassert its agency in the face of intensifying competition between the United States and China have not necessarily led to concrete results.

3. The Transition and Current State of Europe-China Relations: The Broadening Meaning of "Strategic Autonomy"

(1) The Beginning and Development of the Sino-European Relationship

The year 2020 was the 45th anniversary of diplomatic relations between the EU and China. Diplomatic ties were formally established on May 6, 1975, and since then, the relationship between the two sides has developed mainly in economic terms, especially trade relations. In 1998, the EU identified one of the priorities of its relations with China as: "engaging China further, through an upgraded political dialogue, in the international community."[86] In 2003, the EU established the aim to strengthen relations with China based on the "Comprehensive Strategic Partnership."[87] Ten years later, in 2013, the "EU-China 2020 Strategic Agenda for Cooperation" (hereinafter, "2020 Strategic Agenda") was unveiled.[88] The 2020 Strategic Agenda outlines a total of 92 cooperation initiatives in four priority target areas: "Peace and Security"; "Prosperity"; "Sustainable Development"; and "People-to-People Exchanges." The largest number of initiatives was allocated to "Trade and Investment" under "Prosperity," which includes economic cooperation. Thereafter, EU-China ties continued to develop mainly in the economic field, rather than in legal and political frameworks where there

Figure 1.1. Chinese FDI in the EU

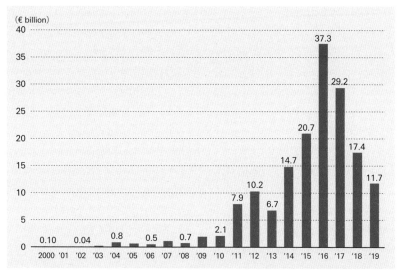

Source: Agatha Kratz, Mikko Huotari, Thilo Hanemann, and Rebecca Arcesati, "Chinese FDI in Europe: 2019 Update," Mercator Institute for China Studies and Rhodium Group (April 2020), 9.

are noted differences between the two sides in their perceptions of human rights and the rule of law.

Alongside the growth in trade between the EU and China, it is worth giving attention to the sharp increase in foreign direct investment (FDI) from China to the EU from around this time in 2010. This increase in China's outward FDI was initially driven by domestic factors. Since 1997, in addition to introducing foreign capital, China has set forth the "Go Global" policy that encourages Chinese companies to expand their overseas operations, articulated as a national strategy in 2001.[89] From then on, China gradually increased its outward FDI, and in around 2008, began to make outward FDI into mega markets, such as the United States and the EU.[90]

Notably, Chinese FDI in the EU has grown at a remarkable rate, increasing about 15-fold from 2008 to 2012, as seen in Figure 1.1. This is attributed to the global economic crisis in September 2008. Moreover, in Europe, the sovereign debt crisis from October 2009 worsened the fiscal situation. Despite the significant stagnation in global FDI activity during this period, Chinese FDI in the EU surged, as mentioned above. Against this backdrop, cooperation on investment was also given focus in the 2020 Strategic Agenda, and negotiations on the EU-China Comprehensive Agreement on Investment (CAI) were launched in 2014.

Sophie Meunier of Princeton University points out that the series of economic crises contributed to the increase in Chinese FDI in the EU.[91] The reason: China had the world's largest foreign exchange reserves and had the economic capacity to continue outward FDI, while the economic crisis originating in the United States made China aware of the need to diversify assets denominated mostly in dollars.[92] Based on these circumstances, it is believed that China proceeded to acquire real assets in Europe, such as infrastructure and corporations, which it considered to have high returns.

On the other hand, Meunier notes that political changes in the EU also contributed to the surge in China's outward FDI. First, following the economic crisis, European countries, including the United Kingdom, France, and Germany, all pinned hopes for Chinese FDI and began to appeal to China to invest in their countries. As a result, by around 2012, most EU countries had relaxed their regulations on inward FDI.[93] With regard to regulations on inward FDI, their implementation at the EU level was discussed from before, and in fact, the Treaty of Lisbon which entered into force in 2009 stipulated the regulations at the EU level.[94] However, as Chinese FDI became essential due to the economic crisis, European countries scrambled to ease regulations to attract FDI from China, and the implementation of inward FDI regulations at the EU level was delayed.[95]

Around Europe, the expansion of China-led economic cooperation with Central and Eastern European (CEE) countries (including the Baltic and Balkan countries) has attracted particular attention. Reeling from stagnant economies due to the spillover effects of the sovereign debt crisis, CEE countries were looking for partners with which to establish new economic ties to revitalize their economies. That was when China was flagged as a candidate partner.[96] The first summit between China and CEE countries was held in Poland in 2012, and since then, the framework has evolved into the 16+1 framework between China and 16 CEE countries (became 17+1 after Greece joined in 2019; hereinafter referred to as "17+1") aiming to promote trade and investment relations.

The deepening of EU-China ties can also be observed in other major initiatives. First, the Belt and Road Initiative (BRI) proposed by President Xi Jinping in 2013 extends westwards to Europe, and as is evident, the initiative became a core concept for the subsequent development of Sino-EU relations. In addition, the Asian Infrastructure Investment Bank (AIIB) for infrastructure investments in Asia, including projects related to BRI, was established under China's leadership, and European countries, including the United Kingdom, France, and Germany, announced their accession in March 2015. European countries were believed to have joined for good governance of the bank, including ensuring the transparency of loan procedures.[97] In that sense, Europe's membership in the AIIB can be seen as a continuation of the EU's efforts in the 1990s for "engaging China further...in the international community." On the other hand, Europe's participation can also be understood as a manifestation of the growing strength of the Chinese economy and the development of relations between China and the EU or European countries, which in turn facilitated or even compelled European countries to participate in the AIIB.

(2) Europe's Reconsideration of Its Stance toward China: The COVID-19 Factor

EU-China relations deepened during the global economic crisis in around 2010 on the one hand. On the other, it is a fact that caution prevailed on China's initiatives from their inception. For example, 12 of the 17 CEE countries in the 17+1 are EU member states, raising suspicions that China was pursuing a "divide and rule" strategy in Europe.[98] Similar to when European countries joined the AIIB, skepticism pervaded the narratives of the media, namely, that China aims to leverage the differences in countries' stances on building relations with China and encourage divisions in the EU. In contrast, the announcements made by the governments of CEE countries at the dawn of the 17+1 expressed favorable perceptions of China overall and visible intent to welcome opportunities that would arise from close cooperation with China.[99]

Nonetheless, the EU raised problems with 17+1 from the beginning. Anticipating the EU's doubts, China shared with it the draft joint communique of the China-CEE summit in 2012 when the 17+1 was formed. However, the EU still expressed opposition to the 17+1 becoming permanent or institutionalized.[100] The EU's concerns may stem from the following reasons. Firstly, China's current engagement in the CEE is ostensibly carried out in economic terms, with BRI being a leading means.[101] If CEE countries become economically dependent on China, this would inevitably increase China's political influence in the region which consists of many EU member states, and by extension, expand China's influence on the EU itself. Simply put, the EU has concerns that 17+1 would make CEE countries a "Trojan horse" for China to enlarge its political and economic presence in the region.

Secondly, the EU is concerned about not only China but also CEE countries. CEE countries have tended to disregard rules on competitive bidding, such as procurement in single markets. These are rules to be prioritized by EU member states when attracting business from China, and the stance of CEE countries was heightening the EU's caution.[102] Other reasons discussed include the fear of a "debt trap," where a country receives huge loans from China and has trouble repaying the debt and the creditor country applies diplomatic pressure on the debtor country. A leading example in Europe is the highway construction project in Montenegro, a candidate for EU membership.[103] However, some studies suggest it is too early to conclude that this case is a "debt trap," taking into account the financial situation and borrower liability.[104] In any event, it is a fact that not only the EU's member states but also member state candidates are becoming dependent on Chinese funding, and the EU has begun taking a more aggressive stance toward expanding membership to the Western Balkans.

In reality, the projects that China has committed to the 17+1 countries have not progressed as much as the CEE countries had expected, and many of the infrastructure projects in the region that China has financed are behind schedule or have not even begun construction work. The reasons for this situation are a combination of the following factors. First, several of the projects financed mainly by China may be in violation of EU regulations on procurement processes, requiring investigations and tenders.[105] It has also been pointed out that the original project plans themselves were unrealistic.[106] Furthermore, the expected Chinese FDI for the 17+1 countries has been limited, and the lack of progress is gradually becoming apparent.[107]

Chinese FDI in Europe is destined mainly for Western European countries. The countries themselves had favorable views toward the large increase in Chinese FDI in the first half of the 2010s.[108] By around 2016, however, when China's annual FDI in the EU reached €37.3 billion, investments tended to shift from infrastructure, which traditionally received FDI, to acquisitions of companies with advanced technologies. The acquisitions of KUKA, a manufacturer of industrial robots, and AIXTRON, a manufacturer of semiconductor deposition equipment, are often cited in this context. KUKA manufactures robots for military use in Europe and the United States, and the acquisition was agreed upon despite an investigation into the acquisition at one point. Conversely, the acquisition of AIXTRON by Fujian Grand Chip Investment Fund was blocked after intervention by the Barack Obama administration on the grounds that the technology may be used for military purposes.[109] Such expansion of Chinese outward FDI and changes in investment areas have raised concerns among European countries. China also worried about excessive capital outflows and imposed tighter control over outward FDI. Under these influences, China's FDI in Europe has been declining since 2017, as can be seen from Figure 1.1.[110]

As illustrated, China's use of economic instruments has generated political concerns. Given China's stance, the EU and its member states have recently showed a marked inclination to reconsider their stance toward China. In September 2017, the European Commission proposed the establishment of an EU-wide framework for screening FDI inflows, which had previously not made strides due to member states' conflicting stances toward China. The proposal warned that, if state-owned or government-controlled companies in third countries acquire European companies with advanced technologies, it would allow the countries to use such technologies, which could be harmful to the EU security and public order.[111] Subsequently, the establishment of an EU system for screening FDI was agreed upon in November 2018, and it entered into force as FDI Screening Regulation on April 10, 2019.

It can be said that Western Europe's wariness of China's political influence through its economic leverage, coupled with CEE's frustration with the lack of progress in Chinese economic support, gradually converged to the EU's reconsideration of its stance toward China. In April 2018, the EU ambassadors to China signed a document that contained criticism of BRI.[112] However, it was never made public, partly because the Hungarian ambassador alone refused to sign it.[113] In any case, it suggests that most EU member states have a negative view of BRI and China's growing political and economic clout. On the other hand, the EU indeed attaches importance to connectivity with Asia. In September 2018, it formulated a policy document called, "Connecting Europe and Asia: Building Blocks for an EU Strategy," which has since become known as the EU's Connectivity Strategy.[114] This strategy aims to contribute to connectivity between the two regions, including in the infrastructure, energy, and digital sectors. Nonetheless, the document unmistakably had China's BRI in mind.

Tensions in EU-China relations can also be observed at recent summits and in policy documents. For example, the 2016 EU-China summit failed to produce a joint statement of the summit for the first time due to significant differences, mainly over issues relating to the South China Sea and non-market economy status.[115] A similar situation occurred in the following year at the 19th EU-China summit. The failure to produce a joint statement for the second year in a row made the confrontation between the EU and China more conspicuous.[116]

Furthermore, in March 2019, the European Commission and the high representative of the Union for foreign affairs and security policy/vice president of the European Commission (hereinafter, "HR/VP") formulated a policy document on China entitled, "EU-China: A Strategic Outlook," presenting the view that the balance of "challenges and opportunities" offered by Sino-European relations is shifting.[117] It even noted that, while China is a "cooperation partner," it is an "economic competitor" and "systemic rival."[118] Zhang Ming, China's ambassador to the EU, argued against the term "systemic rival," saying it creates a worse impression than during the Cold War.[119] Put differently, some assess that China increasingly accepts that it is a competitor of the EU, though it emphasizes "healthy competition."[120] As demonstrated, the EU-China relationship has been in a state of tension since around the latter half of the 2010s.

This situation was spurred by the spread of COVID-19 in 2020 and China's subsequent response. The coronavirus took hold in Europe to the extent that by March, WHO said it was "now epicenter of the pandemic." However, the EU was initially unable to take effective measures against it. This was because the EU's authority over health services and medical care is limited to promoting cooperation among member states in the procurement of supplies, and the primary responsibility for response lies with the government of each member state.[121] Therefore, as the outbreak spread in member states, their governments were busy dealing with COVID-19 in their own countries, including France and Germany that temporarily banned the export of masks. Hence, it took time to achieve a coordinated response at the EU level. As a result, strong criticism erupted over the EU, especially in southern Europe where COVID-19 was spreading.

That was when China came forward to support the European countries. Even before the global outbreak of COVID-19, China had a large share of the global market for personal protective equipment (PPE), including masks and protective clothing. Already as of 2018, Chinese products accounted for 43% of the global PPE market, and 50% of the PPE distributed in the EU was imported from China.[122] In addition, since the pandemic began, China had expanded its domestic mask production capabilities 12-fold over the pre-pandemic level by the end of February 2020, with daily production reaching 116 million masks.[123] From February to March, Chinese PPE, which had become capable of further mass production, was sent to Europe, the epicenter of the pandemic. Furthermore, medical experts and others who had responded to the situation in Wuhan, where the virus spread earlier, were sent to Europe along with PPE.[124] The media prominently reported that China's so-called "mask diplomacy" was received favorably, especially in Italy and the Western Balkans which initially did not receive support from the EU.[125]

Contrary to China's motive, however, the perception of the country continued to deteriorate in Europe. The main reason given is China's hostile diplomatic stance toward the pandemic. China rejects criticism that concealment of information and other factors may have delayed its initial response in the early stages of the COVID-19 outbreak. Instead, China emphasizes that it is playing a constructive role, providing support to the international community. As demonstrated in the text posted by the Chinese embassy in France, China asserts that the spread of the coronavirus was a European blunder.[126] China's stance has resulted in a deterioration of sentiment toward China in the EU. HR/VP Josep Borrell condemned that China's support and narratives related to the pandemic in Europe are causing a rift in the EU, and stressed that it needs to prepare for a "struggle for influence" in the battle of narratives. President of the European Commission Ursula von der Leyen called attention to the fact that a number of EU countries have also provided support and urged caution in the narrative being shaped by China.[127]

(3) The Broadening Meaning of the EU's "Strategic Autonomy"

European Commissioner for Trade Phil Hogan stated that the EU needs to think about how to ensure its "strategic autonomy," recognizing that the EU faces the above-mentioned challenge of correcting the external dependence that has been elicited as a result of the COVID-19 crisis.[128] Moreover, autonomy in this context does not mean self-sufficiency and seems to be primarily concerned with reducing dependence on China. The commissioner referred to, for example, resilient supply chains based on diversification and strengthening strategic stockpiling.[129]

The "strategic autonomy" concept itself is not a new one and is a term that originally appeared in discourse on relations with the United States, especially in the field of security.[130] "Strategic autonomy" came into use in the EU due to its inability to deal with the conflict in the former Yugoslavia in the 1990s for institutional and capacity reasons. The EU recognized then that it needed capabilities to act autonomously. Moreover, the outbreak of the Iraq War in 2003 caused a rift in the U.S.-EU relationship, and the need for the EU's "strategic autonomy" became a subject of discussion once again. In the same year, the discussion paved the way for the realization of the European Security and Defence Policy (ESDP), the predecessor of the current Common Security and Defence Policy (CSDP).[131]

The United States did not oppose Europe having capabilities to take a more autonomous approach to security policy, although conditions were attached, such as avoiding duplication with the North Atlantic Treaty Organization (NATO). As a result, the debate on "strategic autonomy" between the United States and the EU, as well as even within the EU, fell into a temporary disarray. But as the U.S.-EU relationship recovered, the debate on "strategic autonomy" appeared to have settled down. However, this was only because it was difficult for European countries to adopt a unified security or defense industrial policy, and because CSDP and capability development had stagnated under defense spending cuts caused by the economic crisis and other factors. Meanwhile, in the United States, there were constant calls for European countries to develop self-reliance in defense.

The debate on "strategic autonomy" resurfaced in the EU in around 2016. The trigger was the release of the EU's strategy document, the "EU Global Strategy" (EUGS), in June 2016, which makes repeated references to the pursuit of "strategic autonomy."[132] Among its various definitions, Special Advisor to HR/VP Nathalie Tocci, who was in charge of drafting the EUGS, defines "strategic autonomy" as: "[t]he ability of the Union to decide autonomously and have the means to act upon its decisions."[133] Subsequently, the EUGS philosophy resulted in the launch of the EU's own security policy, the Permanent Structured

Cooperation (PESCO).

The following two variables, which occurred around the same time as the formulation of the EUGS, also helped to drive the EU's pursuit of "strategic autonomy." The first was the United Kingdom's withdrawal from the EU (Brexit). The United Kingdom was traditionally opposed to the EU's moves to pursue "strategic autonomy," and the country's decision to leave the EU inevitably increased the momentum for the pursuit of "strategic autonomy" enshrined in the EUGS. The second factor was the establishment of the Trump administration in the United States. As the Trump administration was initially critical of NATO, the EU could not fully trust the U.S. commitment, forcing them to pursue "strategic autonomy" as Plan B.[134] In addition, U.S.-European relations were still not outright favorable in light of the impact on NATO internal politics of the planned reduction of U.S. forces in Germany announced in June 2020.[135]

Rather than the security context, U.S.-EU relations deteriorated in practice under the Trump administration in areas such as trade and climate change where international cooperation is important. The Trump administration, a promoter of protectionist trade policies, did not participate in the negotiations on the Transatlantic Trade and Investment Partnership (TTIP) with the EU launched in 2013. Furthermore, tensions persisted, including trade frictions. On the issue of climate change, President Trump formally notified in November 2019 that the United States would withdraw from the Paris Agreement, an international framework that came into effect in 2016.[136] It is clear these policies of the Trump administration based on the America First doctrine sparked the deterioration of U.S.-European relations.

These upheavals in U.S.-European ties led to an emphasis on Sino-European cooperation in some areas. For example, shortly after the United States formally notified its withdrawal from the Paris Agreement, President Emmanuel Macron of France visited China. He and President Xi Jinping adopted a joint statement on coordinating efforts to address climate change, including the Paris Agreement, underscoring Europe-China cooperation.[137] At the EU-China summit, which failed to produce a joint statement in 2016 and 2017, the two sides reached an agreement to issue a joint statement that contains an anti-protectionism provision in 2018 and 2019. Such joint statements by the EU and China of recent years reveal their intention to resist the Trump administration's unilateralism in trade and climate change.[138] Thus, as the United States continues to put itself first and withdraws from international frameworks, China's aim seems to be to emphasize that it is Europe's true partner with shared values.[139]

Notwithstanding this, Commissioner Hogan urged in April that the EU needs to ensure "strategic autonomy" in light of the COVID-19 pandemic and the subsequent deterioration of relations with China, as was already mentioned. And in June, Commissioner Hogan reiterated the importance of autonomy via the concept of "open strategic autonomy."[140] This is a vague concept and may not sound attractive, as the commissioner admitted, but at the very least it shows that the EU is newly pursuing a diversified trade policy. The commissioner's speech also referred to the proposal for the €750 billion "Next Generation EU" recovery plan from COVID-19 that was agreed in July, and emphasized recovering the economy from the pandemic.[141] In short, the key points of "open strategic autonomy" going forward will be EU unity, represented by self-recovery through the EU's recovery instrument, and the revival of the economy through strengthened trade policies aimed at diversification.

In addition, the commissioner mentioned that "open strategic autonomy" is in line with the objectives of a "geopolitical" European Commission. "A geopolitical commission" was described by President von der Leyen in her pre-inauguration speech in September 2019 as a "a geopolitical Commission committed to sustainable policies," and is a term that has since come into vogue.[142] The president also mentioned building the EU's partnership with the United States and redefining its relations with an increasingly self-assertive China. The EU's stance to redefine its position in Sino-U.S. relations is evident in the EU's external policy in 2020.

For example, the 22nd EU-China summit was held online in June 2020. This was the first summit meeting held with China since the new EU leadership took office, including European Commission President von der Leyen. However, the meeting ended with little result and without the adoption of a joint statement. This can be attributed to differences between the EU and China around the coronavirus discourse and China's hardline diplomatic posture toward Europe.[143] In particular, China's decision at the end of May to enforce the Hong Kong National Security Law clearly factored into the hardened stance of the EU.

The leaders of China and 27 EU member states would have held a special meeting in Leipzig, Germany in September, had it not been for the COVID-19 outbreak, and may have signed the EU-China CAI under negotiations since 2014. Instead, an EU-China summit was held online in September. There were serious differences between the two sides concerning the pandemic and the situation in Hong Kong, and no real progress was made. Nonetheless, the EU and China sought to conclude the negotiations on the CAI by the end of the year and reached an agreement in principle on December 30, 2020.[144]

In terms of investment, the EU framework for screening of FDI, which entered into force in April 2019, became fully operational on October 11, 2020.[145] While the framework is not binding, Executive Vice-President of the European Commission Valdis Dombrovskis explained that the EU needs to work together in line with the framework if it is to achieve an "open strategic autonomy."[146]

European Council President Charles Michel (right) and European Commission President Ursula von der Leyen (left) who attended the 22nd EU-China summit held online (Pignatelli/ROPI via ZUMA Press/Kyodo News Images)

Having taken measures for inward FDI, the EU is likely to pursue a fairer investment and trade regime with China. In addition, the EU has agreed with the United States to commence a senior officials' dialogue on China issues. The EU's stance may reflect expectations for cooperation with the United States on policies toward China.

Apart from "open strategic autonomy," Europe has been

considering the concept of "digital strategic autonomy" as a region caught in the middle of the U.S.-China confrontation in the digital sector. This is a theme that had already begun to gain widespread recognition in Europe by around 2018 to 2019, when the U.S.-European rift on Huawei grew more serious. In the rollout of 5G networks, European countries determined that they ought to consider the use of Chinese products, which the United States advocate banning based on cybersecurity risks. These circumstances have reaffirmed Europe's vulnerability to "digital strategic autonomy," and discussions have unfolded on the need for Europe to retain its own digital capabilities.[147]

This issue has become even more contentious after the United States imposed additional sanctions on Huawei, including a tighter embargo, in May 2020, causing European countries to change their stances. Since July, European countries have shifted their policies to exclude or restrict Huawei from their 5G networks, make the screening process more rigorous seemingly with Huawei in mind, or give preferential treatment to European companies. This move started in the United Kingdom and France and has spread to Germany and Scandinavia.[148] The main underlying reason for this shift is the additional U.S. sanctions and the resulting technical issues. However, it may also be an outcome that took into account the European sentiment toward China, which has worsened as a result of the pandemic. If the United States and Europe remove Huawei, they will be relying primarily on two companies, Nokia and Ericsson, for 5G products. In fact, in October 2020, it was reported that the government of Belgium, where the EU and NATO are headquartered, decided to procure 5G-related products from the two companies.[149] Similar moves are expected to be seen in European countries in the future as well. If Europe pursues "digital strategic autonomy," it is anticipated to make Nokia and Ericsson the core suppliers for its 5G networks.

(4) The EU's Modus Operandi in U.S.-China Relations

Up to this point, this section has analyzed the EU's actions relating to U.S.-China relations from the perspectives of "open strategic autonomy" and "digital strategic autonomy" of recent years. Here, the EU's policy on China is outlined from the standpoint of foreign affairs and security, an essential area of the original "strategic autonomy" concept of the EU. As noted at the beginning of (3), the EU has traditionally continued to pursue "strategic autonomy" in its relations with the United States. However, this did not ultimately work. The reason is that the principle of unanimity is basically applied to decision-making in foreign affairs and security, despite the obvious significant differences in member states' perception of national interests and strategic cultures in this area. As a result, differences in vision, especially between the United Kingdom, which has left the EU, and France and Germany often led to the EU's foreign and security policy failing in significant situations.

And this is now being observed in the Europe-China relationship. The EU's joint statement condemning China's stance on the 2016 South China Sea arbitration award failed to materialize due to opposition from Hungary and Greece. Furthermore, opposition from Hungary prevented the EU from issuing a joint statement in response to the 2017 UN report on the human rights situation in China.[150] The idea of reviewing unanimous decision-making in foreign affairs and security has been discussed for some time. Recently, President von der Leyen reiterated that a review was needed, given the time that was required to decide on sanctions against Belarus.[151] The possibility of introducing EU Qualified Majority Voting (QMV) for foreign affairs and security decisions has been discussed in the past. However, it has not materialized because of the EU's tendency to emphasize unity in foreign policy, among other reasons. Even if QMV were introduced, the EU would still seek consensus, leaving difficulties such as coordinating with member states that oppose a decision. This issue will have a major impact on the fate of not only traditional "strategic autonomy" but also "open strategic autonomy" and "digital strategic autonomy," and future developments will be closely watched.

Based on the previous discussion, this chapter lastly examines how the EU's behavior amidst the U.S.-China confrontation can be understood. This section described that, since 2016, the EU's pursuit of "strategic autonomy" due to deteriorating U.S.-Europe relations led to the launch of EU security initiatives, such as PESCO. In terms of foreign policy, it explained that it resulted in highlighting cooperation with China with which the EU has established favorable economic relations since around 2010. These outcomes, at the same time, signify that economic powerhouse China has an inevitably larger degree of political influence on the EU. Accordingly, the EU's "strategic autonomy" unavoidably pertains not only to the United States but now also to China. In addition, disputes in areas where the EU cannot make concessions, including democracy and human rights, became more manifest in 2020 than ever before.

This format though is not a new one. In the past, the EU has gotten closer to China when the United States appeared to be positioning itself against multilateral cooperation. In particular, the EU-U.S. and EU-China relationships around 2003 were very similar to the relations after 2016. When the United States adopted a notably unilateralist stance during the Iraq War in 2003, the EU pursued "strategic autonomy" and realized its own CSDP, as was described above. In addition, in terms of its policy on China, as mentioned at the beginning of this section, the EU sought to strengthen its relations with China based on a "Comprehensive Strategic Partnership" in 2003, a move that some believe was the result of the EU and China joining hands in the face of the threat of U.S. unilateralism.[152] However, even at that time, the difference in perceptions between the EU and China regarding norms was already hindering the development of their relations.

The fundamental factor that nonetheless made EU-China cooperation possible is that they both implement foreign and security policies by observing the world through the prism of multipolarity or pluralization. Both the EU and China have promoted multipolarity in the post-Cold War world where the East-West bipolarity has eroded, and precisely this factor has made it possible for the EU and China to approach each other if the United States tended to adopt a unilateralist or America First approach. However, there is a structural problem: the development of EU-China relations will reach its limits when China's behavior seriously challenges EU norms. Even then, the EU can be understood as acting as a single pole, not necessarily as a U.S.-European bloc against China.

This attitude of the EU is exemplified in the recent comment by HR/VP Borrell: "in the European Union there is not apparent tendency towards a strategic rivalry that could lead to a kind of new 'Cold War.'"[153] Therefore, there is room for the EU and China to continue to cooperate depending on the area if the United States positions itself against multilateral cooperation.

While such similarities exist, there are also marked differences between the past and now. First, as was expressed in the "responsible stakeholder" speech in 2005, the United States at the time accepted China's growth, and simultaneously, expected China as a great power to contribute to international stability and security. This was similar to the EU's perception around that time of "engaging China further, through an upgraded political dialogue, in the international community." Both the United States and Europe still perceived that rising China could be integrated into the existing international order. Now, however, the confrontation between the United States and China is more intense, while the EU has decided not to join the new Cold War. It cannot be denied that their deep down view of China as a "systemic rival" has not been dispelled and has even gained greater traction.

Second, the composition of EU member states is different. Most of the states in the 17+1 became EU members after 2004. From this time, there have been concerns that increasing the number of member states could lead to a loss of speed and flexibility in the external actions of the EU, which requires security decisions to be made unanimously in principle. However, this arrangement may not have envisioned the penetration of Chinese influence into the member states of CEE. With such a situation emerging, the EU, which aims to expand its membership to the Balkans, will be sought to continue to pursue policies that balance expansion and unity. In addition, in terms of the composition of member states, the withdrawal of the United Kingdom from the EU has brought about changes. The United Kingdom's standing as a permanent member of the UN Security Council and its close relationship with the United States were no doubt important assets for EU diplomacy. In particular, with the Hong Kong issue becoming a matter of concern between the EU and China, it is clear that the withdrawal of the United Kingdom, which has historical ties with Hong Kong, was a major loss for the EU's diplomacy with Asia.

The third difference, related to the second point, is the engagement of European countries in the security of the Indo-Pacific. The United Kingdom has not formulated an official government strategy for the Indo-Pacific but is making strides in security cooperation with the Gulf States, Southeast Asia, and Japan. In the EU, France established its first policy document containing Indo-Pacific in the title in May 2018, Germany in September 2020, and the Netherlands in November 2020.[154] Furthermore, in June 2019, France formulated a strategy document named, "France's Defence Strategy in the Indo-Pacific." Where these documents are positioned and the format of the documents vary by country; however, at the very least, they reveal that European countries have showed an intention to engage in the Indo-Pacific with a certain vision and have begun to actually demonstrate readiness to dispatch assets to the region, representing a new trend of recent years.[155] In the meantime, the EU has not yet released a document on the Indo-Pacific, and its involvement in the region is concentrated in the Gulf States and off the coast of Somalia. The EU is expected to become more engaged through the above-mentioned connectivity strategy and the "EU Maritime Security Strategy" that enshrines the protection of freedom of navigation.[156]

Fourthly, the fundamental cause of the above differences lies in considerable variations in the degree of internationalization. This can be seen in a wide range of areas, such as trade and investment among the United States, China, and the EU as well as in the development of the digital sector and security linkages. As a consequence, the EU's concept of "strategic autonomy" has expanded to include "open strategic autonomy" and "digital strategic autonomy."

Needless to say, these changes from the past have made it difficult for the EU and European countries to find a simple balance between the United States and China in an era of great power competition. While the EU has said publicly that it will not join the U.S.-China confrontation, it likely has not been able to shake off its perception of China as a "systemic rival" either. Whether the U.S.-Europe relationship can be maintained on good terms and what kind of U.S.-Europe cooperation on China is possible will also depend on the relationship with the next U.S. administration.

At the time of this writing on December 31, 2020, preparations are under way for transitioning to the Joseph Biden administration to take office on January 20, 2021. In general, the Biden administration is expected to stand for multilateralism, including returning to the Paris Agreement. As for the U.S.-Europe relationship, momentum is building for the United States to withdraw the proposed troop reductions in Germany, coupled with expectations that the U.S.-Europe alliance will be strengthened through NATO. In terms of trade relations with the EU, it is speculated that the limited sectoral negotiations already under way will continue, even without returning to negotiations for comprehensive free trade agreements (FTAs), such as the TTIP. In anticipation of the incoming Biden administration, the EU formulated a document about its policy toward the United States on December 2 entitled, "A New EU-US Agenda for Global Change," which reaffirms the need for EU-U.S. cooperation on a wide range of areas, including climate change, trade, technology, and security.[157]

However, the document, while espousing the need to jointly deal with an increasingly assertive China, also noted that Europe and the United States have different ways of addressing this. Such differences had already begun to be pointed out before the Biden administration. For example, there are reports that U.S. officials criticized the EU-China CAI agreed upon in principle on December 30, noting that the accord could strengthen the state-led Chinese economy.[158] The EU has responded by claiming that the investment agreement with China does not interfere with EU-U.S. cooperation. Nonetheless, it cannot be denied that it underscored the subtle differences between Europe and the United States in their stance toward China, and that there was a problem of timing given how the CAI was reached just as the Biden administration was expected to restore U.S.-Europe relations. Furthermore, because Germany rushed to conclude the agreement, there were reportedly discrepancies between Germany and other EU member states skeptical of the accord. As such, the agreement also sheds light on the longstanding differences among European countries.[159]

The EU's posture can be understood in the context of its pursuit of "strategic autonomy" and related challenges in great power competition. Under the Trump administration, the extreme deterioration of Europe-U.S. relations at times put the spotlight on Europe-China relations. Under the Biden administration, the Europe-U.S. relationship may be restored, and opportunities for cooperation between the two sides may increase in relative terms. However, this does not necessarily mean that the EU will be in step with the United States, and it cannot be denied that the EU will give consideration to relations with China in some sectors. Whether this is a reflection of the EU's intention or the result of a compromise due to discrepancies among member states will depend on the situation. It is not realistic to eliminate differences in foreign and security policies among member states, which has been a longstanding problem. Nonetheless, it remains that "strategic autonomy" is a necessary means of achieving a delicate balance in great power competition, and for this purpose, the search for ways to minimize policy differences among member states is needed more than ever before.

NOTES

1)   Richard Haass, "The Pandemic Will Accelerate History Rather than Reshape It," *Foreign Affairs*, April 7, 2020.

2)   Richard Haass, "How a World Order Ends: And What Comes in Its Wake," *Foreign Affairs* 98, no. 1 (January/February 2019): 22.

3)   C. Raja Mohan, "Putting Sovereignty Back in Global Order: An Indian View," *Washington Quarterly* 43, no. 3 (2020): 81–98; *Times of India*, May 1, 2020; *India Express*, April 7, 2020.

4)   Japanese Political Science Association, ed., *Kiki no nihon gaiko: 1970 nendai (nenpo seijigaku)* [Japanese diplomacy in crisis: 1970s (The Annuals of Japanese Political Science Association)] (Tokyo: Iwanami Shoten, 1997).

5)   World Bank, "World Development Indicators (1960–2019)," World Bank website.

6)   [Japan] Defense Agency, *Defense of Japan 1979*, Part 1.

7)   Tanaka Akihiko, *Posuto modan no "kindai"* [Postmodern "modernity"] (Tokyo:

Chuokoron-Shinsha, 2020).

8) World Bank, "World Development Indicators (1960–2019)."

9) [U.S.] Director of Intelligence, Central Intelligence Agency, "A Comparison of the US and Soviet Economies: Evaluating the Performance of the Soviet System," SOV 85-10175 (October 1985).

10) *Buenos Aires Times*, August 7, 2020.

11) Organisation for Economic Co-operation and Development (OECD), "G20 GDP Showed a Strong Recovery in the Third Quarter of 2020, but Remained Below Pre-pandemic High" (December 14, 2020).

12) International Monetary Fund (IMF), "World Economic Outlook, October 2020: A Long and Difficult Ascent" (October 2020).

13) [U.S.] Department of State, "Update on U.S. Withdrawal from the World Health Organization" (September 3, 2020).

14) Reuters, September 23, 2020.

15) *Nikkei Shimbun*, September 8, 2020.

16) Ashley J. Tellis, "Overview: The Return of U.S.-China Strategic Competition," in *Strategic Asia 2020: U.S.-China Competition for Global Influence*, eds. Ashley J. Tellis, Alison Szalwinski, and Michael Wills (Washington, DC: The National Bureau of Asian Research, 2020), 1–43; Michael A. Witt, "Prepare for the U.S. and China to Decouple," *Harvard Business Review*, June 26, 2020; Carla Hobbs, ed., "Europe's Digital Sovereignty: From Rulemaker to Superpower in the Age of US-China Rivalry," European Council on Foreign Relations (July 30, 2020); Robert S. Ross, "It's Not a Cold War: Competition and Cooperation in US-China Relations," *China International Strategy Review* 2 (2020): 63–72.

17) Jonathan D. Pollack, "There Are No Winners in US-China Technology Divide," Brookings Institution (September 14, 2020); *Washington Post*, April 28, 2020.

18) Yan Xuetong, "Bipolar Rivalry in the Early Digital Age," *Chinese Journal of International Politics* 13, issue 3 (Autumn 2020): 313–341; Yan Xuetong, "A Bipolar World Is More Likely than a Unipolar or Multipolar One," *China-US Focus*, April 20, 2015.

19) Yuen Foong Khong, "Looking to 2020: Southeast Asian Countries to Choose between US and China," National University of Singapore (January 23, 2020).

20) Volker Perthes, "Dimensions of Strategic Rivalry: China, the United States and Europe's Place," in *Strategic Rivalry between United States and China: Causes, Trajectories, and Implications for Europe*, eds. Barbara Lippert and Volker Perthes (Berlin: German Institute for International and Security Affairs, April 2020), 5–8.

21) Morton A. Kaplan, *System and Process in International Politics* (New York: John Wiley & Sons, Inc., 1957), 23–36.

22) Bilahari Kausikan, "Why the Future Will Be Multipolar (and Why This Is Good News)," *Global Brief*, September 21, 2020.

23) Nakanishi Hiroshi, "Sogo anzen hoshoron no bunmyaku: Kenryoku seiji to sogo izon no kosaku" [The context of comprehensive security theory: The intersection of power politics and interdependence], in *Kiki no nihon gaiko*, 97–115.

24) Hosoya Yuichi, "Kokusai chitsujo no tenbo: 'Kyotsu no rieki to kachi' wa kano ka" [Prospects for international order: Are "common interests and values" possible?], in *Shorai no kokusai josei to nihon no gaiko: 20 nen teido mirai no shinario puranningu* [The international situation and Japan's diplomacy in the future: Scenario planning 20 years into the future], eds. Yamauchi Masayuki and Nakayama Toshihiro (Tokyo: Japan Institute of International Affairs, 2011), 7–22; Hosoya Yuichi, "Riberaru na kokusai chitsujo to nihon gaiko" [Liberal international order and Japanese diplomacy], *International Affairs* 690 (April 2020): 5–12.

25) Bruce W. Jentleson, "The Post-Trump World in Context: The US and the Northeast Asian Strategic Order," *Global Asia* 11, no. 4 (December 2016); Kuik Cheng-Chwee, "Hedging in Post-Pandemic Asia: What, How, and Why?" *The Asan Forum*, June 6, 2020; Korea National Diplomatic Academy, "The Post-Pandemic World: Reinventing Multilateralism amidst Geopolitical Rivalries" (August 31–September 1, 2020).

26) *Guardian*, May 18, 2020.

27) *New Zealand Herald*, July 10, 2020.

28) WHO, "More than 150 Countries Engaged in COVID-19 Vaccine Global Access Facility" (July 15, 2020).

29) The Asan Institute for Policy Studies, "[Asan Plenum 2019] Session I: 'ROK-U.S. Alliance,'" YouTube Video, 1:29:05, May 16, 2019, https://www.youtube.com/watch?v=uSnFvYb1cLk.

30) Congressional Research Service, *The Pacific Islands*, by Thomas Lum and Bruce Vaughn, IF11208 (May 10, 2019).

31) [Australia] Department of Defence, "Exercise Croix Du Sud 2014," Department of Defence website.

32) [France] Ministry for the Armed Forces, *France and Security in the Indo-Pacific*, 2018 edition (May 2019).

33) [U.S.] Department of the Interior, "Statement of Douglas Domenech, Assistant Secretary, Insular and International Affairs, Department of the Interior, before the Senate Committee on Energy and Natural Resources to Examine the United States'

Interests in the Freely Associated States" (July 23, 2019).

34) *U.S. Naval Institute (USNI) News*, October 22, 2020.

35) *Defence Connect*, April 1, 2020; New Zealand Government, *Strategic Defence Policy Statement 2018* (July 2018).

36) Marcus Hellyer, "The Cost of Defence 2020–2021. Part 1: ASPI 2020 Strategic Update Brief," Australian Strategic Policy Institute (August 12, 2020); World Bank, "GDP (current US$)—Australia," World Bank website.

37) Frank R. Beasley, "Problems of Federation in Australia," *Foreign Affairs* 13, no. 2 (January 1935): 328–338.

38) [Australia] Department of Defence, *Defence 2000: Our Future Defence Force* (2000).

39) [Australia] Department of Defence, "20th Anniversary INTERFET Reception: Timor-Leste" (September 21, 2019).

40) ABC News, August 29, 2019.

41) [Australia] Department of Defence, "Operation Anode," Department of Defence website.

42) Nautilus Institute for Security and Sustainability, "Pacific Patrol Boat Program," Nautilus Institute for Security and Sustainability website.

43) [Australia] Department of Defence, *Defending Australia in the Asia Pacific Century: Force 2030* (2009).

44) Nautilus Institute for Security and Sustainability, "Australian Government Rationale for RAMSI," Nautilus Institute for Security and Sustainability website.

45) Lowy Institute for International Policy, "Pacific Aid Map," Lowy Institute for International Policy website.

46) *Guardian*, September 20, 2019.

47) ABC News, April 19, 2018.

48) Interview by author, Canberra, September 2018 and February 2020.

49) Lowy Institute for International Policy, "Pacific Aid Map."

50) [Australia] Prime Minister, Minister for Foreign Affairs, and Minister for Defence, "Strengthening Australia's Commitment to the Pacific" (November 8, 2018).

51) ABC News, July 18, 2018.

52) [Australia] Department of Foreign Affairs and Trade, "Tropical Cyclone Harold," Department of Foreign Affairs and Trade website.

53) Goroku Tsuyoshi, "Furansu no boei anzen hosho kyoryoku: Sekaidai no gunji nettowaaku wo dodai to shita kiki kanri" [Defense and security cooperation of France: Crisis management founded on the world's largest military network], Sasakawa Peace Foundation (2018).

54) *Sydney Morning Herald*, April 10, 2018.

55) *Islands Business*, May 8, 2019.

56) *Sydney Morning Herald*, March 10, 2020.

57) Qin Sheng, "Zhongguo yu taipingyang daoguo xieshou dazao 'kangyi zhi lu'" [China and Pacific Island countries join hands to carve out a "path for combating the epidemic"], *World Affairs* no. 22 (November 16, 2020): 64.

58) [Australia] Department of Foreign Affairs and Trade, *Partnerships for Recovery: Australia's COVID-19 Development Response* (May 2020).

59) [Australia] Department of Foreign Affairs and Trade, "Australia Stepping-up to Address COVID-19 in the Pacific," Department of Foreign Affairs and Trade website.

60) [U.S.] Department of State, "U.S. Engagement in the Pacific Islands: 2020 Pacific Pledge, Fact Sheet" (October 1, 2020).

61) *Nikkei Asian Review*, October 28, 2020; *Offshore Energy*, May 11, 2020.

62) [U.S.] Embassy in Fiji, Kiribati, Nauru, Tonga, and Tuvalu, "Remarks by Sandra Oudkirk, Deputy Assistant Secretary of State for Australia, New Zealand and the Pacific Islands, U.S.-Taiwan Pacific Islands Dialogue" (October 7, 2019).

63) ABC News, June 3, 2019.

64) [Australia] Minister for Foreign Affairs, "Interview with David Speers, ABC Insiders" (April 19, 2020).

65) ABC News, April 28, 2020.

66) Tony Walker, "China-Australia Relations Hit New Low in Spat over Handling of Coronavirus," *Conversation*, April 28, 2020.

67) *Guardian*, May 19, 2020.

68) ABC News, June 8 and June 9, 2020.

69) Budget Direct, "Australian Tourism Statistics 2020," Budget Direct website.

70) Tourism Australia, "International Tourism Snapshot as at 31 March 2019."

71) [Australia] Department of Education, Skills and Employment, "International Student Data Monthly Summary" (December 2019).

72) *Sydney Morning Herald*, November 3, 2020.

73) Ibid.

74) *Guardian News*, June 14, 2020.

75) ABC News, June 26, 2020.

76) ABC News, September 15, 2020.

77) Consulate General of the People's Republic of China in Sydney, "Australian Agents Raid Chinese Journalists' Residences, Seize Computers 'in Violation of Legitimate Rights': Source" (September 9, 2020). First published in *Global Times* on September 8,

2020.

78) ABC News, November 5, 2020.

79) Ibid.

80) [Australia] Minister for Foreign Affairs, "Statement on Hong Kong" (August 10, 2020); *Guardian*, November 17, 2019.

81) ABC News, August 31, 2020.

82) BBC News, September 8, 2020.

83) [Australia] Prime Minister, "UK Policy Exchange Virtual Address" (November 23, 2020); Prime Minister of Australia, "Q&A, Aspen Security Forum: Transcript" (August 5, 2020).

84) [Australia] Minister for Foreign Affairs and Trade, "Australia-United States Ministerial Consultations (AUSMIN): Joint Transcript, E&OE" (July 29, 2020).

85) *Sydney Morning Herald*, November 18, 2020.

86) Commission of the European Communities, *Building a Comprehensive Partnership with China* (March 25, 1998), 4.

87) European Commission, "EU-China: Commission Adopts New Strategy for a Maturing Partnership" (September 10, 2003).

88) European Commission, *EU-China 2020 Strategic Agenda for Cooperation* (November 23, 2013).

89) Kamata Fumihiko, "Chugoku kigyo no kaigai shinshutsu: 'Zouchuqu' senryaku no rinen to jissai" [Overseas expansion of Chinese companies: The "Go Global" strategy philosophy and practice], in *Gijutsu to bunka ni yoru nihon no saisei: Infura, kontentsu to no kaigai tenkai* [Japan's revitalization through technology and culture: Overseas promotion of infrastructure and contents], ed. Research and Legislative Reference Bureau, National Diet Library (Tokyo: National Diet Library, 2012), 217–218.

90) David Shambaugh, *China Goes Global: The Partial Power* (New York: Oxford University Press, 2013), 174–183.

91) This section's information related to Chinese FDI in the EU (up to 2014) draws mainly on: Sophie Meunier, "'Beggers Can't Be Choosers': The European Crisis and Chinese Direct Investment in the European Union," *Journal of European Integration* 36, no. 3 (March 2014): 283–302.

92) Ibid., 292–293.

93) Ibid., 297.

94) Sophie Meunier, "Integration by Stealth: How the European Union Gained Competence over Foreign Direct Investment," *Journal of Common Market Studies* 55, no. 3 (January 2017): 593–610.

95)   Sophie Meunier, "Divide and Conquer? China and the Cacophony of Foreign Investment Rules in the EU," *Journal of European Public Policy* 21, no. 7 (June 2014): 996–1016.

96)   Richard Turcsányi, "Central and Eastern Europe's Courtship with China: Trojan Horse within the EU?" *EU-Asia at a Glance*, European Institute for Asian Studies (January 2014).

97)   Deutsche Welle (DW), March 18, 2015.

98)   European Parliament Research Service, *One Belt, One Road (OBOR): China's Regional Integration Initiative*, by Gisela Grieger (July 2016), 10.

99)   Dragan Pavlićević, "A Power Shift Underway in Europe? China's Relationship with Central and Eastern Europe under the Belt and Road Initiative," in *Mapping China's 'One Belt One Road' Initiative*, ed. Li Xing (London: Palgrave Macmillan, 2018), 251–252.

100) Masuda Masayuki, "China's Eurasian Diplomacy: Regionalism, Balancing, and Pragmatism," in *NIDS China Security Report 2020: China Goes to Eurasia*, ed. National Institute for Defense Studies (NIDS) (Tokyo: NIDS, 2019), 17.

101) Sijbren de Jong, Willem Th. Oosterveld, Michel Roelen, Katharine Klacansky, Agne Sileikaite, and Rianne Siebenga, "A Road to Riches or a Road to Ruin? The Geo-economic Implications of China's New Silk Road," The Hague Centre for Strategic Studies (August 15, 2017), 27.

102) Higashino Atsuko, "Yooroppa to ittai ichiro: Kyoi ninshiki, rakutan, kitai no kyozon" [Belt and Road Initiative (BRI) and Europe: Sense of threat, disappointment, and expectation], *The Journal of International Security* 47, no. 1 (June 2019): 38.

103) IMF, "Motenegro: 2014 Article IV COnsulation Staff — Staff Report; Press Release; and Statement by the Executive Director for Montenegro," IMF Country Reports, no. 15/26, (February 2015).

104) Austin Doehler, "How China Challenges the EU in the Western Balkans," *Diplomat*, September 25, 2019; Tsuchida Yosuke, "Ittai ichiro to chutoo keizai: Monteneguro no kosoku doro kensetsu keikaku no jirei kenkyu" [The Belt and Road Initiative & Central Eastern Europe: The case study of highway project in Montenegro], *Russian and East European Studies* 48 (2019): 41–54.

105) Richard Q. Turcsányi, "China and the Frustrated Region: Central and Eastern Europe's Repeating Troubles with Great Powers," *China Report* 56, no. 1 (February 2020): 69; Dragan Pavlićević, "'China Threat' and 'China Opportunity': Politics of Dreams and Fears in China-Central and Eastern European Relations," *Journal of Contemporary China* 27, no. 113 (May 2018): 701.

106) Andreea Budeanu, "The '16+1' Platform: China's Opportunities for Central and Eastern

Europe," *Asia Focus*, Institut de Relations Internationales et Stratégiques (October 2018), 12.

107) Turcsányi, "China and the Frustrated Region," 66–67.

108) Agatha Kratz, Mikko Huotari, Thilo Hanemann, and Rebecca Arcesati, "Chinese FDI in Europe: 2019 Update," *Merics Paper on China*, Mercator Institute for China Studies (MERICS) and Rhodium Group (April 2020), 10.

109) Bas Hooijmaaijers, "Blackening Skies for Chinese Investment in the EU?" *Journal of Chinese Political Science* 24 (February 2019): 451–470.

110) Tamai Yoshino, "Henyo suru chugoku no taigai chokusetsu toshi" [Transformation of China's foreign direct investment], *Mizuho Insight*, Mizuho Research Institute (March 4, 2020), 4.

111) European Commission, "State of the Union 2017 – Trade Package: European Commission Proposes Framework for Screening of Foreign Direct Investments" (September 14, 2017).

112) *Handelsblatt*, April 17, 2018.

113) Steven Blockmans and Weinian Hu, "Systemic Rivalry and Balancing Interests: Chinese Investment Meets EU Law on the Belt and Road," *CEPS Policy Insights*, Centre for European Policy Group (CEPS) (March 21, 2019), 32.

114) European Commission and High Representative of the Union for Foreign Affairs and Security Policy, *Connecting Europe and Asia: Building Blocks for an EU Strategy* (September 19, 2018).

115) Hayashi Daisuke, "Oshu no chugoku ninshiki to taichugoku seisaku wo meguru kessoku to bundan" [Europe's perception of China and unity and division in its China policy], in *Chugoku no taigai seisaku to shogaikoku no taichu seisaku* [China's Foreign Policy and Other Countries' China Policies], ed. Japan Institute of International Affairs (JIIA) (Tokyo: JIIA, 2020), 294.

116) Ibid.

117) European Commission, *EU-China: A Strategic Outlook* (March 12, 2019).

118) Ibid.

119) *Politico EU*, April 8, 2019.

120) Matthias Hackler, "Rapprochement amid Readjustment: How China Sees Issues and Trends in its Changing Relationship with the EU," *Asia Europe Journal* 18 (May 2020): 253.

121) The Treaty on the Functioning of the European Union, Title XIV Public Health, Article 168.

122) Chad P. Bown, "COVID-19: China's Exports of Medical Supplies Provide a Ray of

Hope," *Trade and Investment Policy Watch*, Peterson Institute for International Economics (March 26, 2020).

123) Jiji Press, March 3, 2020.

124) Sylvain Kahn and Estelle Prin, "In the Time of COVID-19 China's Mask Has Fallen with Regard to Europe," *European Issues 569*, Fondation Robert Schuman (September 8, 2020); Raj Verma, "China's 'Mask Diplomacy' to Change the COVID-19 Narrative in Europe," *Asia Europe Journal* 18 (May 2020): 206.

125) Brian Wong, "China's Mask Diplomacy," *Diplomat*, March 25, 2020.

126) Yamaguchi Shinji, "Chugoku no tatakau gaikokan no taito?" [The rise of Chinese warrior diplomats?], *NIDS Commentary* 116, NIDS (May 26, 2020), 1–2.

127) Verma, "China's 'Mask Diplomacy' to Change the COVID-19 Narrative in Europe," 208.

128) European Commission, "Introductory Statement by Commissioner Phil Hogan at Informal Meeting of EU Trade Ministers" (April 16, 2020).

129) Ibid.

130) The discussion on "strategic autonomy" in U.S.-Europe relations is based on the following: Tanaka Ryosuke, "Kiki kanri to noryoku kojo ni okeru EU eikoku kankei: Buregujittogo no oshu no 'senryakuteki jiritsu' no yukue" [EU-UK relations in crisis management and capability development: European "strategic autonomy" after Brexit], *Security & Strategy* 1, no. 1 (August 2020): 83–100.

131) Daniel Fiott, "Strategic Autonomy: Towards 'European Sovereignty' in Defence?" *Brief Issue*, European Union Institute for Security Studies (November 30, 2018), 1.

132) European External Action Service (EEAS), *Shared Vision, Common Action: A Stronger Europe; A Global Strategy for the European Union's Foreign and Security Policy* (June 2016).

133) Nathalie Tocci, "Interview with Nathalie Tocci on the Global Strategy for the European Union's Foreign and Security Policy," *International Spectator* 51, no. 3 (October 2016): 3.

134) Margriet Drent, "European Strategic Autonomy: Going It Alone?" *Clingendael Policy Brief*, The Netherlands Institute of International Relations (August 8, 2018), 4.

135) Judy Dempsey, "Judy Asks: Will U.S. Troop Pullouts Accelerate European Defense Integration?" Carnegie Europe (June 11, 2020).

136) *Guardian*, November 5, 2019.

137) [France] Ministry for Europe and Foreign Affairs, "Beijing Call for Biodiversity Conservation and Climate Change" (November 6, 2019).

138) A number of publications make this point. For example, Andrew Cottey, "Europe and

China's Sea Disputes: Between Normative Politics, Power Balancing and Acquiescence,"
European Security 28, no. 4 (2019): 480–481; Stewart M. Patrick and Ashley Feng,
"Trading Places: How the EU-China Summit Underlined U.S. Isolationism in Trade
under Trump," Council on Foreign Relations (July 19, 2018).

139) Tsuruoka Michito, "Beio kankei no tenkai to nihon: Henyo suru nichibeio kankei
no dainamizumu" [The evolution of U.S.-Europe relations and Japan: The changing
dynamism of Japan-U.S.-Europe relations], *International Affairs* 688 (January/
February 2020): 35.

140) European Commission, "Speech by Commissioner Phil Hogan at Launch of Public
Consultation for EU Trade Policy Review – Hosted by EUI Florence" (June 16, 2020).

141) Ibid.

142) European Commission, "The von der Leyen Commission: For a Union that Strives for
More" (September 10, 2019).

143) Suzana Elena Anghel, "Outcome of EU-China Video-Summit of 22 June 2020,"
European Parliamentary Research Service Blog, European Parliamentary Research
Service (July 30, 2020).

144) European Commission, "EU and China Reach Agreement in Principle on Investment"
(December 30, 2020).

145) European Commission, "EU Foreign Investment Screening Mechanism Becomes Fully
Operational" (October 9, 2020).

146) Ibid.

147) European Political Strategy Centre, "Rethinking Strategic Autonomy in the Digital
Age," *EPSC Strategic Notes* (July 2019).

148) Shannon Tiezzi, "Sweden Becomes Latest – and Among Most Forceful – to Ban Huawei
from 5G," *Diplomat*, October 21, 2020.

149) Reuters, October 9, 2020.

150) Leonard Schuette, "Should the EU Make Foreign Policy Decisions by Majority Voting?"
Policy Brief, Centre for European Reform (May 15, 2019).

151) European Commission, "State of the Union Address by President von der Leyen at the
European Parliament Plenary" (September 16, 2020).

152) Richard Maher, "The Elusive EU-China Strategic Partnership," *International Affairs*
92, no. 4 (2016): 961.

153) EEAS, "China, the United States and Us" (July 31, 2020).

154) [France] Ministry for the Armed Forces, *France and Security in the Indo-Pacific* (May
2018); [Germany] Federal Government, *Policy Guidelines for the Indo-Pacific Region*
(September 2020).

155) As of the end of December 2020, the format of the Indo-Pacific documents formulated by European differs as follows. The French documents are a pamphlet and a strategic document prepared by the Ministry for the Armed Forces. Germany's is a government document approved by the cabinet. The Netherlands' is a document attached to a letter from the Minister of Foreign Affairs to the parliament.

156) Giulia Iuppa, "An 'Indo-Pacific' Outlook for the European Union," *Briefing Paper*, European Institute for Asian Studies (October 2020).

157) European Commission, *A New EU-US Agenda for Global Change* (December 2, 2020).

158) *Wall Street Journal*, December 31, 2020.

159) *Politico EU*, December 29, 2020.

Chapter 2

China

The Xi Administration's Accelerating Hardline Stance
due to COVID-19

IIDA Masafumi

DF-26 anti-ship
ballistic missiles of
the PLA (Beijing,
October 2019)
(Kyodo News)

Summary

The explosive outbreak of the novel coronavirus disease (COVID-19) in Wuhan, Hubei Province infected and killed many people and fueled economic stagnation, bringing to the fore the public's dissatisfaction with the Xi Jinping leadership. In response, the Xi government sought to resume economic activities and at the same time tighten control over society to weather the situation. President Xi further expanded his political authority following the fifth plenary session of the 19th Chinese Communist Party (CCP) Central Committee.

As it tightened its control, the Xi leadership directed its hardline stance also at Hong Kong and Taiwan. In Hong Kong, the Xi government imposed the Hong Kong national security law, hollowed out "one country, two systems" that promised a high degree of autonomy to Hong Kong, and used force to silence the Hong Kong people's calls for freedom and democracy. In Taiwan, President Tsai Ing-wen who rejects the "One China" principle demanded by China was reelected, and Taiwan's successful response to the COVID-19 pandemic elevated its reputation in the international community. In addition, the United States strengthened its relations with Taiwan by sending high-ranking government officials and selling many weapons to the island. China responded with strong intimidation tactics, stepping up military drills in waters and the airspace around Taiwan.

The Xi government took a hardline stance toward other countries as well. While relations between China and the United States had already been deteriorating, criticism of each other intensified over responsibility for the pandemic, raising the level of U.S.-China confrontations to that of "New Cold War." China's hardline diplomatic stance was also directed at Australia and India, increasing the alarm of many countries, including European countries, toward China.

Amid the COVID-19 crisis, the People's Liberation Army (PLA) played a role in promoting vaccine development and providing assistance to countries, along with sending medical personnel and transporting medical supplies. At the same time, the PLA ramped up exercises in the South China Sea, including firing anti-ship ballistic missiles, and strengthened vessel forays into the Pacific with a view to countering the U.S. Forces. Furthermore, China put more pressure on Japan, intensifying the activities of China Coast Guard (CCG) vessels in the waters surrounding the Senkaku Islands, an inherent territory of Japan, and approaching Japanese fishing vessels in Japanese territorial waters.

1. The Xi Government's Heightened Anxiety amidst COVID-19

(1) The Regime Draws Increasing Criticism due to the Pandemic

The year 2020 started out with a nightmare for China. In January, there was an explosive outbreak of COVID-19 centered in Wuhan, Hubei Province. It not only spread across China but also triggered a pandemic globally in Asia, Europe, America, and other parts of the world. In China, more than 96,600 people were infected, and the death toll exceeded 4,700 as of the end of 2020,[1] leaving a devastating impact on Chinese society. As discussed later, the global spread of the coronavirus also led to a deterioration in China's relations with the United States and other Western industrialized countries.

In response to the COVID-19 pandemic in Wuhan, President Xi Jinping instructed relevant departments on January 20 to focus efforts on curbing infection and release information on infections in a timely manner. On the same day, Premier Li Keqiang held a State Council executive meeting, where the following was announced: relevant departments would study countermeasures; the Wuhan municipal government would enforce quarantine measures; efforts would be made for the treatment of patients and prevention of infection among healthcare workers; information would be released appropriately; and research on the virus would be bolstered. On January 23, the Xi government decided to effectively seal off Wuhan by suspending all public transportation connecting the city to other parts of the country and prohibiting people from entering or leaving Wuhan. Nonetheless, COVID-19 cases surged through mid-February under the city's lockdown, and the number of deaths increased correspondingly. According to an official announcement of the Wuhan municipal government, there were 49,122 cases and 2,195 deaths as of the end of February.[2]

As the epidemiological situation in Wuhan became more serious and the virus spread to other cities including Beijing, the people became increasingly dissatisfied with the COVID-19 responses taken by local governments and the Xi Jinping leadership. Local authorities were particularly criticized for not taking immediate measures despite confirming cases of pneumonia caused by COVID-19, and even trying to conceal this information. According to an official announcement of the Chinese government, the Wuhan municipal government had

"送别李文亮!" [Farewell Li Wenliang!] is written in snow to mourn the death of Li Wenliang (Beijing, February 2020) (Kyodo News)

confirmed cases of viral pneumonia of unknown cause as of December 27, 2019.[3] However, the municipal government did not take proactive measures to prevent infection and failed to disseminate accurate information on the epidemiological situation by January 20, when President Xi Jinping gave his instructions. In addition, it was discovered that the public security authorities of Wuhan had issued a reprimand against a doctor who posted a message on social media, warning about the spread of pneumonia due to COVID-19. Dr. Li Wenliang of the Central Hospital of Wuhan learned about the several cases of pneumonia caused by COVID-19 in Wuhan and posted a message on WeChat on December 30, 2019 to alert fellow doctors. In response, the Wuhan Public Security Bureau summoned Dr. Li to a police station on January 3, 2020 for spreading false rumors and made him sign a letter of admonition.

Later, this fact came to light, and on February 7, Dr. Li died after contracting COVID-19. Following his death, an outpouring of condolences for Dr. Li and severe criticism of the authorities' cover-up circulated primarily on the Internet. "I think there should be more than one voice in a healthy society," Dr. Li is said to have stated before his death.[4] It brought to the fore dissatisfaction with the strict control of speech by the CCP government. A letter signed by hundreds of university professors, lawyers, and others was disclosed; it advocated that the spread of pneumonia due to COVID-19 was a man-made disaster resulting from restrictions on free speech.[5] With criticism rising, the Xi government announced that the National Supervisory Commission would investigate Wuhan's response to Dr. Li. The findings of the investigation, released on March 19, concluded that the Wuhan Public Security Bureau's reprimand against Dr. Li was unjustified and called on the Wuhan municipal government to withdraw the reprimand and hold those involved accountable.[6] On April 2, the Hubei provincial government announced its decision to confer Dr. Li the title of "advanced individual" and designate him a martyr for his sacrifice in dealing with COVID-19.[7]

Furthermore, the worsening of the pandemic prompted calls for President Xi to be held responsible. In early February, Professor Xu Zhangrun of Tsinghua University published an article criticizing that the tighter control of speech by the Xi government blocked out society's warnings against the growing epidemic and resulted in the spread of COVID-19. Professor Xu strongly criticized the concentration of power in the hands of the "Leader." He called for achieving freedom of speech by ending state control of the press and monitoring of the Internet, and for respecting the political rights of the people, including holding universal suffrage.[8] Ren Zhiqiang, a prominent businessman whose father was a senior official of the CCP during the revolutionary era, followed suit by publishing an essay in late February. Ren ridiculed President Xi for concentrating power in his hands, likening him to an emperor clinging to power, and criticized that the "emperor's" disregard for the interests of the people was a factor in the spread of COVID-19. He stressed that freedom of speech must be established in China and hoped that a movement for reform emerges from within the CCP.[9]

The spread of COVID-19 took a heavy toll on the Chinese economy. With people's movements restricted, consumption fell sharply, factories shut down, and retail stores and restaurants ceased operations. Due to the significant economic slowdown in society, China's economic growth rate in the first quarter of 2020 decreased 6.8% year-on-year. This, in turn, has put at risk the achievement of China's vision to "comprehensively build a moderately prosperous society" by doubling the gross domestic product (GDP) in 10 years and eliminating absolute poverty—targets for 2020 that were widely touted by the Xi Jinping leadership. Overall, the explosive outbreak of COVID-19 in China has undermined President Xi's political authority, raised society's doubts over the one-party rule of the CCP, and stalled economic growth, presenting a major threat to President Xi and his leadership.

(2) The Xi Leadership's Attempt to Regain Control

With his grip on power under threat, President Xi Jinping began to take actions in February to turn the situation around. On February 10, President Xi visited Anhuali Community and Capital Medical University Hospital in Beijing to provide on-site guidance for the first time since the pandemic became serious. On January 25, the CCP established the leading group of the CCP Central Committee on the response to the novel coronavirus outbreak, and Premier Li Keqiang was appointed as its head. On January 27, Premier Li visited Wuhan to offer encouragement to healthcare workers who were treating patients at hospitals and to give instructions on infection control. Since then, Premier Li frequently presided over meetings of the leading group and remained at the forefront of the response to COVID-19. On the other hand, President Xi rarely demonstrated initiative in tackling COVID-19, raising criticism over his lack of proactive actions. It is thought that President Xi provided on-site guidance in an attempt to counter these criticisms, albeit the disease being under control in Beijing.

The Xi Jinping leadership successively ousted those who were in charge in Hubei Province and Wuhan, which bore the brunt of the COVID-19 cases. The director of the Hubei Province Health Commission was dismissed on February 11. Jiang Chaoliang, secretary of the CCP Hubei Provincial Committee, and Ma Guoqiang, secretary of the CCP Wuhan Municipal Committee, were dismissed on February 13. It is believed that these dismissals were made to alleviate local residents' dissatisfaction that heightened due to the pandemic. They were also aimed at blaming the inadequate COVID-19 countermeasures on local governments to deflect criticism away from President Xi and his leadership. Jiang Chaoliang was replaced by Shanghai mayor Ying Yong, who had worked under President Xi when he was secretary of the CCP Zhejiang Provincial Committee. This appointment simultaneously strengthened President Xi's political influence in Hubei Province.

Alongside preventing the spread of COVID-19, President Xi began to put emphasis on resuming economic activities. During his on-site guidance in Beijing, President Xi noted, "We need to make greater efforts to raise the level of economic activities, minimize the impact of the epidemic on the economy, and reach this year's goals and tasks of economic and social development," stressing, "The resumption of operations and production by enterprises and businesses should be actively promoted." In his remarks at a meeting of the Standing Committee of the Political Bureau of the CCP Central Committee held on February 12, President Xi underscored "striving to achieve this year's economic and social development goals and tasks." Based on these remarks, the Standing Committee meeting indicated that China would endeavor to minimize the impact of COVID-19, maintain stable economic performance and social stability, and realize the goals and tasks set by the CCP Central Committee.[10] In quickly resuming economic activities, President Xi's aim was likely to restore and strengthen his damaged political authority by overcoming the economic downturn and achieving his economic targets.

Furthermore, President Xi began to assert his leadership in combatting COVID-19. The February 16 issue of the CCP theoretical journal, *Qiushi*, published the full text of the speech by General Secretary Xi at the February 3 meeting of the Standing Committee. At the outset, General Secretary Xi reportedly stated, "When I presided over the meeting of the Standing Committee of the Political Bureau of the CCP Central Committee on January 7 after the outbreak of COVID-19 pneumonia in Wuhan, I issued instructions on responding to the pneumonia."[11] President Xi stressed that he had given instructions on tackling COVID-19 almost two weeks before January 20, when he was thought to have given his first instructions. At the meeting of the Standing Committee held on February 21, General Secretary Xi noted that he had personally directed the work and made arrangements for the measures to prevent the spread of the novel coronavirus.[12] It was emphasized on various occasions thereafter that President Xi "personally directed" the response to COVID-19.

At a meeting held on February 23, President Xi stated, "I have been giving unremitting attention to controlling COVID-19, issuing verbal and written instructions daily." He pointed out that there had been a turnaround in the COVID-19 situation and that the measures to curb infection were delivering outcomes. President Xi contended that such results "have once again demonstrated the notable advantages of the leadership of the CCP and the system of socialism with Chinese characteristics."[13] In short, President Xi underscored his leadership in the fight against the pandemic and claimed that the achievements proved the superiority of the current system of CCP governance. Though the explosive outbreak of COVID-19 gave momentum to criticism of the governance system of President Xi and the CCP, the developments in mid-February indicate that the Xi leadership had begun to recover from the backlash. Subsequently, the number of new cases centered in Wuhan began to decline, and spread of the virus was no longer observed across the country. On March 10, President Xi visited Wuhan, gave instructions on infection control, and comforted hospitalized patients and healthcare workers. On April 8, the lockdown of Wuhan was lifted.

The Xi Jinping leadership tightened control over speech in an effort to contain criticism. In July, Professor Xu Zhangrun of Tsinghua University was detained by public security authorities. Despite Professor Xu's release a week later, Tsinghua University decided to dismiss him. That same month, the Commission for Discipline Inspection of Beijing's Xicheng District stripped Ren Zhiqiang of his party membership, citing, among other reasons, his "failure to maintain unity with the CCP Central Committee on important issues of principle."[14] Ren was later indicted on charges of corruption, and he was sentenced to 18 years in prison on September 22. The Xi Jinping leadership sought to overcome the social dissatisfaction that manifested amidst the pandemic by highlighting the strong leadership of President Xi and the superiority of the socialist system led by the CCP, in addition to further tightening its control over society.

(3) Xi's Ever-growing Political Authority

China has not seen a large-scale spread of the coronavirus since the lifting of Wuhan's lockdown in April, although clusters have occurred in some cities. The Chinese government focused on resuming and strengthening economic activities by introducing major fiscal stimulus packages and support measures for small and medium-sized enterprises. As a result, China's economic growth rate rebounded by 3.2% in the second quarter of 2020 and 4.9% in the third quarter compared to the previous year. In 2020, the economic growth rate reached 2.3%, making China the only country with positive growth among the major powers.[15] At the third plenary session of the 13th National People's Congress (NPC) held in May following postponement, a target for the 2020 economic growth rate could not be set.[16] Nevertheless, the session projected that GDP would exceed 100 trillion yuan in 2020 and absolute poverty would be eradicated, and emphasized that China was on target to achieving the goal to "comprehensively build a moderately prosperous society."[17]

The fifth plenary session of the 19th CCP Central Committee held in October deliberated and adopted the proposals for formulating the 14th Five-Year Plan (2021–2025) for National Economic and Social Development and the Long-Range Objectives through the Year 2035. These proposals presented the goal of raising the per capita GDP to that of a moderately developed country by 2035 to "comprehensively build a modern socialist country," identifying the 14th Five-Year Plan as the first step to achieving this goal.[18] General Secretary Xi Jinping's two-term, 10 year tenure is slated to end at the 20th CCP Congress in 2022. Xi's central role in the formulation of the Long-Range Objectives through the Year 2035[19] demonstrates he is keen to remain as the leader beyond the next CCP Congress. At the fifth plenary session, no new individual who was deemed a candidate for the next-generation leader was elected as a member of the Standing Committee.

Prior to the fifth plenary session, the CCP promulgated the Regulations on Work of Central Committee. The regulations specify operational matters and the authority of each post in the Central Committee, the highest leadership body in the CCP. They stipulate that the general secretary would set the agenda for Standing Committee meetings, and that the CCP Central Committee would use the "Xi Jinping Thought on Socialism with Chinese Characteristics for a New Era" to arm the entire party and educate the people.[20] Both of these measures will lead to strengthening the power and authority of General Secretary Xi Jinping in the CCP. President Xi succeeded in restoring and strengthening his political authority that was damaged by the pandemic.

2. "One Country, Two Systems" at a Deadlock

(1) The Hollowing Out of "One Country, Two Systems" in Hong Kong

In Hong Kong, the proposed amendment to the Hong Kong extradition bill that would allow extraditions of suspects detained in Hong Kong to China triggered a growing opposition movement from mid-2019. Protesters repeatedly staged large-scale demonstrations to demand the withdrawal of the amendment and the realization of universal suffrage. Hong Kongers have become more antagonistic to the Xi Jinping leadership, which has been increasingly interfering in Hong Kong's politics and neglecting "one country, two systems" that allows Hong Kong a wide range of autonomy. In the District Council election held in November 2019, the pro-democracy faction won 80% of the seats, securing an overwhelming victory over the pro-China faction, which held about 70% of the seats before the election. With Hong Kong's legislative body, the Legislative Council, scheduled to hold elections in September 2020, attention was focused on how the Chinese government would respond to the Hong Kong people's heightening calls for freedom and democracy.

The Xi leadership chose to take a hardline approach to ramp up the central government's interference in Hong Kong and silence the Hong Kong people's calls for freedom and democracy. First, the Xi leadership undertook an overhaul of the key posts in charge of Hong Kong affairs. On January 4, 2020, Wang Zhiming, director of the Liaison Office of the Central People's Government in Hong Kong Special Administrative Region (the central government's outpost in Hong Kong), was ousted and replaced by Luo Huining, former secretary of the CCP Shanxi Provincial Committee. On February 13, Zhang Xiaoming, director of the Hong Kong and Macao Affairs Office of the State Council, was demoted to deputy director, and Xia Baolong, former secretary of the CCP Zhejiang Provincial Committee, was appointed as the new director. Both have served as provincial heads and have extensive experience in local administration. Xia Baolong also worked under President Xi when he was head of Zhejiang Province. It is likely that influential personnel were appointed to shore up the departments in charge of Hong Kong policy and strengthen the control of the Xi leadership.

Furthermore, in May, the Xi leadership initiated steps toward enacting the Hong Kong national security law, which would enable the central government to directly crack down on activity in Hong Kong that denounces China. Article 23 of the Basic Law of the Hong Kong Special Administrative Region (SAR), a law that stipulates the system of the Hong Kong SAR, requires the government of Hong Kong to enact laws to prohibit uprisings against the central government and to prohibit political activities by foreign organizations. In 2002, the Hong Kong government attempted to enact the National Security Legislation, aiming to legislate Article 23 of the Basic Law. However, it was met with large-scale protests and abandoned. The Hong Kong government subsequently did not push for the legislation of Article 23 of the Basic Law. In place of the Hong Kong government, the Xi leadership moved to enact a law on national security. At the third plenary session of the 13th NPC held in late May, the draft "decision on the improvement of the legal system and implementation mechanism for the Hong Kong special administrative region to safeguard national security" was proposed[21] and passed.[22] Based on this decision, the Hong Kong national security bill was proposed to a meeting of the NPC Standing Committee.[23] Article 18 of the Basic Law contains the provision that laws can enter into force in Hong

Kong if the NPC Standing Committee adds them to an annex of the Basic Law, confined to national laws relating to foreign affairs, defense, and other matters outside the limits of the autonomy of the Hong Kong SAR. Under this provision, the NPC Standing Committee, which met on June 30, passed the Hong Kong national security law, and at the same time, added it to the annex of the Basic Law. It entered into force in Hong Kong on July 1 without being deliberated at the Hong Kong Legislative Council.[24]

The Hong Kong national security law makes it a criminal offense to endanger national security through acts of secession, subversion of state power, terrorist activities, and collusion with foreign forces, and sets the maximum penalty at life in prison. In addition, it established the Office for Safeguarding National Security in Hong Kong as a branch office of China's public security authorities. The law stipulates that the Office collects intelligence related to national security and provides guidance to the Committee for Safeguarding National Security to be newly established within the Hong Kong government. There is also a clause that could be interpreted to allow for the Office's direct exercise of jurisdiction over serious cases and for a trial to be held in mainland China. Even where a trial is held in Hong Kong, the chief executive is to designate the judges. Furthermore, the law is said to apply to residents outside of Hong Kong, and the possibility of foreign nationals being arrested and prosecuted on suspicion of violating the law cannot be denied.[25] Thus, the Hong Kong national security law gives the Chinese government wide discretion in the interpretation and application of the law, and it can be inferred that the law aims to deescalate the rhetoric and actions of the Hong Kong people and their supporters. And in fact, prominent democracy activists, including Agnes Chow and Jimmy Lai, have been arrested and prosecuted on the grounds of violating the Hong Kong national security law.

China's imposition of the national security law on Hong Kong hollows out the "one country, two systems" that granted Hong Kong a high degree of autonomy. The enforcement of this law without deliberation by the Hong Kong Legislative Council has greatly undermined Hong Kong's legislative authority. The establishment of security bodies by the central government that are not subject

Demonstrators protesting against the enforcement of the national security law in Hong Kong on July 1, 2020 (Getty Images/Kyodo)

to the jurisdiction of the Hong Kong government is in direct contradiction to the purpose of Article 22 of the Basic Law, which prohibits the central government from interfering in the affairs of Hong Kong. The enforcement of the Hong Kong national security law set off demonstrations voicing opposition to the law, despite Hong Kong's ban on gatherings to prevent the spread of COVID-19. In a public opinion poll conducted in August, about 60% responded they were opposed to the law.[26] Many countries have expressed concerns over China's imposition of the law on Hong Kong, and 27 countries, including Japan, the United Kingdom, France, and Germany, issued a joint statement criticizing the law for undermining the high degree of autonomy, rights, and freedoms guaranteed by "one country, two systems."[27] Japan's then chief cabinet secretary Suga Yoshihide stated, "It is regrettable that the law was enacted despite strong concerns from the international community and the people of Hong Kong," and criticized the law for "undermining the international community's trust in the one country, two systems framework."[28]

China forcibly enacted the national security law in Hong Kong despite backlash and concerns from the Hong Kong people and the international community. Underlying this move was the growing freedom and democracy movement in Hong Kong and strong anxiety among the Xi leadership that it could upset the CCP's one-party rule in China. Following the passage of the Hong Kong Human Rights and Democracy Act in the United States in November 2019, the CCP official newspaper *People's Daily* published a commentary, which argued that "anti-Chinese forces in the United States" and "radical forces in

Hong Kong" were colluding to push Hong Kong into chaos and criticized U.S. political forces for plotting to carry out a "color revolution" in Hong Kong.[29] Following the entry into force of the Hong Kong national security law, a commentary in the *People's Daily* accused some external forces of seeking to turn Hong Kong into a "bridgehead" of anti-China activities and a "base camp" of uprisings and riots and instigate a "color revolution."[30] It is believed that the Xi leadership determined it had to significantly tighten control over Hong Kong in order to maintain the CCP's one-party rule.

(2) Taiwan's Rejection of "One Country, Two Systems"

The intransigence of the Xi Jinping leadership in crushing the people's calls for freedom and democracy in Hong Kong and drastically restricting its autonomy, which was supposedly guaranteed under "one country, two systems," has raised strong antipathy and alarm among Taiwanese people. According to a public opinion poll released by Taiwan's Mainland Affairs Council in August 2020, 80.9% of respondents said that the enactment of the Hong Kong national security law violated Hong Kong's democracy, freedom, and judicial independence and damaged "one country, two systems." In addition, 88.8% of respondents objected to the CCP's insistence on "one country, two systems," while 82.4% rejected the Taiwanese version of "one country, two systems."[31] Underlying Taiwanese people's growing rejection of "one country, two systems" was Chinese president Xi Jinping's open desire to unify Taiwan into China based on this principle. In January 2019, President Xi pointed out that "one country, two systems" was the best way to achieve national unification, and insisted on proceeding with concrete considerations of "one country, two systems" to be applied to Taiwan.[32] While proposing the materialization of "one country, two systems" to be applied to Taiwan on the one hand, the Xi leadership hollowed out "one country, two systems" applied to Hong Kong and increased Taiwanese people's distrust of China.

This Taiwanese public sentiment was reflected in the outcome of the presidential election held in January 2020. President Tsai Ing-wen of the

Democratic Progressive Party, who had consistently opposed "one country, two systems," was reelected by securing an overwhelming victory over the Kuomintang candidate Han Kuo-yu, who advocated improving relations with China. In her speech at the inaugural ceremony on May 20, President Tsai emphasized that Taiwan "stand[s] fast by this principle" on not accepting the "one country, two systems" advocated by China. President Tsai also announced Taiwan's position to build a stable relationship with China based on the principles of "peace, parity, democracy, and dialogue." Regarding diplomacy over the next four years, she indicated that Taiwan would strive to join international organizations and deepen partnerships with countries that share its values, such as the United States, Japan, and European countries.[33]

Inaugurated in 2016, the Tsai administration has seen the number of Taiwan's formal diplomatic partners decrease from 22 to 15 as a result of China's diplomatic offensive. Meanwhile, the international community's interest in and appreciation of Taiwan has increased. In particular, the Tsai administration has raised Taiwan's international reputation by successfully combating COVID-19. Taiwan has succeeded in containing the spread of the coronavirus by quickly imposing entry restrictions and implementing thorough infection prevention measures. As of the start of the Tsai administration's second term on May 20, Taiwan had 440 cases and just seven deaths.[34] Such achievements raised calls for permitting Taiwan's involvement in the World Health Organization (WHO), the central actor for international cooperation against COVID-19. Advocating the "One China" principle, China has excluded Taiwan from WHO, an international organization. While China had allowed the former pro-China Ma Ying-jeou administration to participate as an observer in the World Health Assembly, it did not permit the Tsai administration.

Taiwan expressed its strong desire to attend the World Health Assembly in May 2020, and a campaign for Taiwan to participate was supported broadly by the major powers. It has been reported that the United States, Japan, Australia, the United Kingdom, Canada, France, Germany, and New Zealand issued a demarche to WHO requesting Taiwan's participation as an observer at the

World Health Assembly.[35] Taiwan's participation was ultimately not realized due to the strong objection of China. In Taiwan's absence, Japan's then minister of health, labour and welfare Kato Katsunobu mentioned to the assembly that "the consideration should be given to regions which successfully embraced COVID-19 in terms of public health response, such as Taiwan."[36] Izumi Hiroyasu, chief representative of the Japan-Taiwan Exchange Association, Taipei Office, also issued a statement, saying: "We sincerely regret that Taiwan was not allowed to participate as an observer, despite the many voices expressing support for Taiwan. [...] Japan will continue to strongly support Taiwan's participation as an observer at the World Health Assembly."[37]

The Donald Trump administration of the United States accelerated efforts to strengthen relations with Taiwan. On March 26, 2020, President Trump signed the TAIPEI Act into law. The purpose of this law is to support the expansion of Taiwan's international space, such as by requesting the U.S. government to support Taiwan's membership and observer participation in international organizations and requesting the State Department to submit annual reports on the U.S. government's efforts related to Taiwan's foreign affairs.[38] The Chinese government strongly objected to the passage of the TAIPEI Act. A spokesperson for the Ministry of Foreign Affairs stated: "The Taiwan question concerns China's sovereignty and territorial integrity as well as China's core interests. The determination and resolution of the Chinese government and people to safeguard their core interests are firm as rock."[39] The *People's Daily* published a commentary criticizing that the passage of the TAIPEI Act could cross China's "red line" on Taiwan.[40]

Following the passage, the United States continued to steadily deepen its relationship with Taiwan. In August 2020, Alex Azar, secretary of health and human services of the United States, visited Taiwan, becoming the highest-ranking U.S. official to visit Taiwan since the United States broke ties with the island in 1979. Secretary Azar met with President Tsai Ing-wen. He praised Taiwan's democracy and transparency for contributing to its successful response to COVID-19, and discussed ways to deepen the partnership between the United

States and Taiwan.[41] In September 2020, Under Secretary of State Keith Krach, also visited Taiwan. Under Secretary Krach had dinner with President Tsai and attended the memorial service for former president Lee Teng-hui who passed away in July.

Furthermore, the Trump administration bolstered support for Taiwan on the security front. By 2019, the Trump administration had sold weapons, such as interceptor missiles, tanks, and F-16V fighters. In 2020, it decided to sell torpedoes and other weapons in May as well as air-to-surface missiles, multiple rocket launchers, anti-ship missiles, and other weapons in October. In August 2020, the American Institute in Taiwan (AIT) released a declassified document indicating the U.S. position to increase arms sales to Taiwan if China were to become more hostile. The document is related to the 1982 U.S.-China Joint Statement, which sets forth that the United States would scale back its arms sales to Taiwan.[42] Moreover, the U.S. Navy has sent vessels through the Taiwan Strait once a month.

With Taiwan's public further distancing itself from China while the United States enhances its ties with Taiwan, the Xi Jinping leadership has escalated the threat of force to check Taiwan and the United States. A symposium was held on May 29, 2020 to commemorate the 15th anniversary of the enactment of the anti-secession law, which mentions the possibility of using force against Taiwan. In his speech at the symposium, Li Zhanshu, chairman of the NPC Standing Committee, noted that the anti-secession law poses a "great threat" to independence and secessionist forces in Taiwan and praised its threatening effect on Taiwan. Chairman Li stressed that all possible measures, including the use of force, would be taken to crush independence and secessionist forces in Taiwan, depending on the situation, and indicated the possibility of using force against "external forces" that interfere in Taiwanese affairs.[43]

The PLA has also stepped up its military pressure on Taiwan. On February 9 and 10, 2020, the Eastern Theater Command conducted a joint exercise of vessels, aircraft, and other naval and aerial forces in Taiwan's periphery region. According to a *PLA Daily* article about the exercise, airpower including bombers and fighters were deployed from the Bashi Channel and the Miyako Strait to the Pacific Ocean to conduct real combat-oriented training off the southeast coast of Taiwan, and "developed [China's] ability to safeguard the security of national sovereignty and territorial integrity."[44] On March 16, KJ-500 early warning aircraft and J-11 fighters conducted a nighttime flight drill off the southwest coast of Taiwan. A spokesperson for China's Ministry of National Defense noted that this drill was "targeted specifically at 'Taiwan independence' forces and their secessionist activities." The spokesperson went on to condemn the United States' strengthening of relations with Taiwan as interference in Chinese internal affairs, and stated that China would never condone the use of the "Taiwan card" by foreign forces.[45] In addition, in September, coinciding with Under Secretary of State Krach's visit to Taiwan, the PLA conducted a series of daily drills of flights by fighters across the median line in the Taiwan Strait, combined with flights by patrol aircraft and bombers off the southwest coast of Taiwan.

The PLA's intensification of military activities, which seemingly takes into account threats and attacks against Taiwan, not only increases tensions in its periphery region, but also increases the possibility of unintended accidents and collisions with vessels and aircraft of Taiwanese and U.S. forces. Moreover, increased military pressure on Taiwan is expected to further heighten the Taiwanese people's antipathy toward China. The Xi Jinping leadership is urged to respond calmly by squarely facing reality.

3. China Headed toward a "New Cold War"

(1) Intensifying Confrontation with the United States

The United States and China were mutually engaged in a "trade war" of sanctions and tariffs since July 2018. In late 2019, the two countries reached their first agreement to resolve this issue. This is the so-called "Phase One Trade Deal." The "Phase One Trade Deal," signed by President Trump and Vice

Premier Liu He at the White House on January 15, 2020, includes a $200 billion increase in China's imports from the United States over the subsequent two years and a halving of additional tariffs on about $120 billion worth of U.S. imports from China that the United States imposed in September 2019. This agreement, however, did not lead to an improvement in U.S.-China relations in 2020. Trade is only one of many issues over which the United States criticizes China. In his October 2018 speech on U.S. policy toward China, Vice President Mike Pence severely criticized the policies of the CCP government in a wide range of areas, not only trade and the economy, but also politics, such as surveillance of the Chinese people and suppression of the Uyghur people; diplomacy, such as the "debt trap" created by the Belt and Road Initiative; and security, such as the PLA's challenge to the U.S. military presence.[46]

In addition, the outbreak of the COVID-19 pandemic in 2020 has plunged an already deteriorating U.S.-China relationship into deeper hostility. As the coronavirus spread in the United States and the situation grew more serious, the Trump administration stepped up efforts to hold China responsible for the global pandemic. The Xi government strongly objected to the Trump administration's shifting of blame over its failure to control the virus onto China. In the United States, criticism intensified over the authoritarian political system of the CCP for causing delays in controlling COVID-19 in Wuhan. In China, this sparked widespread alarm that the United States sought to weaken the governance system of the CCP. The mutual distrust created by the COVID-19 pandemic was one of the reasons for the rapid deterioration of U.S.-China relations.

In May 2020, the White House released a policy document on China titled, "United States Strategic Approach to the People's Republic of China." This document notes that the CCP seeks to transform the existing international order based on free and open rules to one that is more in line with Chinese interests and ideology, and that this attempt "harms vital American interests." It also asserts that the incumbent U.S. administration has taken a "competitive approach" to respond to China's challenge, which will not shy away from greater bilateral friction. Specifically, it gives examples such as resisting China's attempts by strengthening coordination with allies and partners, pushing back on China's hegemonic assertions and excessive claims in the South China Sea and other areas, and deploying weapons and strengthening capabilities as necessary to deter China's ambitions. Lastly, the document presents the recognition that a "long-term strategic competition between [the] two systems" has begun between the United States and China.[47]

The Trump administration has since taken a series of actions in line with this policy document on China. On July 13, 2020, the State Department issued a statement outlining the U.S. government's position on claims to maritime rights in the South China Sea. The statement condemned China's repeated coercion and intimidation of other countries in the South China Sea. It explicitly rejected China's claims to maritime rights across most of the South China Sea, noting that the claims were completely unlawful.[48] On July 21, the State Department demanded that the Chinese government close its consulate-general in Houston, Texas. On July 23, Mike Pompeo, secretary of state, gave a speech at the Richard Nixon Presidential Library and Museum in California. He noted that the U.S. engagement policy implemented since Richard Nixon's presidency failed to deliver the transformation of China that was expected by strengthening bilateral relations. Secretary Pompeo criticized that President Xi is a true believer in a bankrupt totalitarian ideology and that the CCP is pursuing global hegemony based on communism, and advocated that Chinese communism will change the world unless the United States and the rest of the free world unite against it.[49]

In response to such moves by the Trump administration, the Xi government strongly criticized the United States for attempting to start a "New Cold War" with China, and emphasized its readiness to resolutely counter the words and deeds of the United States where the CCP is the target of criticism. In an interview with the state-run Xinhua news agency on August 5, Wang Yi, state councilor and foreign minister, condemned that rhetoric and actions denigrating China by some U.S. political forces are "reviving the ghost of McCarthyism." He stressed that China is strongly opposed to the artificially created "New Cold War" and that "Anyone who tries to start a new Cold War in the 21st century will be on the wrong side of history."[50] Yang Jiechi, director of the Central Foreign Affairs Commission Office of the CCP, published a commentary in the August 8th edition of the *People's Daily*, stressing that the CCP is supported by the Chinese people and that the United States' attempt to separate the CCP and the Chinese people is doomed to fail. Furthermore, Director Yang noted that Taiwan, Hong Kong, the Tibet Autonomous Region, and the Xinjiang Uygur Autonomous Region were "core interests" for China, and declared that China would "take necessary countermeasures" against any U.S. actions that undermine China's core interests.[51]

On August 26, the PLA fired anti-ship ballistic missiles (ASBM) from the Chinese mainland into the South China Sea. ASBM is a weapon which can be fired from the Chinese mainland and strike aircraft carriers and other vessels sailing at sea. The U.S. Forces views ASBM with wariness, calling it a "carrier killer." China reportedly fired two types of ASBMs that it possesses, one DF-21D and one DF-26B, launching them from Zhejiang and Qinghai Provinces, respectively, into the northern waters of the Paracel Islands in the South China Sea.[52] By demonstrating military capability to constrain U.S. military actions in the South China Sea, where China's core interests are a source of increasing friction between the two countries, China highlighted its firm stance both at home and abroad that it would not compromise in the competition with the United States.

President Xi himself expressed his determination to ultimately win the struggle with the United States. On October 23, 2020, President Xi delivered a speech at a meeting marking the 70th anniversary of the participation of the Chinese People's Volunteer Army in the Korean War. In his speech, President Xi argued that China's participation in the War to Resist U.S. Aggression and Aid Korea was a legitimate countercharge against the U.S. Forces' threat to Chinese security and a just war to help North Korea combat the invasion by the United States. President Xi underscored that the ultimate victory of the Chinese People's Volunteer Army, which was overwhelmingly underpowered compared to the U.S. Forces, "shattered the myth of invincibility of the U.S. army." Furthermore,

President Xi stated that "the Chinese people is sure to inflict a painful blow" if any action undermines China's sovereignty, security, and development interests, or violates and divides Chinese territory.[53]

(2) Hardline Diplomacy Elicits Confrontation with Countries

The Xi government has employed hardline diplomacy involving threats and pressure, not only with the United States but also with countries that criticize China's response to COVID-19 or take issue with China's stance on Hong Kong, Taiwan, or other matters. China's foreign affairs appear to reflect the uncompromising nature of the Xi leadership, which seeks to forcefully contain criticism of itself. Consequently, more countries are adopting a critical view toward China, resulting in China self-handedly worsening the international environment surrounding the country.

In April, Scott Morrison, prime minister of Australia, proposed an international independent investigation into the source of COVID-19 that exploded in Wuhan.[54] In response, the Chinese ambassador to Australia suggested that China may restrict imports of Australian wine and beef and the number of Chinese students and tourists who go to Australia, speaking in an interview with a local newspaper.[55] Later, the Chinese government suspended some beef imports from Australia, imposed additional tariffs on barley imports, and urged its citizens not to visit Australia. In addition, China detained an Australian anchor who worked for a Chinese international broadcaster and de facto expelled two Australian journalists from China.

China has also deepened its confrontation with India over their land border. On June 15, soldiers from both militaries clashed in the Galwan Valley in the Sino-Indian border area, resulting in 20 deaths on the Indian side and four deaths on the Chinese side. This was the first instance since 1975 that a conflict between the two countries resulted in fatalities, although neither side used firearms in the latest incident.[56] Thereafter, dialogue continued between the two countries to ease tensions. However, in September, one of the two sides opened fire, leading both sides to accuse the other of firing. A standoff also took place between the two

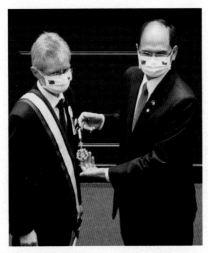

Senate President Milos Vystrcil of the Czech Republic being conferred a medal by You Si-Kun, president of the Legislative Yuan of Taiwan (right) (Taipei, September 1, 2020) (Kyodo News)

militaries near Pangong Lake in the same area.[57]

China's hardline diplomatic stance was directed at European countries as well. In late August, Czech Senate president Milos Vystrcil, visited Taiwan. President Vystrcil delivered a speech on the theme of "unity of democracies" to the Taiwanese parliament known as the Legislative Yuan, calling on the two sides that have achieved democracy to work together to protect shared values.[58] The Chinese government strongly objected to President Vystrcil's visit to Taiwan. On August 31, Foreign Minister Wang Yi, who was visiting European countries, stated that President Vystrcil's visit to Taiwan challenged the "One China" principle and threatened that President Vystrcil would "pay a heavy price."[59] In response to this remark, the French Foreign Ministry issued a statement, which noted that "any threat to the EU's member state is unacceptable" and emphasized solidarity with the Czech Republic. At a joint press conference with Minister Wang, Heiko Maas, federal minister for foreign affairs of Germany, also criticized China's threat against the Czech Republic as inappropriate. Minister Wang, in a speech at the French Institute of International Relations, criticized U.S. unilateralism and urged China and the European Union (EU) to cooperate to promote multilateralism.[60] Minister Wang's visit to Europe, however, resulted in increasing European countries' distrust of China.

Negative views of China are on the rise around the world spurred by COVID-19 that originated in Wuhan and spread across the globe, coupled with the hardline political and diplomatic stance of the Xi leadership. According to

Figure 2.1. Confidence in President Xi Jinping's actions regarding world affairs

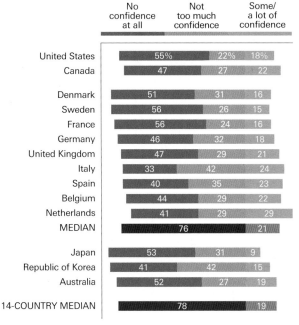

Source: Pew Research Center, "Unfavorable Views of China Reach Historic Highs in Many Countries" (October 6, 2020), 15.

a survey on perceptions of China in 14 countries released by the Pew Research Center in October, sentiment toward China worsened in all countries compared to the previous year, and more than 70% in 12 countries had negative views of China. In particular, since the survey began, distrust of China reached its highest level in Australia, Canada, Germany, the Netherlands, the Republic of Korea, Spain, Sweden, the United Kingdom, and the United States. Many expressed negative views of China's response to COVID-19 and President Xi's role in solving global issues.[61]

Moreover, cooperation is deepening between countries that are highly criticized and pressured by China. On June 4, Prime Minister Morrison of Australia and Narendra Modi, prime minister of India, held a telephone talk and issued a joint statement that labeled their bilateral relationship as a "Comprehensive Strategic Partnership." The leaders agreed, among other things, to share a common "Free and Open Indo-Pacific" (FOIP) vision and to promote defense cooperation.[62] On October 27, the United States and India held a 2+2 foreign and

Ships from the Royal Australian Navy, Indian Navy, Japan's Maritime Self-Defense Force, and the U.S. Navy participating in Malabar 2020 in the North Arabian Sea on November 17, 2020 (U.S. Navy photo by Mass Communication Specialist 3rd Class Keenan Daniels)

defense ministerial dialogue in New Delhi. The two countries agreed to cooperate to maintain free and open Indo-Pacific and to conclude an agreement on mutual sharing of geographic data that would contribute to defense cooperation.[63] With regard to multilateral cooperation among the four countries of Japan, Australia, India, and the United States, on October 6, Motegi Toshimitsu, minister for foreign affairs; Marise Payne, minister for foreign affairs; Subrahmanyam Jaishankar, minister of external affairs; and State Secretary Pompeo held a Japan-Australia-India-U.S. Foreign Ministers' Meeting in Tokyo. The foreign ministers of the four countries concurred on further developing practical cooperation to promote FOIP.[64] In addition, the four countries conducted the Malabar 2020 joint exercise in the Bay of Bengal from November 3 and in the North Arabian Sea from November 17.

4. The PLA's Stepped-up Activities

(1) The Military's Actions amid COVID-19

As COVID-19 spread across the country, especially in Wuhan, the PLA played a role in combatting the virus while steadily conducting military exercises, highlighting both at home and abroad the PLA's advanced capacity to respond to the pandemic. Based on President Xi's January 20 instructions to contain the virus, the Joint Prevention and Control Mechanism was established, comprised of entities under the Central Military Commission (CMC), the Joint Logistic Support Force, the People's Armed Police Force, and the Academy of Military Science.[65] On January 24, with the ratification by the CMC, the Logistic Support Department of the CMC mobilized a total of 450 medical personnel from military medical universities of the Army, Navy, and Air Force and sent them to Wuhan on military transport aircraft from Shanghai, Chongqing, and Xi'an.[66] On February 3, some 950 medical personnel were mobilized from hospitals nationwide affiliated with the Joint Logistic Support Force and sent to the hastily built Huoshenshan Hospital to specialize in treating COVID-19 patients.[67] Most of the mobilized medical personnel flew separately on eight Air Force transport aircraft from Shenyang, Lanzhou, Guangzhou, and Nanjing to Wuhan.[68] On February 13, an additional 2,600 medical personnel were sent to Wuhan from the Army, Navy, Air Force, Rocket Force, Strategic Support Force, Joint Logistic Support Force, and People's Armed Police Force, bringing the total number of military medical personnel dispatched to Wuhan to 4,000.[69] Chen Jingyuan, health division director of the Logistic Support Department under the CMC, praised the role of the PLA in responding to COVID-19, saying at a press conference, "All military units unwaveringly carried out President Xi Jinping's important instructions, swiftly took preventive control actions against COVID-19, and played the role of guardians and defenders of the safety of the life of the people and their physical health."[70]

The PLA is also playing an important role in the development of COVID-19 vaccines. A research team led by Chen Wei, academician at the PLA Academy of Military Medical Sciences, was among the first to begin developing a vaccine against COVID-19, starting the first phase of clinical trials in March and beginning the second phase of clinical trials for the first time in the world in April. In September, the team initiated the final third phase of clinical trials, taking the lead in the global race to develop COVID-19 vaccines. At an award ceremony for China's fight against COVID-19 held on September 8, President Xi conferred the Medal of the Republic on Dr. Zhong Nanshan and the national honorary title on three individuals, including Dr. Chen. Speaking at the award ceremony, President Xi stressed that the significant strategic achievements made in the fight against COVID-19 attest to the CCP's strong leadership and to the superiority of the system of socialism with Chinese characteristics.[71] The PLA's contribution to combating COVID-19 has been touted by the Xi Jinping leadership as proof of the superiority of the Chinese system.

Meanwhile, the PLA has steadily carried out various drills and exercises to strengthen its combat capability even amidst the pandemic. A spokesperson for the Ministry of National Defense noted that the Chinese military is focusing on controlling infectious diseases, as well as prioritizing trainings and combat readiness, working to minimize the impact of infectious diseases on military trainings.[72] Indeed, in March, the PLA participated in a joint drill with Cambodia as scheduled. In April, a fleet of six ships, led by the aircraft carrier *Liaoning,* was deployed from the East China Sea to the Western Pacific via the Miyako Strait, advanced to the South China Sea via the Bashi Channel, and then sailed back to the East China Sea via the Western Pacific. At around the same time, COVID-19 spread within the U.S. military, and the aircraft carrier USS *Theodore Roosevelt* was unable to conduct operations for a long period. The *Liaoning* drill in the Western Pacific left an impression on people in China and abroad that the PLA had COVID-19 under control and had maintained its normal operational capabilities.

(2) Continued Hardline Stance in the Seas

Even as China was hard pressed to respond to COVID-19, it continued to make hardline forays into the seas aimed at expanding its maritime interests and increasing its ability to counter U.S. military presence. China has disputes with Vietnam, the Philippines, Malaysia, and other countries over territorial rights and maritime interests to the Spratly (Nansha) and Paracel (Xisha) Islands in the South China Sea. In 2012, China established Sansha City under Hainan

Figure 2.2. Number of China Coast Guard vessels that entered Japan's
contiguous zone around the Senkaku Islands

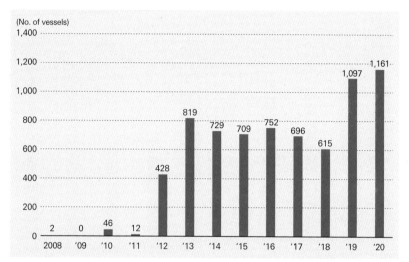

Province as an administrative unit with jurisdiction over the entire South China Sea. Then, in April 2020, it announced the establishment of Nansha District and Xisha District under Sansha City to serve as administrative districts with jurisdiction over the Spratly and Paracel Islands, respectively. It is believed that China sought to strengthen the basis for its de facto control by establishing administrative districts with jurisdiction over the two disputed groups of islands.

On April 2, a vessel from the China Coast Guard (CCG) and a Vietnamese fishing boat collided in the vicinity of the Paracel Islands, a territory disputed by China and Vietnam, resulting in the sinking of the fishing boat. The Vietnamese government strongly condemned China, asserting that the CCG vessel deliberately collided with the fishing boat and detained eight crew members. The Chinese government, on the other hand, claimed that the Vietnamese fishing boat, which was operating illegally in Chinese waters, suddenly changed course to evade crackdown by CCG vessels and caused the collision. Although China

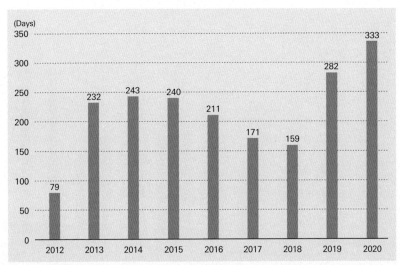

Source: Compiled by the author based on data released by the Japan Coast Guard.
Note: The year 2012 covers the period from September 14 onwards only.

handed over the eight detained crew members to the Vietnamese side, criticism of China intensified in Vietnam.[73] Also in April, CCG vessels interfered with a Malaysian company's offshore drilling operation in the waters around the Spratly Islands. As government vessels sent by Malaysia continued to monitor the situation, the U.S. Navy and the Royal Australian Navy dispatched vessels to the surrounding sea area to conduct exercises and act as a check on China's moves.[74]

In the East China Sea as well, China continues to make aggressive forays to expand its interests. China, which makes its own claims to the Senkaku Islands that are an inherent territory of Japan, has CCG vessels frequently intrude into Japan's territorial waters. In May 2020, CCG vessels approached a Japanese fishing boat that was operating in Japanese territorial waters near the Senkaku Islands, and they appeared to be tracking it. The Japan Coast Guard's patrol vessels intervened between the two sides to protect the fishing boat, but the CCG vessels persistently pursued the boat. In July, CCG vessels attempted again to approach a fishing boat in Japanese territorial waters and intruded into the waters for more than 39 hours continuously. A spokesperson for China's Ministry of Foreign Affairs asserted based on Beijing's own position that the "China Coast Guard followed and monitored this ship in accordance with law and demanded it immediately leave China's waters."[75] Japan has sovereignty over the territorial waters of the Senkaku Islands, as a matter of course. The Japanese government has made a stern protest to the Chinese side, stating that the activities of CCG vessels are unacceptable. The Xi Jinping government is increasingly challenging Japan's sovereignty by relying on force. Incidents of CCG vessels approaching Japanese fishing vessels have occurred sporadically since then, and the October incident was the longest-ever incursion into Japanese territorial waters, lasting more than 57 hours. The number of days that CCG vessels sailed in Japan's contiguous zone in 2020 reached a record high of 333. Furthermore, China has enacted and entered into force the new Coast Guard Law. Japan has conveyed strong concern to China that the law contains provisions that have problems with consistency with international law, including ambiguity over applicable waters and authority to use weapons. There are acute concerns warranting caution that China may further arm its ships and take more provocative actions in waters surrounding the Senkaku Islands.

China has also accelerated efforts to strengthen anti-access/area denial (A2/AD) capabilities against the United States. From January to February 2020, a fleet of four vessels including destroyers belonging to the Chinese Navy's South Sea Fleet conducted a far-sea exercise for deployment to the Western Pacific. The fleet advanced into the Western Pacific by transiting the Bashi Channel from the South China Sea, crossed the date line, and approached 300 kilometers off the western coast of Hawaii.[76] It then turned westward, sailed past waters near Guam, and headed for the South China Sea, where a Chinese vessel irradiated a military laser at a U.S. Navy P-8A patrol aircraft during a surveillance flight. The U.S. Navy's Pacific Fleet issued a statement strongly criticizing the laser irradiation by the Chinese vessel, calling it "unsafe and unprofessional actions."[77] In response, a spokesperson for China's Ministry of National Defense condemned the actions of the P-8A patrol aircraft that had been monitoring Chinese vessels for a long period as "unfriendly in intention and unprofessional by operation."[78] The PLA aims to interdict U.S. military forces' approach toward China via the Pacific Ocean, which is anticipated in case of emergency. It is expected that the military rivalry between China and the United States in the East Asian seas, including the Western Pacific, will become even more intense in the U.S.-China "New Cold War."

NOTES

1) World Health Organization (WHO), "WHO Coronavirus Disease (COVID-19) Dashboard," WHO website; Johns Hopkins University, "COVID-19 Dashboard by the Center for Systems Science and Engineering (CSSE) at Johns Hopkins University (JHU)," JHU website.

2) Wuhan Municipal Health Commission, "2 yue 29 ri xinxing guanzhuang bingdu feiyan yiqing zuixin qingkuang" [February 29 Update on COVID-19 pneumonia] (March 1, 2020).

3) *People's Daily*, June 8, 2020.

4) *Yomiuri Shimbun*, February 8, 2020.

5) Voice of America (Chinese), February 25, 2020.

6) Xinhua Net, March 19, 2020.

7) *People's Daily*, April 3, 2020.

8) *Hong Kong Citizen News*, May 2, 2020; *Asahi Shimbun*, February 5, 2020; NHK, February 7, 2020.

9) IPK Media, March 6, 2020.

10) *People's Daily*, February 13, 2020.

11) *Qiushi*, February 15, 2020.

12) *People's Daily*, February 22, 2020.

13) *People's Daily*, February 24, 2020.

14) Chinese Communist Party (CCP) Beijing Municipal Commission for Discipline Inspection, "Beijingshi Huayuan jituan yuan dangwei fu shuji, dongshizhang Ren Zhiqiang yanzhong weiji weifa bei kaichu dangji" [The former chairman and deputy party secretary of Huayuan Group Ren Zhiqiang was expelled from the party for

15) *People's Daily*, January 19, 2021.

16) *People's Daily*, May 30, 2020.

17) Xinhua Net (Japanese), November 4, 2020.

18) *People's Daily*, November 4, 2020.

19) *People's Daily*, November 4, 2020.

20) *People's Daily*, October 13, 2020.

21) *People's Daily*, May 23, 2020.

22) *People's Daily*, May 29, 2020.

23) *People's Daily,* June 21, 2020.

24) *People's Daily*, July 1, 2020.

25) *People's Daily*, July 1, 2020.

26) Reuters, August 31, 2020.

27) AFPBB, July 1, 2020.

28) [Japan] Prime Minister's Office, "Naikaku kanbo chokan kisha kaiken" [Press conference by the Chief Cabinet Secretary] (June 30, 2020).

29) *People's Daily*, December 3, 2019.

30) *People's Daily*, July 5, 2020.

31) [Taiwan] Mainland Affairs Council (MAC), "Over 80% of the Public Oppose CCP's Hong Kong National Security Law and Military and Diplomatic Suppression of Taiwan," MAC Press Release No. 43 (August 6, 2020).

32) *People's Daily*, January 3, 2019.

33) [Taiwan] Office of the President, "Inaugural address of ROC 15th-term President Tsai Ing-wen" (May 20, 2020).

34) Taiwan Centers for Disease Control, "CECC Reports No New Confirmed Cases: 402 Patients Released from Isolation" (May 20, 2020).

35) CBC, May 9, 2020.

36) [Japan] Ministry of Health, Labour and Welfare, "The Statement of Mr. Kato Katsunobu, Minister of Health, Labour and Welfare, in Seventy Third World Health Assembly" (May 19, 2020).

37) Japan-Taiwan Exchange Association, "Taiwan no WHO sokai sanka ni tsuite" [About Taiwan's participation in the World Health Assembly] (May 19, 2020).

38) Taiwan Allies International Protection and Enhancement Initiative (TAIPEI) Act of 2019, Pub. L. No. 116-135, 134 Stat. 278.

39) *People's Daily*, March 28, 2020.

40) *People's Daily*, March 30, 2020.

Chapter 2 China

85

41) American Institute in Taiwan (AIT), "HHS Secretary Azar Meets with President Tsai of Taiwan and Praises Taiwan's Transparent COVID-19 Response" (August 10, 2020).

42) AIT, "Declassified Cables: Taiwan Arms Sales & Six Assurances (1982)," AIT website.

43) *People's Daily*, May 30, 2020.

44) *PLA Daily*, February 11, 2020.

45) *People's Daily Online*, March 27, 2020.

46) [U.S.] White House, "Remarks by Vice President Pence on the Administration's Policy toward China" (October 4, 2018).

47) [U.S.] White House, *United States Strategic Approach to the People's Republic of China* (May 20, 2020).

48) [U.S.] Department of State, "U.S. Position on Maritime Claims in the South China Sea" (July 13, 2020).

49) [U.S.] Department of State, "Communist China and the Free World's Future" (July 23, 2020).

50) *People's Daily*, August 6, 2020.

51) *People's Daily*, August 8, 2020.

52) *South China Morning Post*, August 26, 2020; Jiji Press, August 27, 2020; *Yomiuri Shimbun,* August 28, 2020.

53) *People's Daily*, October 24, 2020.

54) *West Australian*, May 1, 2020.

55) *Australian Financial Review*, April 26, 2020.

56) BBC News, June 17, 2020.

57) Jiji Press, August 31, 2020.

58) Jiji Press, September 1, 2020.

59) [China] Ministry of Foreign Affairs, "Wang Yi: Those Who Challenge the One China Principle Will Pay Heavy Price" (August 31, 2020).

60) *People's Daily Online*, August 31, 2020.

61) Laura Silver, Kat Devlin, and Christine Huang, "Unfavorable Views of China Reach Historic Highs in Many Countries," Pew Research Center (October 6, 2020).

62) [Australia] Department of Foreign Affairs and Trade, "Joint Statement on a Comprehensive Strategic Partnership between Republic of India and Australia" (June 4, 2020).

63) [U.S.] Department of State, "Joint Statement on the Third U.S.-India 2+2 Ministerial Dialogue" (October 27, 2020).

64) [Japan] Ministry of Foreign Affairs, "The Second Japan-Australia-India-U.S. Foreign Ministers' Meeting" (October 6, 2020).

65) *PLA Daily*, January 27, 2020.

66) *PLA Daily*, January 25, 2020.

67) [China] Ministry of National Defense, "Jundui chou zu yiliao liliang chengdan Wuhan Huoshenshan yiyuan yiliao jiuzhi renwu" [Select medical personnel from the military to undertake medical assistance mission at Huoshenshan Hospital in Wuhan] (February 2, 2020).

68) [China] Ministry of National Defense, "Kongjun ba jia feiji jinji kongyun jundui zhiyuan Hubei yiliaodui dida Wuhan" [Air Force hastily airlifts the military's Hubei medical assistance team to Wuhan on eight transport aircraft] (February 2, 2020).

69) *People's Daily*, February 14, 2020.

70) [China] Ministry of National Defense, "Quan jun kaishe shouzhi chuangwei jin 3 qian zhang, 1 wan yu ming yihu renyuan touru yixian jiuzhi" [From across the military, nearly 3,000 beds opened for treatment and more than 10,000 medical personnel mobilized to provide frontline emergency treatment] (March 3, 2020).

71) *People's Daily*, September 9, 2020.

72) *PLA Daily*, February 29, 2020.

73) *South China Morning Post*, April 3, 2020.

74) Asia Maritime Transparency Initiative, "Update: Chinese Survey Ship Escalates Three-way Standoff," Center for Strategic and International Studies (May 18, 2020).

75) [China] Ministry of Foreign Affairs, "Foreign Ministry Spokesperson Zhao Lijian's Regular Press Conference on July 6, 2020" (July 6, 2020).

76) *Yomiuri Shimbun*, March 29, 2020.

77) U.S. Pacific Fleet Public Affairs, "People's Liberation Army Navy Lased a U.S. Navy P-8A in Unsafe, Unprofessional Manner" (February 27, 2020).

78) Xinhua Net, March 6, 2020.

Chapter 3

The Korean Peninsula

Wavering North-South Relations

WATANABE Takeshi

Summary

On March 3, 2020, a day after the Democratic People's Republic of Korea (DPRK, or North Korea) fired the first of a series of short-range ballistic missiles (SRBMs), it denounced the Republic of Korea (ROK, or South Korea) for considering its alliance with the United States dearer than its own countrymen. In June, through statements by Kim Yo Jong, first vice department director of the Central Committee of the Workers' Party of Korea (WPK), the North pressured the South to correct its "flunkeyism," or subservience to the United States. North Korea's external actions were not directed at DPRK-U.S. relations, which had an uncertain future with the coming American presidential election. According to the DPRK's Foreign Ministry, the United States should not interfere in inter-Korean relations because it is an internal ethnic issue of the Korean people. Meanwhile, North Korea adopted the stance that it might back down from elevating tensions if "flunkeyism" was not corrected. This included imposing on South Korea the option of abrogating the agreement in the military domain, which was announced at the 2018 inter-Korean summit, and blowing up the inter-Korean joint liaison office. Prior to the inauguration of the new U.S. administration, North Korea focused on withdrawing the ROK from its cooperation with the United States.

The Moon Jae-in administration in South Korea was strongly resolved to improve inter-Korean relations following North Korea's actions and appeared to distance itself from the United States. For example, South Korea has been engaged in a growing debate about limiting the discussion matters at the U.S.-ROK working group for coordinating the two countries' policy toward North Korea, and promoting cooperation with the North more autonomously. Furthermore, the Standard Missile-3 (SM-3) sea-based ballistic missile interceptor, a component of the missile defense system, was not mentioned in the Mid-term Defense Plan released in August. Although the Navy insisted on the need for a multilayered defense system to cope with North Korea's development of SRBMs, the SM-3 was not adopted for this purpose. On the other hand, the ROK vowed to become "a nation that cannot be shaken" and to achieve "complete missile sovereignty." By relaxing the U.S.-ROK missile guidelines, which was a framework with the United States to restrict missile development by South Korea, the ROK demonstrated readiness to expand its missile capabilities. No significant progress was made in the transfer of wartime Operational Control (OPCON) Authority, a priority of the Moon Jae-in administration, and this will be a focal point of U.S.-ROK relations under the new U.S. administration, along with the unresolved issue of host nation support.

The inter-Korean joint liaison office (foreground) in Kaesong blown up by North Korea (KCNA/Kyodo)

1. Inter-Korean Relations Spearheaded by North Korea

(1) North Korea's Threats

On June 4, 2020, First Vice Department Director of the WPK Central Committee Kim Yo Jong, the supposed younger sister of Kim Jong Un, chairman of the WPK (chairman of the State Affairs Commission), issued a statement condemning the distribution of anti-North Korea leaflets by North Korean defectors. (Although Chairman Kim assumed the post of general secretary of the WPK at its Eighth Congress on January 10, 2021, this chapter covers events up to the end of 2020 and uses "Chairman Kim," his title as of 2020.) In the statement, Kim Yo Jong noted that the distribution of leaflets was a violation of the Panmunjom Declaration (April 27, 2018) signed by President Moon Jae-in and Chairman Kim, in which they agreed to completely cease all hostile acts including broadcasting through loudspeakers and distribution of leaflets, and warned that North Korea would abrogate the Agreement on the Implementation of the Historic Panmunjom Declaration in the Military Domain (September 19, 2018) that was reached between North and South Korea for implementing the Panmunjom Declaration.[1] Gradually, North Korea's demands shifted to correcting South Korea's "flunkeyism" (meaning the habit of being subservient to a great power).[2] A statement by Kim Yo Jong, published in the June 17, 2020 edition of the *Rodong Sinmun*, expressed loathing for the message delivered by South Korean president Moon Jae-in on the 20th anniversary of the South-North Joint Declaration (June 15, 2000), criticizing that the message reflected "deep-rooted flunkeyism." Kim's statement singled out the U.S.-ROK working group on North Korean affairs and rebuked South Korea's stance toward the United States: "It is a tragedy produced by the persistent and deep-seated pro-U.S. flunkeyism and submission of the South Korean authorities that the North-South ties reduced into the plaything of the U.S."[3] It suggests that the ceasing of loudspeaker broadcasting and leaflet distribution themselves were not necessarily North Korea's main purpose in condemning the ROK's "flunkeyism." In other words, North Korea's demand was for South Korea to withdraw its cooperation with the United States. When a U.S. State Department spokesperson expressed concern over the situation to the ROK media,[4] Kwon Jong Gun, director general of the Department of U.S. Affairs of the DPRK Foreign Ministry, issued a statement rebutting that the United States had no right to interfere in North-South relations, which were "the internal affairs of the Korean nation from A to Z."[5]

It could be thought that North Korea raised issues of loudspeaker broadcasting and leaflet distribution as a starting point for imposing demands on South Korea and creating conditions which would force the ROK to accept them in negotiations with the South. Such North Korean attempts date back to at least 2015. In August 2015, the two Koreas issued a Joint Press Statement aimed at ending tensions between North and South Korea along the Military Demarcation Line (MDL). The version of the statement released by North Korea stated that the ROK would stop loudspeaker broadcasts and the DPRK would "lift the semi-war state at that time."[6] It can be construed that North Korea would cease actions which heighten military tensions on the condition that South Korea ceases loudspeaker broadcasting. On the other hand, the wording "at that time," which gives rise to such an interpretation, was not included in the version released by the ROK.[7] If North Korea had intended to make the cessation of loudspeaker broadcasting a condition in exchange for the lifting of the semi-war state, the Park Geun-hye administration would not have accepted it at that time.

In contrast, the 2018 Panmunjom Declaration committed both the North and South to cease hostile acts, including loudspeaker broadcasting and leaflet distribution. It made it possible to assert that ceasing such hostile acts was a prerequisite for North Korea to avoid military tensions (according to Article 2.1 of the Panmunjom Declaration, the two Koreas, for the present, have an obligation to cease all hostile acts, including broadcasting through loudspeakers and distribution of leaflets, in order to alleviate the military tension and eliminate the danger of war on the Korean Peninsula).[8] Because the DPRK acquired the latitude to make such an interpretation of the Panmunjom Declaration, certain legitimacy was given to the North's insistence that South Korea would be made to pay a price for violating "the articles of the Panmunjom Declaration and the agreement in the military field in which both sides agreed to ban all hostile acts including leaflet-scattering." That was seen in the aforementioned statement of First Vice Department Director Kim Yo Jong. In the statement, North Korea indicated that, if hostile acts were not corrected, it reserved the option to close the inter-Korean joint liaison office (established in September 2018 in the Kaesong Industrial Complex) or to abrogate the September 19 agreement in the military domain, and attempted to put pressure on the ROK which wished to avoid such situations.[9] Soon after, North Korea emphasized its intention for military action, with the General Staff of the Korean People's Army (KPA) considering the actions (June 13),[10] and then blew up the inter-Korean joint liaison office (June 16).[11] On the following day, June 17, the KPA General Staff announced that plans for military action against the ROK would be submitted to the WPK Central Military Commission.[12]

The strong impression created by the bombing of the joint liaison office may reflect North Korea's intention to signal it would not hesitate to increase military tensions. If so, it would mean North Korea sought to conduct coercive diplomacy. Coercive diplomacy refers to presenting options that can inflict pain on the other country without defeating its troops necessarily, and forcing policymakers of the other country to choose an action that is preferable to the coercer.[13]

At this point in time, Chairman Kim Jong Un held a "preliminary meeting" of the WPK Central Military Commission and temporarily suspended the military action plans against the South (June 23).[14] It was announced two days before the anniversary of the outbreak of the Korean War (June 25). June 25 was also the anniversary of the ROK's alliance with the United States that fought the Korean War together. North Korea may have made the announcement shortly before the anniversaries to suggest it was ready to avoid escalation of the situation, depending on the stance of the South, and pressed the ROK to indicate whether it would maintain or correct its "flunkeyism."

Less than a week later, senior officials in the Moon Jae-in administration announced that the South wishes to limit the content discussed at the U.S.-ROK working group, which North Korea had accused as subjecting people to "flunkeyism." For example, Moon Chung-in, special advisor to the president on unification, foreign affairs and national security, criticized that the working group had become a forum where the United States restricts South-North cooperation.[15] At around the same time, Lee In-young, the former parliamentary leader of the Democratic Party (ruling party) who was nominated minister of unification by President Moon Jae-in, vowed that the ROK would separate what the South can decide on its own from the agenda of the U.S.-ROK working group, i.e., narrow the scope of U.S.-ROK discussions regarding policy on the North.[16]

President Moon Jae-in nominated former leader Lee In-young as minister of unification since his predecessor resigned in the wake of inter-Korean tensions caused by the bombing of the joint liaison office and other factors. The new minister of unification is expected to reflect the Moon administration's policy toward North Korea. Immediately after taking office, Minister Lee invited U.S. ambassador to South Korea Harry Harris to the ministry and told him that there were "positive and negative assessments of the working group." He said there were "negative assessments" in the ROK and conveyed that the functions of the working group must be "readjusted and rearranged" so that it can play a "role in promoting the development of inter-Korean relations and the consolidation of peace."[17] On this occasion, the minister of unification made clear to the U.S. ambassador that South Korea would distinguish what can be discussed with the United States at the working group and what the ROK can do on its own and proceed with them.[18]

(2) The Moon Administration Seeks to Improve Relations with North Korea

In 2020, the ROK made a salient attempt to resolve the confrontation with the

DPRK, even in the face of Pyongyang's hardline stance which was almost synonymous with intimidation. The ROK's conciliatory attitude toward the North was already evident in a speech made on March 1, 2019 (100th anniversary of the independence movement against Japanese colonial rule). In this speech, President Moon Jae-in offered his historical perspective that "pro-Japanese" conservative factions regarded the "independence activists" as siding with North Korea, which created "ideological" stigmas in South Korea. President Moon drew linkages between the ideological stigmas and the South's policy toward North Korea, rephrasing it as "the 38th parallel drawn through our minds." The president expressed his intent to resume tours of Mt. Kumgang and the Kaesong Industrial Complex as well as complete the railroads running the length of the Korean Peninsula.[19] In 2020, President Moon delivered an address to the people and the North on June 25, shortly after North Korea blew up the inter-Korean joint liaison office on June 16 and suspended military actions on June 23. In this speech, the president spoke about the significance of ending the war (ending the Korean War in a state of armistice), which the North could consider as an opportunity for the withdrawal of the U.S. Forces in Korea.

In addition, on June 30, 12 lawmakers from the Democratic Party proposed an amendment to the Development of Inter-Korean Relations Act.[20] The amendment would regulate acts, such as leaflet distribution, loudspeaker broadcasting, and visual materials posting, on the pretext that they could threaten the safety of residents in areas along the MDL and of the ROK people. Contrary to previous regulations of leaflet distribution, the latest amendment makes the ban on leaflet distribution legally binding by adding "Prohibition of Violation of the Inter-Korean Agreement" (Article 24) and "Penalty Provisions" (Article 25). The government of the ROK asserts that this was a necessary security measure, while it could have been put in place out of consideration for its relations with North Korea. The amendment was passed by the plenary session of the National Assembly on December 14 and promulgated on December 29.[21]

South Korea has also been consistent in its conciliatory approach to the Northern Limit Line (NLL) issue. In a speech delivered on West Sea Defense

Day (March 27, 2020) to mourn the victims of the conflicts with North Korea over the NLL, President Moon Jae-in underscored that "Not a single armed conflict has occurred along the Northern Limit Line" since the signing of the September 19 agreement in the military domain.[22] Yet North Korea has engaged in military actions in areas along the NLL. For example, under the leadership of Chairman Kim Jong Un, North Korea conducted artillery firing on an island off the coast near the NLL in the Yellow Sea on November 23, 2019 (officially reported by the North's media on November 25),[23] and then had its vessels cross the NLL and sail southward.[24] Although President Moon stressed that armed conflict had been avoided in waters around the NLL also including the period of the drill, the artillery firing was an act that the South Korean military considered as violation of the September 19 agreement.[25]

In the incident in September 2020, it showed similar behavior with previous North Korean acts like using as leverage the avoidance of armed conflict, emphasized by the Moon administration. According to an announcement by the ROK Joint Chiefs of Staff, on September 21, a North Korean fisheries inspection vessel discovered a missing crew member of the South Korean Ministry of Oceans and Fisheries in the North's waters area near the NLL, and North Korea conducted "an act of brutality by shooting at him and burning his body."[26] Nevertheless, two days after the incident, President Moon reiterated in a speech at the United Nations (UN) General Assembly that the ROK was committed to declaring an end to the war with North Korea and opening the door to peace regime on the Korean Peninsula.[27] President Moon's reiteration of the "end-of-war declaration" shortly after the incident was preceded by an exchange of letters between the leaders of the North and South around two weeks earlier (on September 12, State Affairs Commission Chairman Kim Jong Un replied to President Moon's September 8 letter).[28] Even after the incident, the Moon administration had showed its readiness to ease inter-Korean tensions toward North Korea.

In fact, the ROK's Presidential Office (Blue House) and Joint Chiefs of Staff disclosed the incident on September 24, after President Moon had delivered his speech at the UN. The Blue House issued a statement that "strongly condemns" "shooting and killing our citizen and burning his body" as a violation of "international law and humanitarianism" and states that "those responsible must be severely punished."[29] The Blue House explained the reason the incident was not disclosed sooner was because it occurred in waters hardly visible from the ROK side, and therefore, it took time to obtain reliable information.[30]

A message reportedly sent by the United Front Department of the WPK Central Committee to the Blue House on September 25 conveyed Chairman Kim Jong Un's view to the South, namely, that he felt "very sorry" for disappointing President Moon Jae-in and fellow countrymen in the South over an "awful incident." This message was not released directly by the DPRK but was read out on its behalf by the Blue House.[31] It can be said that the North Korean message, which contained wording that could be interpreted as an apology, was intended to incentivize the Moon administration to avoid taking a hard line response by hinting at an opportunity to ease tensions. On September 28, the Blue House explained that it would be difficult for South Korea to establish sufficient facts. So the government proposed a joint investigation of the incident to North Korea and then softened its condemnation of the incident.[32]

However, the message from North Korea's United Front Department also condemned the South Korean military for unilaterally describing the incident as "barbaric" without having any "evidence" and "without asking for [an] account of the crackdown process." The Department said that the incident should not destroy "the relations of trust and respect" between North and South Korea. On the day the message was read out by the Blue House, North Korea's Korean Central News Agency (KCNA) reported that ROK vessels, searching for the crew member who was shot, "intruded" into "our territorial waters," despite the "security measures" taken by the North to ensure that "the relations of trust and respect" would not be spoiled. The KCNA added that this foreshadowed the outbreak of a new "awful incident."[33] Shortly thereafter, Chairman Kim gave a speech at the 75th anniversary of the foundation of the WPK on October 10 and expressed "hope [that] the day would come when the North and South take each other's hand again."[34]

In response to the North's wavering messages, on October 11, the day after the 75th anniversary celebration, the National Security Council of the Moon administration stated it would take note of the DPRK's stance to "restore inter-Korean relations." Likewise, the ROK Ministry of National Defense commented on Chairman Kim Jong Un's speech, saying it would take note of the North's position that military force "will never be abused or used as a means for preemptive strike."[35] As discussed later, Chairman Kim Jong Un mentioned that military force "will never be abused or used as a means for preemptive strike," and went on to say, if there is infringement upon North Korea's security, it "will enlist all our most powerful offensive strength in advance to punish [it]," leaving room for interpretation. It is hard to imagine that this latter remark went unnoticed by the Ministry of National Defense. The Ministry's comment, which focused only on the first part of Chairman Kim Jong Un's speech, may reflect the Moon administration's strong desire to improve inter-Korean relations.

Minister of Unification Lee In-young insisted on the need for South-North cooperation being separated from the U.S.-ROK working group discussions to some extent. He reiterated the ROK's willingness to cooperate in the humanitarian and economic fields, including provision of medical and food assistance in the wake of flood damage in North Korea and cooperation for tackling the novel coronavirus disease (COVID-19), such as supplying COVID-19 vaccines.[36] However, the response from North Korea has not been positive, and it is unclear whether the offer of cooperation has contributed to improving inter-Korean relations as the Moon Jae-in administration had intended.[37]

2. Different Preferences for Military Capabilities between the Two Koreas

(1) North Korea: Continuation of Threats

Any decrease in the functions and activities of the KPA due to the spread of

COVID-19 would put the North Korean regime's very survival at risk. This can be said from the standpoint of both the North's use of military tensions as leverage to sway the ROK and manifestation of its deterrence. North Korea is believed to have begun taking measures against COVID-19 in early January 2020. North Korean authorities put everyone who crossed the border into the North after January 13 under "medical supervision."[38] At the end of January, the Non-Permanent Central Public Health Guidance Committee declared that the Hygienic and Anti-epidemic System would be converted into the State Emergency Anti-epidemic System until COVID-19 no longer posed a risk.[39] According to a briefing held in mid-March by Gen. Robert Abrams, commander of United Nations Command (UNC), U.S.-ROK Combined Forces Command (CFC), and United States Forces Korea (USFK), the KPA were placed on lockdown for approximately 30 days, and no military aircraft activity by the North was observed for 24 days.[40]

North Korea has not acknowledged any outbreak of COVID-19 within its borders. Even as the virus spread worldwide, North Korea took actions that increased military tensions, including firing SRBMs into the Sea of Japan four times in March. The first SRBMs fired on March 2 from the vicinity of Wonsan into the Sea of Japan are thought to have flown 240 kilometers.[41] Analysis suggests these SRBMs are the same type launched by North Korea in the previous year, which was called a "super-large" multiple rocket launcher (MRL).[42] On March 9, North Korea again fired missiles (flight range of about 200 kilometers), which are believed to be the "super-large" MRL, from the Sea of Japan side.[43] This was followed by another firing on March 21 of missiles (flight range of about 400 kilometers), which are said to be similar to the United States' Army Tactical Missile System (ATACMS), from the Yellow Sea side in the west, flying over North Korea and into the Sea of Japan,[44] and still another firing on March 29 of SRBMs (flight range of about 250 kilometers),[45] which it called a "super-large" MRL, from the Sea of Japan side.[46]

On March 3, the day after the first launch, Kim Yo Jong, first vice department director of the Central Committee, criticized that South Korea considers "the alliance with the U.S. dearer than its own fellow countrymen," and that consideration for the spread of COVID-19 was the only reason for refraining from the U.S.-ROK combined training in March.[47] North Korea urged the ROK to suspend drills with the United States on its own initiative rather than because of external factors such as the pandemic. The DPRK heightened military tensions and also imposed demands on the ROK. It is believed that North Korea perceives it has retaliatory deterrence capabilities that deter the United States and the ROK from taking a military response and that this is behind North Korea's posture. Any military action taken by the United States and the ROK against North Korea would raise fears of the North's retaliation by deploying MRLs and long-range artillery in large numbers to areas along the MDL and include the South Korean capital and surrounding areas in their range. Because North Korea has the military capability to turn Seoul into a "sea of fire,"[48] it has not faced preventive attacks from the United States and South Korea, even if the North's development of nuclear weapons is unveiled. Moreover, that allowed the DPRK to take actions provoking military tensions.[49]

Since the previous year, the DPRK has continued to develop SRBMs and enhance other capabilities to enlarge the coverage of the "sea of fire." The 300-millimeter caliber MRL launched by North Korea in 2019[50] is estimated to have a range (about 170 kilometers) that reaches U.S. Army Garrison Humphreys, located south of Seoul, where the U.S.-ROK CFC is to relocate.[51] The USFK concentrated facilities in Camp Humphreys partly for allowing more families to accompany personnel as U.S. bases relocate southward.[52] In addition, the South Korean government continues to develop the surrounding urban areas.[53] After the USFK was relocated away from the range of the traditional "sea of fire," North Korea has continued to pursue them and attempts to maintain the option of engulfing the camp and its periphery into armed conflict.

Following the series of SRBM launches and an inspection of an air unit drill in the western area,[54] Chairman Kim Jong Un held an Enlarged Meeting of the WPK Central Military Commission in May 2020. In its announcement about the meeting, North Korea referred to strengthening "nuclear war deterrence" and released photos of Chairman Kim pointing to a blurred-out image in front of senior military officers, suggesting that a major weapon was under development confidentially (May 24).[55] The images and the chairman's remarks released by North Korea may have been intended to hint to the United States, the ROK, and other countries that progress was being made in nuclear weapons development that could trigger a new crisis. Less than 10 days later, North Korea issued a statement announcing it would abrogate the September 19 agreement in the military domain, which had been marked as an achievement of the Moon Jae-in administration (June 4; see previous section). As discussed above, the South Korean administration sought to distance itself from the United States after North Korea's intimidation.

On October 10, at the military parade on the 75th anniversary of the establishment of the WPK, Chairman Kim Jong Un referred to "dear fellow countrymen in the South" and raised issues that could be related to North Korea's strategy toward the United States or nuclear doctrine. According to the speech, North Korea intends to strengthen its military capability based on "[its] timetable" and build a "war deterrent" to contain all dangerous attempts, including nuclear threat.[56] This is in line with the commentary published in the *Rodong Sinmun*

Chairman Kim Jong Un delivering a speech at the military parade on the 75th anniversary of the WPK's founding on October 10, 2020 (KCNA/Kyodo)

in 2018, which noted that the suspension of nuclear testing was "an important process for the worldwide nuclear disarmament" and the DPRK would "advanc[e] along the path taken by itself according to its timetable."[57] The concept of non-proliferation precludes non-nuclear weapon states from possessing nuclear weapons, i.e., countries other than the United States, Russia, the United Kingdom, France, and China, which are designated as nuclear-weapons states in the Treaty on the Non-Proliferation of Nuclear Weapons (NPT). It is not a concept that permits North Korea to possess nuclear weapons until "worldwide nuclear disarmament" is achieved.[58] Nevertheless, the speech by Chairman Kim Jong Un strongly suggests that the DPRK rejects denuclearization.

In the same speech, Chairman Kim Jong Un stated that "our war deterrent" "will never be abused or used as a means for preemptive strike," but that "if, and if, any forces infringe upon the security of our state and attempt to have recourse to military force against us, I will enlist all our most powerful offensive strength in advance to punish them." The following points can be noted. First, although Chairman Kim did not make it explicit, "most powerful offensive strength" may refer to nuclear weapons. Second, it is unclear what is meant by a situation which threatens North Korea's security and enlists all of North Korea's most powerful offensive strength in advance. It appears to leave room for the preemptive use of strength, depending on North Korea's perception of the situation. Third, the aim of preemptive strike is to "punish." The intention could be to threaten to destroy value targets, such as densely populated areas and industrial centers, rather than targeting the source of an imminent attack by the other country. If it cannot be ruled out that North Korea will use nuclear weapons as a means for preemptive strike in a countervalue strike rather than a counterforce strike, then Kim Jong Un's speech could be understood as a strong message, even if it is ambiguous in wording.

(2) South Korea Seeks Self-Reliance, Facing the U.S.-China Competition

With North Korea launching the Pukguksong-3 submarine-launched ballistic missile (SLBM)[59] on October 2, 2019, the ROK Navy reiterated the need to equip its next-generation Aegis ships with interceptor missiles equivalent to the SM-3 ballistic missile defense interceptor. The SLBM, launched from the Sea of Japan side, flew 450 kilometers and reached an altitude of about 900 kilometers, which was considerably higher than usual. The SLBM is believed to have been on a lofted trajectory that makes interception difficult.[60] A missile on a lofted trajectory is hard to intercept by the conventional Korea Air and Missile Defense (KAMD) system, which intercepts missiles at an altitude no higher than 100 kilometers, far below the SLBM's maximum altitude.[61] Originally, the KAMD focused on terminal-phase, lower-tier missile defense and was designed to deal with situations on the Korean Peninsula without relying on the missile defense of the U.S. Forces. In an emergency, it detects an enemy missile with an early warning radar or an Aegis radar, analyzes the information, and then promptly intercepts the missile. While South Korea's Ministry of National Defense stresses that it constructs its own KAMD system, it is also enhancing interoperability with the U.S. Forces.[62]

A week later, on October 10, the ROK chief of naval operations told the National Assembly that the Navy was working to procure SM-3-class interceptors, citing their effectiveness in defending against SLBMs or high-altitude ballistic missiles.[63] A missile equivalent to the SM-3 would have an altitude of well over 100 kilometers. According to materials submitted by the Navy Headquarters to the National Assembly at that time, SM-3-class missiles would be needed for developing the KAMD from a lower-tier-focused system into a multilayered one. This would expand the range of intercepts to an altitude of 100 kilometers or higher to deal with improvements in North Korea's ballistic missile capabilities.[64]

The introduction of interceptors against ballistic missiles has raised controversy in South Korea since several years ago. On October 15, 2013, the ROK Ministry of National Defense limited the range of the KAMD to an altitude of 100 kilometers, while at the same time denying the introduction of SM-3 interceptors and the acceptance of Terminal High Altitude Area Defense (THAAD) system deployment.[65] This was followed by South Korea's decision not to introduce THAAD but to introduce its replacement,[66] the indigenously manufactured long-range surface-to-air missile (L-SAM; not yet developed).[67] About four months earlier, President Park Geun-hye of the ROK had vowed to establish a "strategic cooperative partnership" with President Xi Jinping of

China.[68] However, South Korea has also agreed to a "comprehensive strategic alliance"[69] with the United States. In 2015, debate arose over the deployment of THAAD to the USFK, prompting China's Defense Minister Chang Wanquan to express concerns over it. Defense Minister Han Min-goo of the ROK explained to Defense Minister Chang that South Korea would harmonize its "comprehensive strategic alliance" with the United States and its "strategic cooperative partnership" with China.[70] The ROK explicitly stated that it would harmonize each of the strategic partnerships with the United States and China for the purpose of alleviating China's concerns over the introduction of THAAD. When the Park Geun-hye administration decided to accept the deployment of THAAD to the USFK in July 2016, the Chinese Foreign Ministry stated that it was "strongly dissatisfied with and firmly opposes to this."[71]

About a year later, in late October 2017, the newly inaugurated Moon Jae-in administration engaged in negotiations with China, aiming to end the economic retaliation that China had been launching against the ROK for accepting THAAD deployment.[72] The ROK agreed not to change its three existing positions as demanded by China, which were: (i) not make an additional deployment of THAAD; (ii) not join the U.S. missile defense system; and (iii) not develop the ROK-Japan-U.S. trilateral cooperation into a military alliance ("three no-policies").[73] The "three no's" constitute red lines for China, and it can be said that the ROK accepted China's insistence on not crossing the red lines if South Korea does not want to be disadvantaged.[74]

The ROK Navy pressed for the introduction of SM-3-class interceptors, noting that "neighboring countries should not interfere in the decisions of a sovereign nation."[75] However, at the South Korean National Assembly in 2019, legislators from the Democratic Party on the side of the Moon Jae-in administration expressed concern over the ROK Navy's assertion, stating that SM-3-class missiles violated the three no-policies.[76] The ruling party also expressed concern that the SM-3 exceeded the altitude for intercepting missiles targeting the Korean Peninsula area.[77]

The 2021–2025 Mid-term Defense Plan, unveiled by the Moon Jae-in administration in August 2020, aims for "comprehensive multilayered defense." It mentions the introduction of additional Aegis ships but does not refer to SM-3-class missiles, which the Navy had insisted were necessary for this purpose. The Mid-term Plan focuses on improving defense capabilities, including the Korean version of the Iron Dome air defense system to protect the capital Seoul from North Korea's long-range artillery. They also include the deployment of additional surface-to-air missiles, such as the Patriot and the indigenously manufactured Cheolmae II to complement the KAMD. SM-3-class missiles, however, were removed from the plan.[78]

In August 2020, Suh Hoon, director of national security at the Blue House, held talks with Yang Jiechi, director of the Central Foreign Affairs Commission Office of the Chinese Communist Party. According to Director Suh's explanation, the ROK elicited the comment of China that South Korea was "a priority country to visit" for Chinese president Xi Jinping.[79] The Chinese announcement, however, mentioned neither this comment nor President Xi's visit to South Korea.[80] The Moon Jae-in administration hoped President Xi would visit South Korea, giving China the ability to leverage the visit to extract concessions from South Korea on certain issues. In fact, there was a comment of the ROK released unilaterally by China. According to China, Director Suh of the ROK is said to have stated that it was "jointly building lasting peace on the Korean Peninsula" with China. However, this was not mentioned in the South Korean announcement.[81] The 2018 South-North Panmunjom Declaration contains text suggesting that discussions toward a peace regime may be held without China. China's announcement may suggest that it would ensure its participation in the discussions.

On August 15, 2019, President Moon Jae-in called for building "a nation that cannot be shaken."[82] About a month and a half after this speech, in October 2019, President Moon instructed negotiations to revise the U.S.-ROK missile guidelines. The guidelines, while undergoing revisions since 1979, constrain the development of rockets and ballistic missiles by South Korea. On July 28, 2020, Kim Hyun-chong, deputy national security advisor, announced that restrictions on the development of solid-propellant space rockets were lifted as a result of the negotiations. He explained that this was significant in bringing South Korea closer to becoming "a nation that cannot be shaken."[83] On the one hand, the ROK removed the acquisition of SM-3 interceptors from the Mid-term Defense Plan as if to give in to pressure from China. On the other hand, the administration strongly supported the development of missiles exceeding the existing restrictions imposed by the United States in order to become "a nation that cannot be shaken."

On July 23, shortly before the announcement of the revised missile guidelines, President Moon visited the Agency for Defense Development (ADD). Successfully developing the indigenously manufactured SRBM Hyunmoo-2, President Moon praised ADD for serving as the fountainhead of the defense capabilities of "[t]he Republic of Korea [which] ranks 6th globally in military strength."[84] During the Park Chung-hee administration in the 1970s, ADD developed the first indigenously manufactured ballistic missile, the Baekgom, Nike Hercules Korea-1 (NHK-1), using technology secretly acquired through a project related to the Nike surface-to-air guided missile of the United States.[85] The U.S.-ROK missile guidelines originated from a promise made by the South Korean defense minister to restrict the development of NHK-1, responding to a request from the USFK commander to suspend the development following the test firing of the missile in 1978.[86]

During the visit to ADD, President Moon referred to an "indigenous ballistic missile capable of carrying one of the world's heaviest payloads" and is said to have told others to secure "complete missile sovereignty" in the future.[87] The president likely had in mind the Hyunmoo-4 ballistic missile, which was developed after the previous revised missile guidelines (2017) abolished restrictions on payload weight and is said to have a payload weight of two tons. South Korea reportedly test fired the missile in March 2020.[88] The Hyunmoo-4 has a range of 800 kilometers, which can strike all of North Korea from a city south of central South Korea and is the upper limit of the range that continues to be restricted under the missile guidelines.[89]

In September 2020, the Moon Jae-in administration proposed a 52.9 trillion-won defense budget for FY2021. This was an increase of 5.5% over the previous year, even as the South Korean economy was hit by the COVID-19 pandemic. The budget priorities included a military satellite communication system project (2.2296 trillion won) to enable the transfer of wartime OPCON Authority held by the CFC commander (U.S. Army general) to a general of the ROK Armed Forces.[90] In his Armed Forces Day speech on September 25, President Moon underscored capabilities, such as the development of ballistic missiles with a range of over 800 kilometers, a 30,000-ton "light aircraft carrier," and submarines. However, it is unclear whether these capabilities are necessary based on South Korea's role in the U.S.-Republic of Korea Combined Operations envisioned against North Korea. The president did not specifically mention North Korea in his speech.[91]

With regard to the U.S.-ROK Alliance, host nation support (South Korea's share of the cost for stationing the USFK) has been debated between the two countries. The ROK's share has continued to increase from 790.4 billion won in 2010 to 1,038.9 billion won in 2019.[92] The Special Measures Agreement (SMA) for 2020 was still being negotiated at the start of the year, and on March 20, the ROK disclosed that "the two sides have differences in their positions" and the talks were temporarily suspended. The USFK furloughed more than 4,000 Korean National employees who should have been paid under the SMA since April 1, and this situation continued until the South Korean government offered to shoulder their salaries in June. After the SMA ceased to be effective at the end of December 2019, the United States is said to have had to unilaterally bear the costs of the USFK.[93]

In the October 14, 2020 Security Consultative Meeting (SCM) Joint Communique between the U.S. and ROK defense ministers, the United States noted that the current lack of an SMA could have lasting effects for Alliance readiness. On the other hand, in the same Joint Communique, the United States and the ROK discussed ways to transfer the OPCON of the CFC (commanded by a U.S. Army general) to the Future Combined Forces Command (commanded by a ROK Armed Forces general), and also committed to continue U.S.-ROK-Japan defense cooperation, including information sharing for the security of Northeast Asia.[94] At the SCM, the ROK reportedly stated that it would "thoroughly prepare for a combined defense posture under the South Korean military's leadership by fulfilling the conditions as early as possible," while the United States responded that "Fully meeting all the conditions for the transition of operational control to the Republic of Korea commander will take time."[95] The comments reveal a gap between the United States and South Korea over the timing of the OPCON transfer. In 2013, during the previous Park Geun-hye administration, the two countries were said to have considered the ROK assuming the commander's position for a new command similar in size to the CFC after the OPCON transfer.[96] However, a specific transfer date was no longer mentioned in 2014. Since then, it has been decided that the OPCON transfer would proceed under a "conditions-based" approach.[97]

In 2020, unlike the previous two years, no major progress related to the Korean Peninsula was seen at the summit level, in part because the United States was preparing for a presidential election and in part because of the global spread of COVID-19. The North's testing of the South was thus all the more salient in 2020, as seen in the bombing of the inter-Korean joint liaison office. Nevertheless, Japan-ROK and U.S.-ROK bilateral efforts as well as Japan-U.S.-ROK trilateral efforts are important for peace and stability in East Asia, alongside improving inter-Korean relations. Attention will be focused on how South Korea will work together with the administration of Suga Yoshihide, Abe Shinzo's successor, and the new President Joseph Biden.

NOTES

1) KCNA, June 4, 2020.
2) KCNA, June 17, 2020.
3) *Rodong Sinmun*, June 17, 2020.
4) Yonhap News, June 10, 2020.
5) KCNA, June 11, 2020.

6)   *Rodong Sinmun*, August 25, 2015.

7)   [ROK] Ministry of Foreign Affairs, "Joint Press Release from the Inter-Korean High-Level Meeting" (August 25, 2015); *Rodong Sinmun*, August 25, 2015.

8)   Watanabe Takeshi and Koike Osamu, "The Korean Peninsula: Prospects of the 'Denuclearization' Negotiations," in *East Asian Strategic Review 2019*, English edition, ed. National Institute for Defense Studies (NIDS) (Tokyo: NIDS, 2019), 86.

9)   KCNA, June 4, 2020.

10) KCNA, June 13, 2020.

11) KCNA, June 17, 2020.

12) *Rodong Sinmun*, June 17, 2020.

13) Thomas C. Schelling, *Arms and Influence*, revised edition (New Haven: Yale University Press, 2008), 21–23; Todd S. Sechser and Matthew Fuhrmann, *Nuclear Weapons and Coercive Diplomacy* (Cambridge: Cambridge University Press, 2017), 28.

14) KCNA, June 24, 2020.

15) Yonhap News Television, July 1, 2020.

16) *Dong-A Ilbo*, July 7, 2020; *Chosun Ilbo*, July 7, 2020; [ROK] National Assembly, *Foreign Affairs and Unification Committee Record*, 280th Session (Extraordinary Session), July 23, 2020, 15.

17) [ROK] Ministry of Unification, "'Minister of Unification Rejected U.S.-ROK Working Group' Not True: Statement regarding August 19 Article in *Munhwa Ilbo*" (August 19, 2020).

18) [ROK] Ministry of Unification, "Unification Minister Lee Meets with US Ambassador to the ROK Harry Harris" (August 18, 2020).

19) [ROK] Presidential Secretariat, *Collection of Speeches by President Moon Jae-in: We Must Live Together*, vol. 2, issue 2 (Seoul: Presidential Secretariat, 2019), 256–263.

20) *Dong-A Ilbo*, June 30, 2020.

21) [ROK] Ministry of Unification, "Information on Amendment to the 'Development of Inter-Korean Relations Act' Related to Regulations on Anti-North Korea Leaflets" (December 18, 2020); Chosunbiz, December 29, 2020.

22) [ROK] Presidential Secretariat, *Collection of Speeches by President Moon Jae-in: Together With Our Great People, I Will Strive to Pave the Way for the Republic of Korea to Take the Lead Globally*, vol. 3, issue 2 (Seoul: Presidential Secretariat, 2020), 323.

23) *Rodong Sinmun*, November 25, 2019; *Kookbang Ilbo*, November 27, 2019.

24) *Kookbang Ilbo*, November 28 and November 29, 2019.

25) *Kookbang Ilbo*, November 27, 2019.

26) [ROK] Joint Chiefs of Staff, "Announcement regarding Position on Missing Fishery

Guidance Official" (September 24, 2020).

27) [ROK] Presidential Office, "Address by President Moon Jae-in at 75th Session of United Nations General Assembly" (September 23, 2020).

28) [ROK] Presidential Office, "Briefing by Director of National Security Suh Hoon regarding the Letters of the South and North Korean Leaders" (September 25, 2020).

29) [ROK] Presidential Office, "Statement by the NSC Standing Committee regarding the Death of Our Fishery Guidance Official" (September 25, 2020).

30) [ROK] Presidential Office, "Written Briefing by Spokesperson Kang Min-seok" (September 28, 2020).

31) [ROK] Presidential Office, "Briefing by Director of National Security Suh Hoon regarding the North's Written Notification" (September 25, 2020).

32) [ROK] Presidential Office, "Written Briefing by Spokesperson Kang Min-seok."

33) KCNA, September 27, 2020.

34) *Rodong Sinmun*, October 10, 2020.

35) *Kookbang Ilbo*, October 12, 2020.

36) *Hankyoreh*, August 22, 2020; Yonhap News, October 23, 2020; [ROK] Ministry of Unification, "Minister of Unification Hosts Debate on Inter-Korean Health and Medical Services Cooperation" (November 20, 2020).

37) *Rodong Sinmun*, November 19, 2020.

38) KCNA, February 3, 2020.

39) KCNA, January 30, 2020.

40) [U.S.] Department of Defense, "Gen. Robert B. Abrams Holds a Press Briefing on U.S. Forces-Korea's Response to COVID-19" (March 13, 2020).

41) [Japan] Ministry of Defense (MOD), "2020 nen no kitachosen ni yoru dando misairu hassha" [North Korea's ballistic missile launches in 2020] (April 2020).

42) *Rodong Sinmun*, September 11 and November 1, 2019.

43) *Janes*, March 10, 2020; [Japan] MOD, *Defense of Japan 2020*, English edition (2020), 98.

44) *Janes*, March 23, 2020.

45) Regarding the flight distances of the missiles fired by North Korea in March 2020, see [Japan] MOD, "2020 nen no kitachosen ni yoru dando misairu hassha."

46) *Rodong Sinmun*, March 30, 2020.

47) KCNA, March 3, 2020.

48) KCNA, March 25 and March 27, 2013 and March 27, 2016; [ROK] Bureau of Public Information, *Change and Reform: Collection of Materials on Five Years of the Kim Young-sam Government*, vol. 1 (Seoul: Bureau of Public Information, 1997), 468.

49) Ashton Carter and William Perry, *Preventive Defense: A New Security Strategy*

for America (Washington, DC: Brookings Institution, 1999), 128–129; Michishita Narushige, *North Korea's Military-Diplomatic Campaigns* (London: Routledge, 2010), 105–107, 193–194; Watanabe Takeshi, "Without Incentives: North Korea's Response to Denuclearization," *NIDS Journal of Defense and Security* 18 (December 2017): 106.

50) *Kookbang Ilbo*, May 7, 2019.

51) [ROK] Joint Chiefs of Staff, *The Situation of North and South Korea, Q&As* (Seoul: Joint Chiefs of Staff, 2015), 55.

52) [U.S.] General Accounting Office, *Defense Infrastructure: Basing Uncertainties Necessitate Reevaluation of U.S. Construction Plans in South Korea*, GAO-03-643 (July 2003), 7; Jon Letman, "USAG Humphreys: The Story behind America's Biggest Overseas Base," *Diplomat*, November 6, 2017.

53) [ROK] Ministry of the Interior and Safety, "This Year, 1 Trillion Won to Be Invested in Pyeongtaek Area Development for Relocation of U.S. Military Base: Ministry of the Interior and Safety Finalizes 'FY2020 Implementation Plan for Pyeongtaek Area Development Project for Relocation of U.S. Military Base'" (March 10, 2020).

54) *Rodong Sinmun*, April 12, 2020.

55) *Rodong Sinmun*, May 24, 2020.

56) Hereafter, the speech on the 75th anniversary of the founding of the WPK is excerpted from: KCNA, October 10, 2020.

57) *Rodong Sinmun*, May 28, 2018; Watanabe and Koike, "The Korean Peninsula," 77–78.

58) Watanabe and Koike, "The Korean Peninsula," 75–78.

59) *Rodong Sinmun*, October 3, 2019.

60) [Japan] MOD, "Boei daijin rinji kisha kaiken" [Extraordinary press conference by defense minister] (October 3, 2019); [Japan] MOD, *Defense of Japan 2020*, Part 1, Chapter 1, Section 3.

61) *Kookbang Ilbo*, October 16, 2013.

62) [ROK] Ministry of National Defense, *2016 Defense White Paper* (2017), Chapter 3, Section 5.

63) [ROK] National Assembly, *National Defense Committee Record*, Audit Session, October 10, 2019, 14.

64) [ROK] National Assembly, *National Defense Committee Record*, Audit Session, Appendix, October 10, 2019, 120.

65) *Kookbang Ilbo*, October 16, 2013.

66) [ROK] National Assembly, *National Defense Committee Record*, 326th Session (Extraordinary Session), no. 6, Appendix, July 7, 2014, 37.

67) *Kookbang Ilbo*, October 16, 2013.

68) *People's Daily*, June 28, 2013; [ROK] Ministry of Foreign Affairs, "ROK-China Joint Statement on the Future Vision" (June 27, 2013).

69) [U.S.] White House, "Joint Vision for the Alliance of the United States of America and the Republic of Korea" (June 16, 2009).

70) *Kookbang Ilbo*, February 5, 2015.

71) Xinhua Net, July 8, 2016.

72) [ROK] National Assembly, *Foreign Affairs and Unification Committee Record*, 354th Session (Regular Session), no. 6, Appendix, November 27, 2017, 28.

73) [ROK] National Assembly, *Foreign Affairs and Unification Committee Record*, 354th Session (Regular Session), no. 6, November 27, 2017, 15; [ROK] Ministry of Foreign Affairs, "Outcome of ROK-China Consultations on Improving Bilateral Relations" (October 31, 2017).

74) Takeshi Watanabe, "Japan-US-ROK Cooperation for Sustaining Deterrence," in *NDA-FOI Joint Seminar: North Korea's Security Threats Reexamined*, eds. Hideya Kurata and Jerker Hellström (Yokosuka: National Defense Academy, 2019), 85–87.

75) [ROK] National Assembly, *National Defense Committee Record*, Audit Session, October 10, 2019, 123.

76) Ibid.

77) Ibid., 122.

78) *Kookbang Ilbo*, August 11, 2020.

79) [ROK] Presidential Office, "Written Briefing regarding Meeting between Suh Hoon, Director of National Security and Yang Jiechi, Member of the Politburo of the Chinese Communist Party Central Committee" (August 23, 2020).

80) *People's Daily*, August 23, 2020.

81) *People's Daily*, August 23, 2020; [ROK] Presidential Office, "Written Briefing regarding Meeting between Suh Hoon, Director of National Security and Yang Jiechi, Member of the Politburo of the Chinese Communist Party Central Committee."

82) [ROK] Presidential Secretariat, *Collection of Speeches by President Moon Jae-in: Together With Our Great People, I Will Strive to Pave the Way for the Republic of Korea to Take the Lead Globally*, vol. 3, issue 1 (Seoul: Presidential Secretariat, 2020), 268–269.

83) [ROK] Presidential Office, "Briefing by Deputy National Security Advisor Kim Hyun-chong regarding the Revised ROK-U.S. Missile Guidelines" (July 28, 2020).

84) [ROK] Presidential Office, "Remarks by President Moon Jae-in at Agency for Defense Development" (July 23, 2020).

85) Ahn Dongman, Kim Byungkyo, and Cho Taehwan, *NHK-1's Endeavors and Victories*

on Record: The Story of the Development of the First Surface-to-Surface Missile of the Republic of Korea (Seoul: Planet Media, 2016), 120–124, 146, 150–182.

86) Ibid., 360–361; *Kookbang Ilbo*, September 25, 2017.

87) [ROK] Presidential Office, "Briefing by Spokesperson Kang Min-seok regarding Outstanding Issues" (July 23, 2020).

88) SBS 8 News, August 2, 2020; Julia Masterson, "South Korea Tests New Missile," Arms Control Association (June 2020); Timothy Wright, "South Korea Tests Hyunmoo-4 Ballistic Missile," International Institute for Strategic Studies (June 10, 2020).

89) *Hankyoreh*, August 3, 2020.

90) *Kookbang Ilbo*, September 2, 2020.

91) [ROK] Presidential Office, "Address by President Moon Jae-in at 72nd Armed Forces Day" (September 25, 2020).

92) ROK e-National Indicators, "Status of Host Nation Support," ROK e-National Indicators website.

93) *Kookbang Ilbo*, June 4, 2020; [U.S.] Department of Defense, "Department of Defense Accepts Korean Ministry of Defense's Proposal to Fund Korean National Employee Labor Costs" (June 2, 2020).

94) [U.S.] Department of Defense, "Joint Communique of the 52nd U.S.-Republic of Korea Security Consultative Meeting" (October 14, 2020).

95) KBS News 9, October 15, 2020.

96) *Kookbang Ilbo*, June 3, 2013.

97) [U.S.] Department of Defense, "Joint Communique of the 46th ROK-U.S. Security Consultative Meeting" (October 23, 2014).

Chapter 4

Southeast Asia

Post-COVID-19 Regional Security Issues

MATSUURA Yoshihide (Lead author, Sections 1 and 2 (3))
TOMIKAWA Hideo (Sections 2 (1) and (2) and 3)

Prime Minister Suga attending the East Asia Summit held online due to the pandemic on November 14, 2020. President Trump of the United States did not attend it even once during his four-year term. (Prime Minister's Office of Japan official website)

Summary

Southeast Asia was impacted greatly by the novel coronavirus disease (COVID-19) in 2020. In Indonesia and the Philippines, infections continued to spread or level off even into the start of 2021. While some countries in the region largely contained new infections, others experienced a resurgence of cases from the second half of 2020. In the region as a whole, there is no sign of the pandemic ending. Measures taken in response to COVID-19, such as border closures, city-wide lockdowns, and other restrictions, had serious repercussions on domestic economies with the poor particularly hit hard. At the same time, some governments resorted to authoritarian approaches under the pretext of the response to COVID-19, raising concerns about the impact on democratic practices that have been implemented in the countries. Although the Association of Southeast Asian Nations (ASEAN) played a role as a platform for international support to deal with COVID-19, its role as an independent actor to deal with problems was limited.

Notwithstanding the pandemic, the situation in the South China Sea remained tense as China's activities to claim its rights unfolded with a greater show of force. Southeast Asian countries responded militarily and diplomatically to the extent possible, taking into account the disparity in their forces with China's and the impact on economic relations. Western countries, on the other hand, became increasingly wary of China's actions, and the United States in particular embraced a more active engagement on this issue. As differences in opinion between the United States and China become prominent in the ASEAN diplomatic arena, the organization appears to be distancing itself from this great power competition.

Despite the effects of COVID-19 spending on national defense budgets, countries are working to reinforce and modernize their naval fleets and boost their capabilities for anti-ship attacks and maritime intelligence, surveillance, and reconnaissance (ISR) for strengthening sea power. As regards military activities, while the first half of 2020 was marked by the postponement of joint exercises due to COVID-19, large-scale exercises resumed in the second half of the year, including by the Indonesian Navy.

1. COVID-19 and Southeast Asia

(1) The Epidemiological Situation in Southeast Asian Countries

COVID-19 spread around the world and is also raging in Southeast Asia. The pandemic has affected the nature of state management in regional countries and even the role of ASEAN as a regional community.

According to the count of the World Health Organization (WHO), the 10 ASEAN member states had about 1.51 million total cases and a death toll of about 34,000 in 2020.[1] Restrictions on movement and economic activities within the countries, coupled with a slowdown in cross-border human mobility and trade, had a significant fallout on the regional economy. In December 2020, the Asian Development Bank (ADB) forecasted Southeast Asia's real growth rate for the year at -4.4%.[2]

Figure 4.1. Cases of COVID-19 in ASEAN member states (2020)

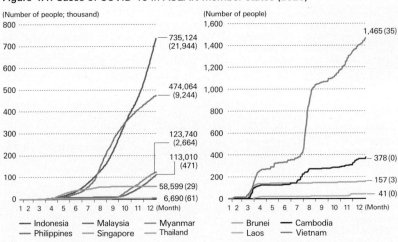

Source: Compiled by the author based on country data from the WHO Coronavirus (COVID-19) Dashboard.

Note: Numbers on the right not in parentheses indicate the total number of confirmed cases, while those in parentheses indicate the number of deaths, both as of the end of December 2020.

Figure 4.1 shows trends in COVID-19 cases in the ten ASEAN member states. Among them, Indonesia and the Philippines accounted for about 80% of the total COVID-19 cases and about 90% of the total deaths in the region as of the end of 2020.[3] Indonesia has seen cases rise almost consistently since the beginning of the

A Philippine military personnel conducting lockdown inspections in Manila (DPA/Kyodo News Images)

outbreak and clearly has not succeeded in containment. The Philippines recorded fewer cases after they peaked in August and September. However, infections have nearly levelled off since then, and containment has not been achieved.

In Indonesia, the Joko Widodo administration issued the "Regulation of Minister of Health Number 9 of 2020 on Guidelines to Large-scale Social Restrictions in Accelerating COVID-19 Mitigation" on April 3. Based on the regulation, local governments imposed restrictions on activities called "large-scale social restrictions" (Pembatasan Sosial Berskala Besar: PSBB). However, strict measures like a city-wide lockdown were not taken in order to balance preventing contagion and sustaining economic activities. During the Ramadhan period from the latter half of April, for example, initially the government only requested people to voluntarily refrain from returning to their hometowns, and this is believed to have contributed to spreading the disease across the country. In the Philippines, President Rodrigo Duterte declared a state of public health emergency on March 8, put Metro Manila in lockdown from mid-March, and applied curfews to the entire island of Luzon. From June, infections surged after restrictive measures were relaxed, and the Philippines has since gone back and forth between tightening and loosening restrictions. In its report, the

International Monetary Fund (IMF) mentions Indonesia and the Philippines as countries that eased restrictions before they had suppressed infection. It notes that the effectiveness of containment was affected by constraints in testing, healthcare, and government capacity to implement lockdowns of densely populated cities, which have both a large informal sector and a high level of poverty, and in the case of Indonesia, also by the delayed start of restrictions.[4]

Until around July, the rest of the countries in the region fell into two categories: those that had a certain number of total cases but avoided the explosive spread of new infections like in Indonesia and the Philippines and had a limited number of deaths (Malaysia, Thailand, and Singapore); and those that had minimal cases and deaths (tens to hundreds of cases and zero or single-digit deaths) (Vietnam, Myanmar, Cambodia, Laos, and Brunei). Subsequently, some countries saw a rise in new cases as restrictions were eased on people's movement and economic activities. At the time of writing, Myanmar and Malaysia have recorded a surge in cases (and deaths in the former) since August and September. A unique example is Singapore, where migrant workers account for more than 90% of the total number of cases. Authorities were slow to catch clusters that occurred in overcrowded dormitories with poor hygiene, and this led to infection spreading from April.[5] The government has contained new outbreaks by testing all migrant workers and taking measures to improve their living conditions, including building new dormitories that take into account infectious diseases.

Vietnam stopped issuing visas to Chinese travelers and suspended flights to and from mainland China as early as the beginning of February.[6] It is reported that Vietnam took very strict measures to quarantine infected persons and their contacts and restrict activities, backed by a strong policy implementation mechanism under the direction of the Communist Party.[7] As a result, until July, new cases were not identified in the country for three months, and no deaths were reported since the outbreak began. However, Vietnam has since confirmed community-acquired cases and deaths. Brunei banned entries into the country and restricted the activities of individuals. Large gatherings were prohibited, and public and commercial facilities were temporarily closed. At the end of Ramadhan in May, mass prayers and open houses at government offices and businesses were banned, although there had been no new cases in the previous two weeks. Individuals, too, were restricted from celebrating in large groups.[8] In Cambodia, travel between Phnom Penh and other provinces during the Khmer New Year period in April was prohibited, and public holidays during this period were moved to August.[9]

(2) State Management Problems

The COVID-19 pandemic has constrained state functions in all countries in Southeast Asia, albeit to varying degrees. This has triggered a major fallout on their people's livelihoods. The economic and political issues are discussed below.

First, the pandemic has had an adverse economic impact especially on low-income groups, including people who work in the informal sector. For example, inability to work due to movement restrictions has a direct bearing on the survival of day laborers and street vendors. Even when government subsidies and other support are available, they may be inadequate or may not be properly delivered. According to reports as of June, in Indonesia, the number of people unemployed reached 6.4 million, and the government's cash payments in response to COVID-19 were reaching only about 30% of the population due to geographical constraints, institutional problems, corruption, and other obstacles.[10] People are thus forced to work to survive, even by breaking the restrictions, which in turn hinders containment. Such circumstances are behind the government's drive to give greater priority to maintaining economic activities over strict infection control restrictions. In particular, according to ADB, the Philippines' real growth rate is projected to drop significantly to -8.5% on an annualized basis, and there are concerns that this will have a serious impact.[11] The World Bank, in an October report, forecast that the number of poor people (those with incomes less than $5.50 per day) in developing East Asian and Pacific countries (including Southeast Asian countries except Brunei and Singapore) will increase by somewhere between 9.5 million and 12.6 million in 2020.[12] The prolongation of the COVID-19 pandemic will continue to push more people into poverty and widen the economic gap in the countries, and this is anticipated to have a major impact on state stability and security.

Secondly, in the political context of each country, the restrictions that have been put in place in response to COVID-19 have led to constraints on political freedoms based on democratic values. A salient example is Thailand. In Thailand, a state of emergency was declared by Prime Minister Prayut Chan-o-cha on March 26 to allow for lockdown as a COVID-19 countermeasure. The declaration was extended twice, at the end of April and the end of May. At the end-of-June deadline, Prime Minister Prayut decided to extend the declaration for another month despite the absence of new cases for more than a month. Since then, the declaration has repeatedly been extended, and the state of emergency is still in place as of the end of 2020. Although the Prayut government was transferred from military to civilian rule in July 2019, factions opposed to Prayut's repressive stance toward opposition parties continue to hold anti-government rallies. Though the government denies it, it is believed that the state of emergency continues to be in place to counter such rallies.[13] In fact, since July 2020, rallies by students and others have not only criticized the government but also advocated for reform of the monarchy, which in turn has led to the emergence of pro-royalist groups and the rise of tensions between the opposing factions. Against this backdrop, when an anti-government rally was staged on October 15, the government declared a state of emergency for Bangkok, banned gatherings of five people or more, and arrested 20 protest leaders and others. In addition, at the November 17 rally, at least 55 people were reportedly injured, including six who were shot by unknown assailants amid violent clashes among dissidents, police, and royal supporters. Anti-regime rallies in Thailand continued until December, when COVID-19 infections began to reemerge across the country.[14]

In Malaysia, the resurgence of infections prompted the government to issue a Conditional Movement Control Order for the state of Selangor and the federal territories of Kuala Lumpur and Putrajaya on October 14. Meanwhile, Malaysian politics continued to be in turmoil due to the struggle for leadership following the resignation of Prime Minister Mahathir Mohamad in February. On October 23, Prime Minister Muhyiddin Yassin appealed to King Al-Sultan Abdullah to declare a proclamation of emergency, citing the need to combat COVID-19 and stabilize the lives of the people. The King, however, did not recognize the necessity and rejected the request.

In Myanmar, State Counsellor Aung San Suu Kyi, the de facto government leader, announced that the general election on November 8, 2020 would take place as scheduled, even as the number of infected people increased rapidly and some opposition parties called for a postponement. It is reported that due to a ban on gatherings of more than 50 people and restrictions on movement to curtail COVID-19, emerging opposition parties were at a particular disadvantage in the election campaign.[15] According to the final election results released on November 14, the ruling National League for Democracy won more votes than in the previous election and maintained its single-party majority.

In Singapore, opposition parties called for the postponement of the general election amidst the COVID-19 outbreak, after speculation emerged in March that the Parliament would be dissolved early.[16] However, the "circuit breaker" measure to restrict social activities was lifted on June 1, and the ruling People's Action Party decided to hold the general election in July. Because large campaign rallies and contact between candidates and voters were restricted in response to COVID-19, the election campaign was expected to be unfavorable to opposition parties.[17] Nevertheless, in the July 10 voting results, the ruling party significantly reduced its share of votes although it still won, while the opposition Workers' Party gained more seats.

The need for infection control may be real, and to some extent it may require authoritarian approaches. Nevertheless, the attempts made by incumbent administrations to use COVID-19 as a pretext to steer policies to their own advantage are undermining public trust in the government, and the resultant backlash is creating political and social turmoil. There are concerns that such a situation may jeopardize democratic practices that have been implemented in Southeast Asian countries, which could affect not only ASEAN countries themselves but also the value of ASEAN as a community.

(3) Regional Diplomacy Issues

The COVID-19 pandemic presented issues for Southeast Asian countries and, understandably, also pressing issues for the region as a whole. Still, ASEAN as a regional organization did not play a marked role in dealing with the issues. On April 14, 2020, the Special ASEAN Summit on COVID-19 was held online. The declaration of the summit called for intra-ASEAN cooperation in areas such as health and hygiene, military medicine, humanitarian assistance and disaster relief (HA/DR), and the economy, as well as cooperation with external partners and international organizations, including WHO.[18] It is unclear, however, if ASEAN was useful in sharing and providing hygiene and medical supplies, personnel, funds, know-how, and other items needed by countries in the region during the spread of the disease at that time.

Take HA/DR under the ASEAN framework as an example. The 2004 Indian Ocean earthquake and tsunami prompted the gradual formation of regional cooperation arrangements and schemes in both the military and civilian sectors. But in the midst of the COVID-19 pandemic, various factors are thought to have made cooperation on tangible supplies difficult, including: all member states were affected nearly simultaneously; the nature of the crisis entailing an infectious disease forced countries to close their borders and stop the flow of people and goods; and necessary supplies were overwhelmed by the demand at home. Against this backdrop, the establishment of the COVID-19 ASEAN Response Fund and the ASEAN Regional Reserve of Medical Supplies for Public Health Emergencies was proposed at the summit in April 2020, and the launch of the latter was confirmed at the ASEAN Summit (online) held on November 12, 2020.[19]

Meanwhile, China has been demonstrating its presence by offering bilateral and multilateral cooperation, known initially as "mask diplomacy" and later as "vaccine diplomacy." On August 20, China reached an agreement with Indonesia to cooperate for the provision of COVID-19 vaccines. Since November, China's Sinovac Biotech has been supplying vaccines to Bio Farma, a state-owned pharmaceutical company in Indonesia, and has been producing vaccines for the Indonesian domestic market. On August 24, at the online summit of the Lancang-Mekong Cooperation (LMC), which is a framework for cooperation between China and the countries of the Mekong River basin (Cambodia, Laos, Myanmar, Thailand, and Vietnam), Premier of the State Council Li Keqiang announced that China would give Mekong countries priority access to vaccines and set up special funds for the promotion of public health under the LMC framework.[20] On September 9, at the ASEAN-China Foreign Ministers' Meeting (online), State Councilor and Foreign Minister Wang Yi stated that China would establish a relationship of "China-ASEAN vaccine friends" by giving priority to the vaccine needs of ASEAN member states and announced the joint building of a reserve pool of emergency medical supplies.[21] On December 6, Indonesia received the first shipment of 1.2 million doses of Sinovac vaccines. On December 31, Thailand announced that it secured two million doses of vaccines to be received from February to April 2021, and later revealed in an official announcement that the vaccines would be Sinovac's.[22] In Cambodia, Prime Minister Hun Sen announced on December 15, 2020 that it would only procure vaccines certified by WHO. Although it was reported that this announcement excluded the acceptance of vaccines directly from China, this view has been disputed.[23]

At the same time, the U.S. pledge of over $87 million in COVID-19 related assistance to ASEAN member states was welcomed at the ASEAN-United States Summit (online) held on November 14.[24] At the Mekong-Japan Foreign Ministers' Meeting held online on July 9, it was agreed that Japan would provide assistance worth 11.6 billion yen, including medical equipment, to the five Mekong countries mentioned above.[25] At the ASEAN-Japan Foreign Ministers' Meeting (online) on September 9, Japan announced that it is contributing $50 million to support the establishment of the ASEAN Center for Public Health

Emergencies and Emerging Diseases (ACPHEED) and that it would contribute $1 million to the COVID-19 ASEAN Response Fund.[26] The establishment of ACPHEED was officially announced at the ASEAN Summit on November 12, and the inaugural event was held at the ASEAN-Japan Summit (online) on the same day.[27]

It is meaningful that ASEAN and other regional frameworks function as a platform for support from external partners in responding to COVID-19. As discussed in the next section, however, it would not be sound if the great powers utilize cooperation, even COVID-19 support, as a means for obtaining Southeast Asian countries' alignment with any of them in the age of U.S.-China rivalry. The regional society's recovery from COVID-19 must be made in a forward-looking manner through intra- and extra-regional cooperation, in a way that fully respects both the shared values of ASEAN member states and the ownership and autonomy of ASEAN.

2. The South China Sea Dispute and Security Developments in Southeast Asia

(1) Responses by Countries: Conflict Avoidance and Countermoves

The situation in the South China Sea remained tense in 2020. China continued activities to assert its rights in the South China Sea, and Beijing is demonstrating a greater show of force against other countries concerned, including parties to the South China Sea dispute. To boost its deployment capabilities, China proceeded to establish military outposts on geological features it effectively controls and on maritime features it has reclaimed since 2014. On the other hand, China's show of force has elicited stronger opposition from other countries and raised the alarm of Western countries, including the United States. This section describes some incidents that occurred between China and Southeast Asian countries concerned with the dispute. In addition, it provides an overview of U.S. and Chinese military operations in the South China Sea and the diplomatic responses taken by ASEAN.

Following President Xi Jinping's 2018 announcement to strengthen energy security, China has become more oriented toward securing its own interests and enhancing exploration activities.[28] It has begun to conduct operations with a greater show of force, targeted at Malaysia and Vietnam's independent development of energy resources in waters overlapping with the claims of the so-called nine-dash line.

In mid-May 2019, a China Coast Guard (CCG) vessel patrolled waters around the Luconia Shoals at the southern tip of the Spratly Islands and sailed through a liquefied natural gas (LNG) mining area, which was set up by Malaysia and operated by the private oil company Sarawak Shell. In July, a Chinese survey ship and a CCG vessel sailed near the development area set up by Vietnam, northwest of Vanguard Bank, putting pressure on the development and exploration activities of Rosneft, a Russian national oil company operating in the area.[29] In August, the Chinese survey ship, *Haiyang Dizhi 8*, escorted by several vessels, including the 12,000-ton CCG 3901 cutter, approached the coast of Vietnam.[30] Vietnam deployed its Border Guard and fishing and other vessels. As a result of diplomatic negotiations, the ships of both sides finally left the waters in October.[31] However, in the same month, the drill ship *West Capella*, which was contracted to Malaysia's national oil company Petronas, began exploration activities, and China sent CCG vessels in December. When the drill ship moved from the area off the coast of Sarawak to the Malaysian-Vietnamese joint development area, China followed the ship with alternating vessels.[32]

In the past, China sporadically attempted to put pressure on Malaysia and Vietnam's exploration and development activities in

LCS USS *Gabrielle Giffords* maintaining presence near the drill ship *West Capella* (U.S. Navy photo by MC2 Brenton Poyser)

Figure 4.2. Main claims by countries over the South China Sea

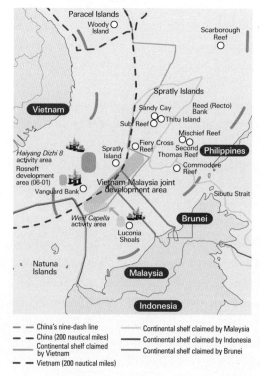

- – – China's nine-dash line
- – – China (200 nautical miles)
- —— Continental shelf claimed by Vietnam
- – – Vietnam (200 nautical miles)
- —— Continental shelf claimed by Malaysia
- —— Continental shelf claimed by Indonesia
- ······ Continental shelf claimed by Brunei

Sources: Compiled by the author based on AMTI, "Maritime Claims of the Indo-Pacific," CSIS, among other sources.

Note: Only the main claims mentioned in this chapter are shown on the map.

gas fields. But, as described above, CCG vessel and survey ship operations from around mid-2019 became more continuous and coordinated.

Under such circumstances, in December 2019, Malaysia made a partial submission for rights in the South China Sea, overlapping with the claims of China and Vietnam, to the Commission on the Limits of the Continental Shelf (CLCS). CLCS makes recommendations based on information received from parties to establish the outer limits of the continental shelf beyond 200 nautical miles from the baselines. In 2009, when Malaysia and Vietnam made a joint submission, China submitted a note verbale attached with a map of the so-called nine-dash line to the United Nations (UN) and asked the UN not to evaluate the joint application.[33] In this light, China submitted another note verbale to the UN strongly protesting the partial submission. It is believed that Malaysia took this measure due to a change in policy under the Mahathir administration, which came to power in May 2018, to proactively address disputes related to rights over the South China Sea. However, political upheaval in February 2020 led to the collapse of the cooperative relationship among the ruling coalition parties, and a new administration headed by Minister of Home Affairs Muhyiddin Yassin was formed.[34]

Vietnam, on the other hand, announced in December 2019 the establishment of maritime militias in 14 provinces, aiming to strengthen response capabilities under military-civilian cooperation.[35] In addition, in April 2020, a collision between a CCG vessel and a Vietnamese fishing boat was reported by the Vietnamese media, ramping up domestic public outcry against China.[36]

In April 2020, it was reported that a Chinese oceanographic survey ship was once again approaching the Vietnamese development area. Subsequently, the survey ship, together with several vessels, sailed southward near the exclusive economic zone (EEZ) claimed by Malaysia and approached the drill ship *West Capella* that was continuing to conduct exploration activities.[37] A Vietnamese ship was also tagging the Chinese survey ship, creating a tense situation with vessels from three countries facing each other in the same waters.[38] In May, *West Capella* completed its scheduled work and left the waters, and later, the *Haiyang Dizhi 8* survey ship also departed. In response to the situation, the United States and Australia sent naval ships and carried out exercises near the waters in late April. In May, the United States sent two vessels, including a littoral combat ship (LCS), to continue surveillance.[39]

The United States, Australia, and other countries carried on with their daily surveillance, including freedom of navigation operations (FONOPs) near maritime features claimed by China. The U.S. action described above, however, can be considered a response tailored more to a particular situation and a new development in U.S. involvement in the South China Sea. Malaysia, on the other hand, could not find effective means other than continuing persistent negotiations, with its ministers and others repeatedly calling for a "peaceful solution" in the face of Chinese pressure. Malaysia sometimes used wordings, including "sea of peace, stability and trade" and "all relevant parties." The new administration's policy toward the South China Sea dispute should be given focus, including the implications of such wordings.[40]

While China had left the area of a standoff with Malaysia, it was confirmed in June that Beijing had sailed an oceanographic survey ship, this time in the EEZ claimed by Vietnam.[41] Even with the ongoing "regular" naval patrols of the United States, a CCG vessel approached a drill ship operating in Vanguard Bank in July as part of China's continued demonstration of force.

The Rodrigo Duterte administration of the Philippines has separated economic development from security in its response to China over the South China Sea dispute, and has actively promoted bilateral cooperation. It appears that this approach basically has not changed. In 2020, the Philippines still fundamentally sought to find a peaceful solution to the dispute; at the same time, though, it made more attempts to counter China's show of force by effectively applying the rule of law in the international framework. This was partially triggered by the continued dispute with China in the area of Thitu Island (Pag-asa Island) that is de facto controlled by the Philippines.

A number of Chinese vessels gathered around Thitu Island and around nearby Sandy Cay, coinciding with the start of the construction of a landing place on Thitu Island in December 2018. A series of incidents then obstructed the sailing of ships and operations of fishing boats.[42] In June 2019, a Philippine fishing boat operating near Reed (Recto) Bank was slammed by a Chinese fishing boat. As a result, public opinion toughened toward China.[43] In July and August, Chinese naval vessels successively sailed in offshore Philippines. Their automatic identification system (AIS) was turned off, and no coastal state was notified, according to reports.[44]

At the beginning of 2020, a CCG vessel paid an official visit to the Philippines for the first time, and a joint drill with the Philippine Coast Guard was conducted, raising an expectation that tensions would ease.[45] However, it was later reported that, in February 2020, a ship believed to be a Chinese naval vessel locked a fire-control radar onto a Philippine navy corvette near Commodore Reef under the effective control of the Philippines; it brought to light the challenges of building trust between the two countries.[46]

In response to China's ambitions to strengthen de facto control over these waters, the Philippines submitted a note verbale in March regarding

Malaysia's submission to CLCS. The note stated that the claims made in China's counterarguments were invalid and appealed for legitimacy based on the Award of the Arbitral Tribunal in the South China Sea Arbitration.[47] China made unilateral decisions related to the South China Sea, announcing the establishment of administrative districts in the Spratly and Paracel Islands in April and a ban on fishing in the waters in May.[48] Indonesia submitted a note verbale in May, and the United States addressed a letter to the UN in June. In July, Secretary of State Mike Pompeo issued a statement on the U.S. position regarding the South China Sea dispute, indicating that the United States would be actively involved in the issue.[49] Moreover, Australia, the United Kingdom, France, Germany, and other countries submitted similar opinions to the UN. Not only countries in Southeast Asia concerned with the dispute but also major Western powers showed clear support for the 2016 Arbitral Award, which President Duterte had not actively referred to after taking office.[50]

The U.S. presence in the South China Sea and its involvement in the dispute are generally thought to favor the Philippine security environment. Since December 2018, Delfin Lorenzana, secretary of national defense, has asked the United States to clarify the scope of application of defense obligations under the Mutual Defense Treaty (MDT) between the Philippines and the United States. In March 2019, he received assurances from Secretary of State Pompeo that "any armed attack [...] in the South China Sea will trigger mutual defense obligations under Article 4 of [the] Mutual Defense Treaty." In reality, however, discussions for clarifying the scope of application have not made progress. When U.S. secretary of defense Mark Esper visited the Philippines in November 2019, Defense Secretary Lorenzana said the Philippines planned to review the MDT by the end of 2019. Nevertheless, discussions were not held by the end of the year. Furthermore, the Philippines' diplomatic stance toward the United States under the Duterte administration has been complicated by the need to move away from over-reliance on the United States and to achieve balance between the United States and China. In February 2020, the Philippines unilaterally decided to abrogate the Visiting Forces Agreement (VFA), a key arrangement for maintaining the Philippines-U.S. alliance.[51] However, in June, a temporary freeze on the abrogation process was announced amidst China's continued show of force in the waters surrounding the Philippines.[52] With U.S.-China tensions in the waters increasing, the Philippines announced in August that it would prohibit its military from participating in joint military exercises with other countries in the high seas of the South China Sea. As such moves illustrate, the Philippines struggled to maintain a balance between the United States and China.[53]

In this way, the Philippines is taking measures to counter China on the South China Sea dispute by utilizing the rule of law in the international framework, alongside asserting its own claims. In August 2019, at the invitation of Beijing, President Duterte made his fifth visit to China since assuming office and raised the Arbitral Award for the first time. However, as Chinese president Xi was steadfast in his refusal to recognize the award, the two sides reaffirmed their differences in opinion and shared the view to resolve the issue peacefully through dialogue and other means. On the occasion of Chinese defense minister Wei Fenghe's visit to the Philippines in September 2020, President Duterte stressed the importance of international law in resolving disputes in the South China Sea, noting, "Any and all disputes must be resolved peacefully in full accord with the UNCLOS [United Nations Convention on the Law of the Sea] and all relevant international instruments." In addition, the Philippine Department of Foreign Affairs in a statement in July 2020 and President Duterte in his speech to the UN General Assembly in September 2020 reiterated the Philippines' commitment to the Arbitral Award. The aforementioned landing place on Thitu Island was completed in June 2020, despite obstructions, and Defense Secretary Lorenzana, who visited the site with senior military officers, stated that work would continue on infrastructure development and runway repairs.[54] In August 2020, the Kalayaan Municipality (town), which has jurisdiction over Thitu Island, gave names to six sandbanks and reefs around the island that have been used as refuge for fishermen, and asserted its de facto control over the waters.[55]

On the other hand, the Philippines has shown an openness to cooperation with China to the extent manageable in energy development in the South China Sea and non-traditional security sectors. For example, during the above-mentioned visit of President Duterte to China, the two countries held talks on joint exploration of resources in the South China Sea. A document describing the members of the Philippines-China Inter-Governmental Joint Steering Committee on Cooperation on Oil and Gas was mutually exchanged, and the committee was established. During Defense Minister Wei's visit to the Philippines in September, the maintenance of peace and stability in the South China Sea was confirmed in a meeting with Defense Secretary Lorenzana, and guidelines were signed for China's financial assistance worth 130 million yuan that could be used by the Philippine military in procuring equipment for HA/DR operations and other supplies.[56]

Indonesia maintains that it is a non-claimant state in the territorial dispute in the South China Sea. Indonesia and China have repeatedly confirmed that there exists no dispute over territorial waters between the two countries. China, on the other hand, contends that the area of the so-called nine-dash line overlaps with Indonesia's claim to maritime rights and interests. In addition, China attempts to make the effect of historic fishing rights in the undemarcated sea area a fait accompli, together with the claim that they precede the exclusive economic activities in the EEZ defined by UNCLOS. There is an ongoing tussle between China and Indonesia, which refuses to accept China's claim.

In December 2019, Prabowo Subianto, defense minister, on his first official visit to China as a minister, met with Chinese officials, including Vice Chairman of the Central Military Commission Xu Qiliang and Defense Minister Wei Fenghe, and discussed strengthening bilateral ties in the defense sector. However, from the latter half of December, it was reported that Chinese fishing vessels accompanied by CCG vessels repeatedly engaged in "illegal, unreported, and unregulated (IUU) fishing" in the EEZ claimed by Indonesia to the north of the Natuna Islands. Indonesia sent a patrol vessel of the Indonesian Maritime Security Agency (Badan Keamanan Laut Republik

Indonesia: BAKAMLA) and lodged a protest through the Chinese embassy.[57] In January 2020, the Indonesian Navy increased the number of ships deployed to the Natuna Islands and conducted monitoring operations with maritime patrol aircraft (MPA). The Air Force also conducted surveillance operations with F-16 fighters in the areas, albeit describing them as part of its routine operation. All these activities demonstrated Jakarta's willingness to take stern responses not only with the maritime security agency but also with the military.[58]

In terms of the political response, Mohd Mahfud MD, coordinating minister for political, legal and security affairs, refused to negotiate on Indonesia's sovereignty. President Joko visited the Greater Natuna Island in January, accompanied by officials including Luhut Binsar Pandjaitan, coordinating minister for maritime affairs and investment, and ACM Hadi Tjahjanto, commander of the Indonesian National Armed Forces. He held a dialogue with fishermen and others regarding the development plan for the Natuna Islands, demonstrating Indonesia's intent to protect its interests to the islands.[59] On the other hand, Coordinating Minister Mahfud, Defense Minister Prabowo, and others sought to defuse the debate, noting that the issues were diplomatic issues.[60] This government policy is believed to be based on Jakarta's realistic perception of the situation, not wanting to escalate the conflict with China, with which there is a difference of military strength.[61]

In the international arena, Indonesia showed clear support for the rule of law in the international framework from the standpoint of a "non-claimant" in the South China Sea dispute, and thereby, squarely opposed China's attempts to make its claims in the waters a fait accompli. In May 2020, the Indonesian government submitted a note verbale to the CLCS in response to China's objections to the Malaysian submission to CLCS. In the note, Indonesia stated that, as a party to UNCLOS, it did not support any claims that violate international law, including UNCLOS, and expressed its support for the 2016 Arbitral Award.[62] In response, China sent a note verbale in June expressing readiness to negotiate with Indonesia. However, Foreign Minister Retno Marsudi refused, stating that Indonesia did not recognize China's claims for neither rights over the Spratly Islands nor historical rights and that negotiation was unnecessary.[63]

In September 2020, a CCG vessel again sailed near the EEZ boundary claimed by Indonesia. Although vessels of all countries enjoy freedom of navigation in the high seas and in the EEZs of other countries, this CCG vessel stayed for many hours and showed suspicious tracks, raising questions about its operations. It was reported that BAKAMLA tracked the vessel and warned that it leave the area.[64]

No significant changes in China's maneuvers were observed despite the rigorous responses taken by Indonesia and the clear show of international public opinion rejecting China's claims. It is anticipated that China's attempts to make its claims a fait accompli in these waters will be continuous. In this regard, Collin Koh, a research fellow at the S. Rajaratnam School of International Studies (RSIS), Nanyang Technological University (NTU) in Singapore, expressed the view that Indonesia may have to rethink its strategy and confront China with a new approach in the future.[65]

(2) U.S. and Chinese Activities in the South China Sea: Deployment Capability and Presence Enhancement

In 2020, as the effects of COVID-19 were felt across the region, China began to conduct a show of force against Malaysia and Vietnam's energy development as described above. The United States, which was considering a more active involvement in the South China Sea dispute, took a stern response toward China, despite temporary constraints on its aircraft carrier operations in the Pacific due to the pandemic.

In March 2020, after USS *Theodore Roosevelt* (CVN-71) made a port call in Da Nang City, Vietnam, crew members were confirmed to have contracted COVID-19 aboard the vessel. It called at Guam and was forced to stay there for a long term.[66] Meanwhile, the Yokosuka-based USS *Ronald Reagan* (CVN-76) and the Naval Base Kitsap-based USS *Nimitz* (CVN-68) were conducting self-quarantine of their crews, leaving the United States without an aircraft carrier deployed in the Western Pacific.[67] Nevertheless, in April 2020, the U.S. Air Force implemented its pulling back schedule as planned for bombers, which had been deployed to Andersen Air Force Base (AFB) in Guam as part of the Continuous Bomber Presence (CBP) missions.[68] Amid these changes in the deployments of the U.S. Forces in the Western Pacific, China stepped up its operations in the South China Sea, timing them as if to test the readiness of the U.S. Forces.

In response, in the same month, the U.S. Navy conducted FONOPs in the Paracel Islands using USS *Barry* (DDG-52), followed by the cruiser USS *Bunker Hill* (CG-52) in the Spratly Islands. In addition, through "dynamic force employment (DFE)" that deploys forces from the U.S. mainland when necessary, B-1Bs of the 28th Bomb Wing (Ellsworth Air Force Base, South Dakota) conducted a Bomber Task Force (BTF) mission over the South China Sea and demonstrated that both the Navy and Air Force had not lost their deployment capability in the Western Pacific (see Chapter 6, Section 2 (2)).[69] In contrast, in May, it was reported that China appears to have sent KJ-500 early warning and control aircraft and MPA KQ-200 (or Y-8 transport aircraft) to Fiery Cross Reef in the Spratly Islands. It was also reported that H-6K bombers conducted takeoff and landing exercises on Woody Island in the Paracel Islands,

B-52Hs participating in an aviation drill with carrier-based aircraft during the dual-carrier exercises (U.S. Navy photo by Lt. Cmdr. Joseph Stephens)

showing China's ability to make deployments in the South China Sea using the features it effectively controls and geographical features reclaimed in these waters.[70]

The United States, on the other hand, deployed four B1-B bombers from the 7th Bomb Wing (Dyess Air Force Base, Texas) to

Andersen AFB in May. In June, it was reported that the United States may have conducted MPA and other aircraft patrols near the Bashi Channel.[71] At the end of June, USS *Ronald Reagan* and USS *Nimitz*, which had returned to duty, joined to conduct dual-carrier exercises in the South China Sea for the first time in six years. B-52H bombers were added to the exercises, and aviation and other drills were carried out.[72]

Drills and deployment of forces by both the great powers, the United States and China, in the South China Sea continued in the months that followed. In early July, China conducted naval exercises in the vicinity of the Paracel Islands, and soon after, the United States again conducted dual-carrier exercises in the South China Sea, which was joined by B-1B BTF. Meanwhile, China deployed J-11B fighters and JH-7 fighter bombers to Woody Island.[73]

Thus, until around mid-2020, the United States continued to demonstrate its presence in the South China Sea with global force projection capabilities, while China demonstrated its deployment capabilities using the geographical features it effectively controls and the geographical features it reclaimed in the South China Sea. Since then, China has begun to demonstrate its ability to strike from longer distances in the course of conducting off-shore drills. From the end of July to early August, China conducted exercises in several sea areas, firing DF-21 and DF-26 ballistic missiles into the South China Sea. Furthermore, the H-6J bomber, which is said to be capable of carrying the YJ-12 long-range anti-ship missile, also reportedly conducted live-fire drills.[74] When USS *Ronald Reagan*, which had returned to the South China Sea upon the completion of its mission in another area, conducted aviation training, China is said to have again fired ballistic missiles into the South China Sea at the end of August.[75]

As shown above, both the United States and China strengthened their presence in the South China Sea. Some believe that China is waging "total competition" encompassing military capabilities against the United States in these waters.[76]

Table 4.1. Major events and activities of countries in the South China Sea

	2019	January (2020)	February	March	April	May	June	July	August	September	October	November	December
Philippines	Chinese vessels pass through Philippines' Sibutu Strait (October)	CCG vessel makes port call	Chinese vessel locks radar on Philippine vessel	CCG vessel sails near Second Thomas Reef					Philippine military's participation in South China Sea joint exercises is banned	Chinese survey ship operates in Reed Bank			Chinese survey ship sails near Natuna coast
Indonesia	CCG and Chinese fishing vessels operate near Natuna Islands; Indonesia sends corvette, etc. (December)			BAKAMLA-related law is amended				1st and 2nd Fleet drills		CCG vessel approaches Natuna coast	Armada Jaya naval exercise	1st Fleet marine drill	
Malaysia	CCG vessel tracks Malaysian survey ship (December)		RMN conducts anti-ship missile drill (July); CCG vessel sails near Luconia Shoals (June)		U.S. and Australian vessels conduct drills in China-Malaysia standoff area	U.S. vessels are sent to China-Malaysia standoff area	Chinese survey ship moves from offshore Vietnam to offshore Malaysia					Malaysia seizes Chinese fishing vessels; CCG vessel sails near Luconia Shoals	
Vietnam	Maritime militias are established; CCG vessel sails near Vanguard Bank (July); Vietnamese frigate is sent (August)				CCG vessel collides into Vietnamese fishing vessel; Chinese survey ship operates in offshore Vietnam		CCG vessels seize Vietnamese fishing vessel	Re-dispatch; Chinese survey ship cruises in offshore Vietnam	Chinese survey ship operates in offshore Vietnam	China-Vietnam new fisheries agreement			Chinese survey ship operates in offshore Vietnam; Vietnamese and Indian navies conduct navigation drill
United States				COVID-19 outbreak on aircraft carrier (CVN-71)	B-52s are withdrawn from Guam			U.S. vessel monitors Chinese survey ship; Dual-carrier exercises (CVN-76/78) / aviation drill (B-52); Dual-carrier exercises (CVN-76/78) (2nd round)	Aircraft carrier (CVN-76) drill; RIMPAC			Aircraft carrier (CVN-76) drill	
BTF mission					B-1B	B-1B	B-1B	B-1B					B-1B
FONOPs (Spratly) Total: 6 times					DDG-85	DDG-52; DDG-89				DDG-89	DDG-56	DDG-56	
FONOPs (Paracel) Total: 3 times			LCS-8			CG-52		DDG-114					
China			Destroyer locks radar on U.S. patrol aircraft (Philippine Sea)	Anti-submarine warfare drill	Naval live-fire drill; Aircraft carrier (Liaoning) sails South China Sea	Bombers to Woody Island		Naval exercise [Paracel area]; Ballistic missile / new bomber drill [Paracel area]	[Incl. Paracel area]; Bombers to Woody Island	Dual-carrier exercises; Bombers to Woody Island; Fighters and fighter bombers to Woody Island	[Incl. Paracel area] Wide-area maritime drill		Aircraft carrier (Shandong) drill [incl. 075 LHD]; Ballistic missile / Wide-area maritime drill / ballistic missile drill; Early warning and control aircraft and maritime reconnaissance aircraft to Fiery Cross Reef

Sources: Compiled by the author based on media reports.

(3) Diplomatic Efforts of ASEAN

The aforementioned issues surrounding the South China Sea and the increased presence of the United States and China have cast a shadow over the workings of ASEAN as a regional organization. Given that the 2020 ASEAN chair was Vietnam, which has taken a strong stance against China, there were preliminary observations that ASEAN may take a stronger stance on the South China Sea dispute than in the past.

The ASEAN Summit, originally scheduled for April in Hanoi, was postponed due to COVID-19 and was held online on June 26. The Chairman's Statement released on the following day, June 27, referred to the South China Sea dispute as follows: "We discussed the situation in the South China Sea, during which concerns were expressed on the land reclamations, recent developments, activities and serious incidents, which have eroded trust and confidence, increased tensions and may undermine peace, security and stability in the region."[77] Compared to the wording at the 2018 and 2019 summits, which "took note of some concerns on the land reclamations and activities in the area," the 2020 wording appears to have elevated the level of concern by mentioning more specific issues, such as those mentioned above, while not identifying the parties by name.

In the same paragraph, a sentence was added reaffirming that UNCLOS was the basis for determining maritime entitlements, sovereign rights, jurisdiction and legitimate interests over maritime zones, and that all activities in the oceans and seas must be carried out in the UNCLOS legal framework. In addition, the paragraph on the Code of Conduct (COC) in the South China Sea removed "warmly welcomed the continued improvement in cooperation between ASEAN and China," which was in the previous statement in terms of Sino-ASEAN relations related to this issue. Regarding the conclusion of the COC, the wording "within a mutually-agreed timeline" (see *East Asian Strategic Review 2020*, Chapter 4, Section 1) was deleted and replaced with "consistent with international law, including the 1982 UNCLOS." These changes, coupled with the increasing support for the Arbitral Award noted earlier, suggest ASEAN's attempt to take a more principled stance toward China on the South China Sea dispute.

From September 9 to 12, meetings originally scheduled for August, including the ASEAN Foreign Ministers' Meeting, the ASEAN Regional Forum (ARF), and the East Asia Summit (EAS) Foreign Ministers' Meeting, were all held online. According to media reports, many countries commented on the South China Sea dispute, including countries noted to have a tilt toward China such as Myanmar, Laos, and Cambodia.[78] In both the Joint Communiqué of the ASEAN Foreign Ministers' Meeting on September 9 and the ARF Chairman's Statement on September 12, the wording on the South China Sea dispute was almost the same as the previous year's but also contained "serious incidents" from the summit in June. In the context of the COC, the statements kept the wording on welcoming Sino-ASEAN cooperation, adopting both "within a mutually-agreed timeline" and "consistent with international law, including the 1982 UNCLOS."[79]

At the EAS Foreign Ministers' Meeting on September 9, U.S. secretary of state Pompeo expressed concerns over China's aggressive actions in the South China Sea and stated that China's expansive maritime claims are unlawful.[80] Also, at the U.S.-ASEAN Foreign Ministers' Meeting on September 10, Secretary Pompeo reportedly called for severing ties with companies that support the construction of military outposts in the South China Sea.[81] Meanwhile, at the EAS Foreign Ministers' Meeting, Chinese foreign minister Wang Yi stated that the acts of U.S. interference in territorial and maritime disputes through enhanced military deployment are becoming the biggest factor fueling militarization in the South China Sea and urged the United States, an external country, to respect the wishes of regional countries.[82]

The Chairman's Statement of the ASEAN Summit on November 12 (online), released on November 18, largely retained the wording of the summit in June and the foreign ministers' meeting in September. However, to the continuously used phrase, "recognized the benefits of having the South China Sea as a sea of peace, stability, and prosperity," it added the wording, "especially during this time in the common fight against COVID-19."[83] The same phrase was also used in the Chairman's Statements of the ASEAN-China Summit on November 12 and the EAS on November 14 (both held online), released on November

20.[84] This could be seen as ASEAN's soft criticism of China's continued provocative activities despite the COVID-19 crisis.

With regard to the COC negotiations, the chair, Prime Minister Nguyen Xuan Phuc of Vietnam, stated at a press conference following the June summit that the negotiations have been suspended and the consultations postponed due to COVID-19.[85] The Chairman's Statement of the ASEAN-China Foreign Ministers' Meeting on September 9 referred to holding the ad-hoc video conference of the Joint Working Group on the Implementation of the Declaration on the Conduct of Parties in the South China Sea (DOC) and confirmed the step-by-step resumption of the negotiations, including continuing the second reading of the Single Draft COC Negotiating Text in spite of the pandemic.[86] The COC was expected to be concluded by the end of 2021, but with no opportunity for in-person negotiations since February 2020, it is unclear whether it will progress as planned. The repeated reference to UNCLOS in chairman's statements of summits could be seen as an attempt to place more emphasis on effective content rather than speed.

As described above, Southeast Asian countries have begun to take measures against China's show of force in the South China Sea using the rule of law in the international framework, in addition to the countries' own efforts. Meanwhile, the regional organization of ASEAN is engaged in COC negotiations with China to maintain ASEAN's centrality and unity. Vietnam's Deputy Prime Minister and Foreign Minister Pham Binh Minh, the chair of the September meeting, stated at a press conference after the meeting that ASEAN countries do not want to be embroiled in the competition among major powers that would affect peace and stability in the region.[87] Likewise, Prime Minister Phuc announced following the November summit that ASEAN and Vietnam in particular expect positive relations and healthy competition among the great powers.[88] It is believed that ASEAN is closely watching how the balance of power in the region will change under the new U.S. administration in 2021.

3. Sea Power Strengthening by Southeast Asian Countries

(1) Malaysia and Vietnam: Establishment of Domestic Production Bases

As the previous section has shown, both the United States and China continued to enhance their presence in the South China Sea in 2020. On the other hand, in the face of difficulties such as budget cuts and activity restrictions due to COVID-19, the militaries of Southeast Asian countries attempted to overcome the capability gap with China. This section provides an overview of the efforts that such countries concerned with the South China Sea disputes are making to strengthen their naval power and maritime ISR capabilities under these circumstances.

The Royal Malaysian Navy (RMN) is currently working to increase and modernize its surface ships under the 15 to 5 Fleet Transformation Programme. As part of this program, the Chinese-built Keris-class littoral mission ship (LMS) KD *Keris* was delivered to RMN at CSOC-Wuchang Shipbuilding Industry in the suburbs of Shanghai at the end of December 2019. This ship is the first of four LMSs to be acquired under the program, and the decision to award the ship building contract to China, the other party to the South China Sea dispute involving Malaysia has been controversial.[89]

Meanwhile, in August 2020, Malaysia's National Audit Department noted delays in the program for acquiring LCSs that are being built domestically. The program (see *East Asian Strategic Review 2019*, Chapter 4, Section 3) was contracted to Boustead Naval Shipyard (BNS) for about 9.1 billion ringgit, and a total of six LCSs were to be delivered from April 2019 to June 2023. As of September 2020, however, none had been completed. BNS stated that it had already spent about 6 billion ringgit and intended to complete at least two LCSs with the remaining budget but an additional 3 billion ringgit was necessary to complete the program.[90] Due to concerns over program management capabilities, in July 2019, the government reviewed plans for the LMS program of which BNS is the lead contractor. Initially, the plan was to build the first two of four LMSs in China and the remainder in Malaysia with technology transfer from China. This plan was revised to build all four ships in China.[91]

In September 2020, it was reported that the evaluation process had begun for the second phase of the LMS acquisition program. According to reports, a total of four teams applied—two Malaysian companies, Preston Shipyard, which has been building and repairing small boats and other vessels, and Destini Shipbuilding & Engineering, which has formed a joint venture team with Damen Schelde Naval Shipbuilding (DSNS) of the Netherlands, as well as one company each from the United States and Germany. Each company submitted a proposal based on a patrol boat.[92]

As for anti-ship capability, in July 2019, under the inspection of Mohamad Bin Sabu, minister of defence, the first Exercise Taming Sari in almost four years was conducted at the same time as Exercise Keris Mas. An SSM Exocet MM40 Block II was fired from the frigate KD *Kasturi*, and ASM Sea Skua missiles were fired from the Super Lynx helicopter.[93] It was also reported that production began in April 2019 of Naval Strike Missiles (NSM) for Malaysia, for which the acquisition plan was announced in 2018. However, the building of LCSs that are planned to be outfitted with the missile is delayed as mentioned above, and the deployment of NSM to troops is expected to be later than the original schedule.[94]

As for maritime ISR capability, in February 2020, a plan was announced to upgrade two of the seven CN-235-200M transport aircraft produced by the Indonesian national aerospace company PT Dirgantara Indonesia (PTDI) to MPA.[95] The mission systems required for the upgrade are to be provided by the United States under the Maritime Security Initiative (MSI). In September, the two aircraft were entrusted to PTDI that is in charge of the conversion work. CN-235 is used by the Indonesian military as an MPA. Furthermore, PTDI has a maintenance, repair and overhaul (MRO) contract with the Royal Malaysian Air Force (RMAF) and has experience implementing a service-life extension program for RMAF's CN-235s in April 2018.

In terms of other U.S. support under the MSI, in February 2020, RMN announced that it had received the first six of 12 unmanned aerial vehicle (UAV) ScanEagles to be supplied along with associated systems. The remaining six ScanEagles are to be delivered in 2022. The support package includes training, maintenance, and sustainment. The aircraft are to be operated by RMN's 601 UAV Squadron, which was established in November 2018.[96]

With regard to Vietnam, no information is available as of September 2020 on the acquisition of a new large surface combatant. As regards other ship types, the *Yet Kieu* MSSARS 9316 multipurpose submarine search-and-rescue ship, built at the Vietnamese state-owned Z189 shipyard in Hai Phong, was commissioned in December 2019, and in the same month, the Song Thu Shipyard in Da Nang City reportedly signed a contract for the constructing of a fourth Roro 5612 landing ship tank (LST).[97] It was also reported in June that the third Roro 5612 was launched. Both ships are designed by DSNS of the Netherlands, and are being produced under license by a shipyard under the General Department of Defense Industry (Cong Nghiep Quoc Phong: CNQP) of the Ministry of Defence, suggesting that the military is working to develop the national industrial base of ship building.

As for anti-ship capability, in November 2019, a Vietnamese corvette (re-commissioned South Korean Pohang-class corvette) is believed to have been equipped with Russian SS-N-25 (Uran-E) anti-ship missile launchers.[98] In May 2020, it was reported that the Z189 shipyard began production of the VCM-01, a domestically produced copy of the SS-N-25.[99] The Military Industry and Telecoms Group (Viettel), the largest mobile telecom operator in Vietnam operated by the Ministry of Defence, is participating in the development of the VCM-01 and is reportedly promoting the domestic production of components including electronics.

(2) Philippines: Review of Military Modernization Program

The Philippine defense budget for FY2020 was initially 191.7 billion pesos. However, the Department of Budget and Management decided to decrease

Table 4.2. The Philippine Navy's original plan for surface ship procurement and revised delivery schedule

Vessel type	Revised number and schedule (Horizon 2 | Horizon 3)	Main equipment	Contractor
Missile frigate	6 vessels (2 | 4)	Anti-ship and anti-air missiles	Hyundai Heavy Industries
OPV	12 vessels (6→0 | 6→?)	———————	Austal's Cebu shipyard
Missile corvette	12 vessels (2→0 | 12→?)	Anti-submarine warfare equipment and missiles	Hyundai Heavy Industries
Fast attack interdiction craft-missile (FAIC-M)	40 vessels (8→0 | 16→?)	Automatic machine guns and short-range missiles	Israel Shipyards
Multipurpose assault craft (MPAC)	42 vessels (12 | 30)	Short-range missiles (some)	Lungteh Shipbuilding (Mk3)
Large transport vessel	4 vessels (4→2 | 2)	———————	PT PAL

Source: Compiled by the author.

the defense budget by 6.7 billion pesos in April and requested an additional reduction of 3 billion pesos in June to allocate additional funds for responding to COVID-19.[100] For FY2021, in contrast, the government requested 209.1 billion pesos in the budget message to the Congress, citing the need for counterterrorism measures and military modernization. The proposed budget included 96.8 billion pesos for the Army, 31.1 billion pesos for the Navy, 29.8 billion pesos for the Air Force, 45.4 billion pesos for the Armed Forces of the Philippines – General Headquarters (AFP-GHQ), and 1.3 billion pesos for the government arsenal buildup. In addition, the budget for the Revised AFP Modernization Program (RAFPMP), which is separate from the general budget, was to be allocated 33 billion pesos in FY2021, 8 billion pesos more than the previous years' 25 billion pesos.[101]

Currently, the Philippine Navy is building surface vessels with a budget of about 75 billion pesos.[102] It also plans to acquire about 100 support vessels and more than 30 fixed and rotary-wing aircraft, which is expected to cost more than 100 billion pesos in total in the long term.

In July 2020, it was announced that the first Philippine missile frigate, BRP *Jose Rizal*, would be commissioned, and the sister ship, BRP *Antonio Luna*, would set sail from South Korea in 2021.[103] Meanwhile, it is anticipated that the corvette acquisition program, which was to acquire two corvettes by 2023 during the second phase of RAFPMP (Horizon 2), would be postponed to Horizon 3 (2023–2028) due to COVID-19's impact on the economic and financial situation. Other acquisition programs are also expected to be delayed by more than a year, and as a result, the replacement plan for older ships is also expected to face delays.[104]

As for training and other activities, the Philippine-U.S. annual exercises Balikatan in May was cancelled in light of the COVID-19 outbreak.[105] RIMPAC conducted at-sea-only trainings for safety considerations. While its scale and participating countries were reduced, the Philippines still sent its newly commissioned BRP *Jose Rizal* to the exercises.[106]

(3) Indonesia: Buildup of Surface Ships

Indonesia's defense budget for FY2020 was originally allocated 131.182 trillion rupiah. However, like other countries, it was reduced to 122.447 trillion rupiah in May and further reduced to 117.900 trillion rupiah in July in order to appropriate more funds for COVID-19 spending.[107] The FY2021 draft budget released by the Finance Ministry approved a budget increase despite fears of an economic slowdown, proposing a defense budget of 136.990 trillion rupiah, about 19 trillion rupiah more than the previous fiscal year, an increase of about 12%, on an execution basis.[108]

The Indonesian Navy is rushing to build up its surface vessels to attain minimum essential forces (MEF). At the end of April, a preamble contract to acquire two Iver Huitfeldt-class frigates from Denmark was reportedly signed between the Indonesian Defense Ministry, Indonesian state-owned shipbuilder PT PAL (Persero), and PT Sinar Kokoh Persada (SKP), a registered supplier to the Indonesian armed forces and the Indonesian agent for Denmark's Odense Maritime Technology.[109] In September, the Defense Ministry sought a budget from the Ministry of National Development Planning (Badan Perencanaan Pembangunan Nasional: BAPPENAS) for the acquisition of two additional R.E. Martadinata-class frigates (SIGMA 10514), developed jointly with DSNS of the Netherlands.[110] At the same time, Indonesia urgently seeks the acquisition of the Interim Readiness Frigate (IRF) to temporarily fill the capability gap, a priority for the third and final phase of Indonesia's long-term modernization program (2020–2024). As part of this effort, it was reported in July that the Defense Ministry showed interest in acquiring the German Navy's Bremen-class frigate *Lubeck*, which is nearing decommissioning.[111]

In terms of anti-ship capability, DSNS and PT PAL announced the successful completion of a sea trial and equipment testing and certifications for the combat systems of two R.E. Martadinata-class frigates from the end of 2019 to March 2020.[112] In March, it was announced that French defense equipment manufacturer Thales and Indonesian state-owned company PT Len Industri plan to modernize the KRI *Usman Harun* multi-role light frigate. The vessel is expected to be equipped with SSM Exocet MM40 Block 3 missiles.[113]

As for maritime ISR capability, it was reported in July that Indonesia plans to build a hangar for the newly established 700 Naval Air Squadron (700 NAS) to operate ScanEagle and other aircraft to be provided by the United States. This facility will be built at Juanda naval air station, Surabaya, where the Naval Aviation Center is located, and will be used primarily for the storage and maintenance of UAVs and their associated equipment.[114]

As for training and other activities, in March, Indonesia and Russia agreed to conduct their first maritime drill, and in December, the naval vessels of the two countries conducted navigation drills in the Java Sea.[115] In July, the 2nd Fleet Command conducted landing drills on the eastern coast of the Java Sea and on the island of Bali, and then the 1st Fleet Command conducted maneuver drills in the Java Sea, including the southern part of the Natuna Islands.[116] In September, following these preparatory drills, the Indonesian Navy conducted Armada Jaya, its most advanced exercise, participated by 181 vessels, including submarines, and about 8,500 personnel.[117]

As shown above, each country is engaged in active efforts to boost its surface ships, provide anti-ship capability, and build maritime ISR capability, aiming to overcome the capability gap necessary to address the South China Sea dispute. Amidst the severe economic and financial situation, countries are striving to achieve these goals not only by procuring the latest equipment, but also through various means such as refurbishing existing equipment, receiving overseas capacity enhancement assistance, and purchasing used equipment.

NOTES

1) World Health Organization (WHO), "COVID-19 Situation in WHO: Western Pacific Region," WHO website; WHO, "COVID-19 Situation in the WHO South-East Asia Region," WHO website.

2) Asian Development Bank (ADB), *Asian Development Outlook (ADO) 2020 Supplement: Paths Diverge in Recovery from the Pandemic* (December 2020), 4.

3) WHO, "COVID-19 Situation in WHO: Western Pacific Region"; WHO, "COVID-19 Situation in the WHO South-East Asia Region."

4) International Monetary Fund (IMF), *Regional Economic Outlook Asia and Pacific: Navigating the Pandemic; A Multispeed Recovery in Asia* (October 2020), 8.

5) [Singapore] Ministry of Manpower, "Ministerial Statement by Mrs Josephine Teo, Minister for Manpower, 4 May 2020" (May 4, 2020).

6) Reuters, January 30 and February 2, 2020.

7) *Asahi Shimbun*, September 23 and September 24, 2020.

8) [Brunei] Ministry of Health, "Media Statement of the Current Situation of the Covid-19 Infection in Brunei Darussalam" (May 21, 2020).

9) *Phnom Penh Post*, April 7, 2020; *Khmer Times*, July 11, 2020.

10) *Nikkei Shimbun*, June 17, 2020; *Nikkei Asian Review*, July 3, 2020.

11) ADB, *ADO 2020 Supplement*, 7.

12) World Bank, *East Asia and the Pacific Economic Update: From Containment to Recovery* (October 2020), 11.

13) *Nikkei Asian Review*, August 20, 2020.

14) *Nikkei Asia*, December 23, 2020.

15) *Nikkei Shimbun*, September 11, 2020; *Asahi Shimbun*, October 26, 2020.

16) *The Star*, March 15, 2020.

17) *The Star*, July 5, 2020.

18) ASEAN Secretariat, "Declaration of the Special ASEAN Summit on Coronavirus Disease 2019 (COVID-19)" (April 14, 2020).

19) ASEAN Secretariat, "Chairman's Statement of the 37th ASEAN Summit" (November 12, 2020); ASEAN Secretariat, "Terms of Reference: ASEAN Regional Reserve of Medical Supplies for Public Health Emergencies," approved November 10, 2020.

20) CGTN, August 24, 2020.

21) [China] Ministry of Foreign Affairs, "Wang Yi Attends a Video Conference of China-ASEAN Foreign Ministers' Meeting" (September 9, 2020); *Asahi Shimbun*, September 17, 2020.

22) *Bangkok Post*, December 31, 2020; Reuters, January 4, 2021.

23) *Nikkei Asia*, December 15, 2020; Sebastian Strangio, "Is Cambodia Really Turning Its Back on Chinese Vaccines?" *Diplomat*, December 22, 2020.

24) ASEAN Secretariat, "Chairman's Statement of the 8th ASEAN-United States Summit" (November 14, 2020).

25) [Japan] Ministry of Foreign Affairs, "13th Mekong-Japan Foreign Ministers' Meeting" (July 9, 2020).

26) [Japan] Ministry of Foreign Affairs, "Japan-ASEAN Ministerial Meeting" (September 9, 2020).

27) ASEAN Secretariat, "Chairman's Statement of the 37th ASEAN Summit"; [Japan] Ministry of Foreign Affairs, "23rd Japan-ASEAN Summit Meeting" (November 12, 2020).

28) Reuters, January 23, 2019.

29) *South China Morning Post*, July 17, 2019; Asia Maritime Transparency Initiative (AMTI), "Update: China Risks Flare-Up over Malaysian, Vietnamese Gas Resources," Center for Strategic and International Studies (CSIS) (December 13, 2019); *South China Morning Post*, July 26, 2019.

30) Reuters, August 24, 2019.

31) Reuters, October 24, 2019.

32) AMTI, "Malaysia Picks a Three-Way Fight in the South China Sea," CSIS (February 21, 2020).

33) Voice of America, December 23, 2019.

34) *South China Morning Post*, September 18, 2019.

35) VietNamNet Global, January 23, 2020.

36) *South China Morning Post*, April 3, 2020.

37) *Benar News*, April 14, 2020.

38) *Benar News*, April 16, 2020; Reuters, April 17, 2020.

39) *U.S. Naval Institute (USNI) News*, April 20 and May 8, 2020; ABC News, April 22, 2020.

40) Reuters, April 23, 2020; *New Straits Times*, June 26, 2020; *Edge Markets*, September 12, 2020.

41) *Benar News*, June 16, 2020.

42) *Philippine Inquirer.net (Inquirer)*, March 4, 2019.

43) *South China Morning Post*, June 13, 2019.

44) CNN Philippines, July 29, 2019.

45) Philippine News Agency (PNA), January 14, 2020.

46) PNA, April 23, 2020.

47) *Inquirer*, March 10, 2020; *South China Morning Post*, March 18, 2020; Harada Yu, "Minamishinakai no ima: Chuhietsu no doko wo shoten ni" [South China Sea now: With focus on China, the Philippines, and Vietnam], *NIDS Commentary* 76, National Institute for Defense Studies (June 18, 2018).

48) *Inquirer*, April 20, 2020; *Benar News*, May 1, 2020.

49) *Benar News*, June 3, 2020; [U.S.] Department of State, "U.S. Position on Maritime Claims in the South China Sea" (July 13, 2020).

50) PNA, September 18, 2020.

51) PNA, January 30, 2020; CNN Philippines, February 11, 2020.

52) PNA, June 3, 2020.

53) *Inquirer*, August 3, 2020; PNA, August 13, 2020.

54) *South China Morning Post*, June 9, 2020.

55) *Philippine Star*, August 17, 2020.

56) PNA, September 11, 2020.

57) Radio Free Asia, December 30, 2019; *Tempo*, December 31, 2019.

58) *Benar News*, January 3, 2020; Reuters, January 7, 2020; *Janes*, January 10, 2020.

59) *Tempo*, January 6, 2020; Reuters, January 8, 2020.

60) *Tempo* (English), January 6, 2020.

61) CNN Indonesia, January 7, 2020.

62) *Benar News*, May 28, 2020.

63) *Benar News*, June 18, 2020.

64) Reuters, September 15, 2020.

65) *South China Morning Post*, September 14, 2020.

66) *USNI News*, March 24, 2020.

67) *USNI News*, May 6, 2020.

68) *Military.com*, April 20, 2020.

69) *Stars and Stripes*, April 28, 2020; [U.S.] Pacific Air Forces (PACAF), "B-1s Conduct

South China Sea Mission, Demonstrates Global Presence" (April 30, 2020).

70) *Global Times*, May 4, 2020; AMTI, "China Lands First Bomber on South China Sea Island," CSIS (May 18, 2018).

71) *Stars and Stripes*, May 28, 2020; *South China Morning Post*, June 26, 2020.

72) *Navy Times*, July 6, 2020.

73) [U.S.] Department of Defense, "People's Republic of China Military Exercises in the South China Sea" (July 2, 2020); *USNI News*, July 17, 2020; PACAF, "B-1s Conduct Bomber Task Force Mission in South China Sea" (July 22, 2020); *Stars and Stripes*, July 23, 2020.

74) *Global Times*, July 30, 2020.

75) *USNI News*, August 17, 2020; [U.S.] Department of Defense, "DOD Statement on Recent Chinese Ballistic Missile Launches" (August 27, 2020).

76) Patrick M. Cronin and Ryan Neuhard, "Total Competition: China's Challenge in the South China Sea," Center for a New American Security (January 2020).

77) ASEAN Secretariat, "Chairman's Statement of the 36th ASEAN Summit" (June 26, 2020).

78) *Nikkei Shimbun*, September 12, 2020.

79) ASEAN Secretariat, "Joint Communiqué of the 53rd ASEAN Foreign Ministers' Meeting" (September 9, 2020); ASEAN Secretariat, "Chairman's Statement of the 27th ASEAN Regional Forum" (September 12, 2020).

80) U.S. Mission to ASEAN, "Secretary Pompeo's Participation in the 10th East Asia Summit Virtual Foreign Ministers' Meeting" (September 9, 2020).

81) *Nikkei Shimbun*, September 12, 2020.

82) [China] Ministry of Foreign Affairs, "Wang Yi: The United States is Becoming the Biggest Factor Fueling Militarization and the Most Dangerous Factor Jeopardizing Peace in the South China Sea" (September 9, 2020).

83) ASEAN Secretariat, "Chairman's Statement of the 37th ASEAN Summit."

84) ASEAN Secretariat, "Chairman's Statement of the 23rd ASEAN-China Summit" (November 12, 2020); ASEAN Secretariat, "Chairman's Statement of the 15th East Asia Summit" (November 14, 2020).

85) *Nikkei Shimbun*, June 30, 2020.

86) ASEAN Secretariat, "Chairman's Statement of the ASEAN Post Ministerial Conference (PMC) 10+1 Session with China" (September 9, 2020).

87) *Nikkei Shimbun*, September 12, 2020; *South China Morning Post*, September 12, 2020.

88) *Hanoi Times*, November 16, 2020.

89) *Janes*, January 6, 2020.

90) *Janes*, August 27, 2020.

91) *Malaysia-kini*, July 23, 2019.

92) *Janes*, September 16, 2020.

93) *Benar News*, July 24, 2019.

94) *Naval News*, April 2, 2019.

95) *Janes*, February 3, 2020.

96) *Janes*, March 27, 2020.

97) *Vietnam Shipbuilding News*, December 19, 2019; *Navy Recognition*, December 29, 2019; *Janes*, June 25, 2020.

98) *Asia Pacific Defense Journal (APDJ)*, November 8, 2019.

99) *APDJ*, May 27, 2020.

100) *Inquirer*, June 8, 2020.

101) *Inquirer*, August 29, 2020.

102) PNA, May 12, 2020; *One News*, May 25, 2020.

103) PNA, July 11, 2020.

104) PNA, July 11, 2020.

105) *Stars and Stripes*, March 27, 2020.

106) PNA, July 7, 2020.

107) *Kompas*, April 13, 2020; *Jakarta Post*, July 6, 2020.

108) *Janes*, August 18, 2020.

109) *Janes*, June 12, 2020.

110) *Janes*, September 4, 2020.

111) *Janes*, July 30, 2020.

112) Damen, "Damen Completes Combat Systems Installation and Trials on Second Indonesian Guided Missile Frigate" (March 18, 2020); TNI-AL, "Tiga KRI dan Tiga Rusia Terlibat Latihan PASSEX RUSINDO-20" (December 20, 2020).

113) Thales, "Len Industri and Thales to Modernise Indonesia's Naval Capabilities" (March 10, 2020).

114) *Janes*, July 7, 2020.

115) TASS, March 13, 2020.

116) TNI-AL. Koarmada II, "Koarmada II Uji Profesionalisme dan Kesiapan SSAT Melalui Glagaspur Tingkat L-3 Terpadu" (July 4, 2020); *Kompas*, July 22, 2020.

117) Kompas TV, August 27, 2020.

Chapter 5

Russia

The Post-Putin Issue and Changes in the 1993 Constitutional System

HASEGAWA Takeyuki (Lead author, Sections 1 and 2)
SAKAGUCHI Yoshiaki (Section 3)

A military parade to commemorate the 75th anniversary of victory over Nazi Germany in World War II, held on June 24, 2020 in Red Square, Moscow (Xinhua News Agency/Kyodo News Images)

Summary

The Russian Federation, which newly emerged after the fall of the Soviet Union in December 1991, governed the nation with the Federal Constitution established in December 1993. The Boris Yeltsin administration in the 1990s was characterized by chaotic socioeconomic conditions, an unstable political order, and increasingly centrifugal federal-regional relations. On the other hand, the Vladimir Putin administration inaugurated in May 2000 opted for "power vertical," executed large-scale political reform, including of the federal system, and worked to stabilize the constitutional system. In this context, problems concerning the Rights and Freedoms of Human and Citizen guaranteed in Chapter 2 of the 1993 Constitution have emerged against the backdrop of strengthened measures to combat terrorism and extremism and legal restraints on the mass media. These problems have become the focus of Russian politics, particularly in recent years.

The process of amending the 1993 Constitution, which began in earnest at the beginning of 2020, has built the basic mechanisms for maintaining the Putin regime. On the other hand, voices of citizens calling for change also grew, ushering Russian society into a period of change. The amendments to the Constitution clarified a prohibition on electing a president three times, but because a provision was established stating that previous terms of incumbent or former presidents are not counted, President Putin and Dmitry Medvedev, deputy chairman of the Security Council, are able to run in the next presidential election under this system. In this chapter, we focus on Russian Constitutional reforms to derive suggestions about the political regime and the Post-Putin issue.

Issues of arms control between the United States and Russia are attracting international interest. These include the termination of the Intermediate-range Nuclear Forces (INF) Treaty and the extension of the New Strategic Arms Reduction Treaty (New START). Moreover, Russia-Europe relations have entered a more difficult phase due to the attempted murder by poisoning of opposition leader Aleksei Navalny.

Amid the global spread of the novel coronavirus disease (COVID-19), the Russian military has taken on new roles, including, for example, the construction of multifunctional medical centers, disinfection operations by the nuclear, chemical and biological protection troops, and emergency assistance to Italy and Serbia. Equipment upgrades and posture strengthening by the military have continued to progress, military cooperation was strengthened through the large-scale exercises Kavkaz 2020, and moves to expand arms exports to African countries were also seen.

1. Transformation of the Constitutional System: The Constitutional Amendment Process and the Inauguration of a New Cabinet

(1) The Essence of the 2020 Amendments and the Post-Putin Issue

In his annual address to the Federal Assembly on January 15, 2020, President Putin proposed major amendments to the 1993 Constitution.[1] During that same day, the Medvedev cabinet resigned *en masse*, and a working group to draft amendments to the Constitution was established by instruction of the president.[2] In light of the fact that in recent years Viacheslav Volodin, chairman of the State Duma, the lower house of the Federal Assembly,[3] and other top officials in the administration have offered many statements and comments about constitutional problems, it can be concluded that elaborate scenarios for recent amendments to the Constitution were formulated in the administrative core. As shown in Table 5.1, the amendment process progressed in an extremely short period of time, but it was difficult to conclude that sufficient discussions regarding the constitutional amendments were held among Russian citizens. That said, as will be discussed below, the elaborately prepared scenarios of the constitutional amendments had to be reshaped because COVID-19 directly affected the political situation.

In the 1993 Constitution, there are major differences in the procedures for making amendments (*popravka*) to Chapter 3 to Chapter 8 of the Constitution and making revisions (*peresmotr*) to the other chapters of the Constitution (Chapter 1, Chapter 2, and Chapter 9).[4] The latter contain provisions stipulating human rights guarantees, the separation of powers, and procedures for amending or revising the Constitution, and their procedural hurdles are higher compared with the former chapters. For example, they include the convening of a Constitutional Assembly and the implementation of a national referendum (*vsenarodnoe golosovanie*). Although this time the amendments to the Constitution do not require implementation of a national referendum, President Putin endeavored to guarantee its legitimacy by seeking the judgment of the Constitutional Court

Table 5.1. The constitutional amendment process (January to July 2020)

January 15	Annual address to the Federal Assembly by the president	President Putin proposed constitutional amendments, including a provision for a prohibition on electing a president three times.
	Resignation *en masse* of the Medvedev cabinet	Head of the Federal Taxation Service Mishustin was proposed to the State Duma (Lower House) as a candidate to be the next prime minister, and officially took up the position on the following day, January 16. Medvedev took up the position of deputy chairman of the Security Council.
	Establishment of the Working Group to draft proposals for amending the Constitution	Composed of 75 members with Andrey Klishas, chair of the Federation Council Committee on Constitutional Legislation and State Building, Pavel Vladimirovich Krasheninnikov, chair of the State Duma Committee on State Building and Legislation, and Talia Khabrieva, director of the Institute of Legislation and Comparative Law under the Government of the Russian Federation, as the joint representatives. The first meeting was held at a presidential residence the following day, January 16.
January 20	Submission of the constitutional amendments bill to the Lower House by President Putin	In the second reading preparatory stage (from February 14 onwards), major amendments were proposed, including a "presidential terms reset provision" for incumbent or former presidents. After the third reading, the amendments were sent to the Federal Assembly's Federal Council (Upper House) on March 11 and were passed the same day.
March 11	Sending of the constitutional amendments bill to the Dumas of the federal subjects of Russia	On March 12 and March 13, all of the (regional) Dumas of the federal subjects of Russia approved the constitutional amendments bill.
March 14	Promulgation of the law and judgment of constitutionality by the Constitutional Court	President Putin signed and promulgated the bill, then made an inquiry to the Constitutional Court regarding its constitutionality. Two days later, on March 16, the Constitutional Court recognized its constitutionality.
March 25	The date of the all-Russian vote is postponed due to COVID-19	Initially, April 22 was set as the date of the vote, but due to the rapid spread of COVID-19, it was decided to postpone the date of the vote.
July 1	Implementation of the all-Russian vote	Average voter turnout nationwide was 67.97%, and 77.92% of the people voted in favor of the amendments.

Sources: Compiled by the author based on Prezident Rossii, "Sobytiia"; Gosudarstvennaia Duma RF, "SOZD: Zakonoproekt No. 885214-7"; Konstitutsionnyi sud RF, "16 marta 2020 goda Konstitutsionnyi Sud RF opublikoval Zakliuchenie po zaprosu Prezidenta RF" (March 16, 2020); RBK, July 3, 2020.

regarding its constitutionality and boldly implementing an all-Russian vote (*vserossiiskoe golosovanie*). Due to the spread of COVID-19 inside Russia, the date of the vote was postponed from April 22 to July 1, and the amendments to the Constitution were established by a majority vote. The essence of the amendments

Table 5.2. Provisions concerning territory and patriotic/conservative aspects in the 2020 constitutional amendments (excerpts)

Chapter 3. Federal structure	
Article 67	**Paragraph 2.1** The Russian Federation ensures protection of its sovereignty and territorial integrity. Actions (except for delimitation, demarcation, re-demarcation of the state border of the Russian Federation with bordering states) aimed at removing a part of the territory of the Russian Federation and incitement to such actions shall not be permitted.
Article 67.1	**Paragraph 2** The Russian Federation, united by a thousand years of history, recognizes the historically developed state unity while preserving the memory of ancestors who gave us ideals, belief in God and continuity in the development of the Russian state. **Paragraph 3** The Russian Federation guarantees that it will honor the memory of defenders of the Fatherland and protect historical truth. Diminishing the significance of the people's heroism in defending the Fatherland shall not be permitted. **Paragraph 4** Children are the most important state policy priority in Russia. The state should create conditions that contribute to the comprehensive spiritual, moral, intellectual and physical development of children, fostering patriotism, civic engagement, and respect for elders. The state, giving priority to family-based care, shall undertake the obligations of a parent with respect to children left without guardianship.
Article 72	The matters under the joint jurisdiction of the Russian Federation and the federal subjects of Russia are as follows. [Omitted] zh.1) Protection of families, motherhood, fatherhood and children; protection of the institution of marriage as the union of a man and a woman; the creation of conditions for appropriate nurturing of children in the home, and for adult children to fulfil their obligations to look after their parents.

Sources: Compiled by the author based on E.Iu. Barkhatova, *Kommentarii k Konstitutsii Rossiiskoi Federatsii novaia redaktsiia s popravkami 3-e izdanie* (Moskva: Prospekt, 2021); *Kommentarii k Konstitutsii Rossiiskoi Federatsii 2-e izdanie* (Moskva: Prospekt, 2020); Ueno Toshihiko, "Roshia ni okeru 2020 nen no kenpo shusei wo meguru shomondai" [Issues regarding the 2020 constitutional amendments in Russia], *Russia & NIS Business Monthly* 65, no. 5 (2020), 80–105; Mizoguchi Shuhei, "Roshia renpo" [Russian Federation], in *Shin kaisetsu sekai kenposhu dai-gohan* [Constitutions of Nations, 5th Edition], eds. Shiyake Masanori and Tsujimura Miyoko (Tokyo: Sanseido, 2020), 281–341.

is as follows.

Firstly, there is the establishment of new conservative provisions (Table 5.2). In Article 67 of Chapter 3, the chapter which stipulates the federal structure, the transfer of territory and actions directed toward the transfer of territory of the Russian Federation were prohibited in paragraph 2.1. Although boundary delimitation (*delimitatsiya*) and demarcation (*demarkatsiya*) were excluded from the scope of the prohibition, the very fact that such provisions were newly established strongly shows the diplomatic stance of the Putin administration, and it is difficult to interpret this text only in terms of the domestic political context. Furthermore, Article 67.1, paragraph 3 stipulates that the state "honors the memory of defenders of the Fatherland and protects historical truth," highlighting the issue of historical perception of World War II. Article 67.1, which includes generally conservative content, emphasizes the results of World War II, specifically, "the significance of the people's heroism in defending the Fatherland," against the backdrop of the basic principle in Russia's foreign policy of protecting the country's status as a permanent member of the United Nations Security Council, one of the guarantors of the post-war international order.[5] It is likely that patriotic policies will be promoted further going forward, through history education and other methods, based on these kinds of provisions in the Constitution.

Moreover, Article 72, which stipulates the matters under the joint jurisdiction of the federal government and the federal subjects of Russia, such as republics and oblasts, has incorporated the "protection of the institution of marriage as the union of a man and a woman." Starting with the establishment of the so-called Law Prohibiting Homosexual Propaganda of 2013,[6] the conservative social policies of the Putin administration have aroused criticism from Western countries and international human rights groups. The new provisions include inherent problems pertaining to human rights guarantees, and their consistency with the foundations of the 1993 Constitution that require "constitutional revision" procedures (the provisions in Chapter 1, Chapter 2, and Chapter 9) will undoubtedly be the focus going forward. The conservative tendencies of the administration, which have grown stronger in recent years, are vividly reflected in the new Constitution. In many of the added parts (the amended sections of the Constitution), the new Constitution presents a view of the nation in conflict with the basic principles of the 1993 Constitution, symbolized by human rights protection and political plurality.

Secondly, there are the amendments to the Constitution pertaining to the political regime.[7] Certain changes have been added to the authority of the president and the Federal Assembly, while the broad framework of semi-presidentialism is maintained. The president has been granted the right to remove the chairman of the government (the prime minister) from office and the right to command the federal government, while the authority of the Federal Assembly in federal government formation procedures (appointing cabinet ministers, etc.) was also strengthened. Previously, appointment of the deputy prime minister and federal ministers after the appointment of the prime minister was substantially a matter under the exclusive jurisdiction of the president and the prime minister. With the amendments to the Constitution, the system of appointing the deputy prime minister and federal ministers was changed so that the prime minister would propose candidates to the Lower House, and the president would appoint only the candidates that the Lower House has approved. On the other hand, in the case that the Lower House refuses to approve a candidate three times, the president can dissolve the Lower House under certain conditions. Therefore, there is no change to the major structure: the ruling bloc which supports the president defines president–parliament relations.

Furthermore, the system was changed so that the president appoints the heads of the ministries and agencies in charge of national defense, internal affairs, foreign affairs, intelligence, and other aspects of national security policy after consultation with the Federal Council, the upper house of the Federal Assembly.[8] Previously, the appointment of the directors of paramilitary and intelligence agencies not included in the cabinet, such as the Federal Security Service (Federal'naia Sluzhba Bezopasnosti: FSB) and the Foreign Intelligence Service (Sluzhba Vneshney Razvedki: SVR), was a matter under the exclusive jurisdiction of the president. The recent system change has enabled the Upper House to be involved in the personnel policies of the paramilitary and intelligence agencies, while eliminating the involvement of the Lower House in the appointment of major cabinet ministers such as the defense minister, internal affairs minister, and foreign affairs minister.

Moreover, in the light of the fact that the president's authority to command the federal government is clearly stated in Article 83, the status of the president as head of the executive body has become clearer. Previously, in the federal constitutional law About Government (hereinafter, "Government Act"), the federal government was positioned as the "supreme executive body."[9] Due to Government Act revisions arising from the amendments to the Constitution, however, its status has been changed

President Putin visiting a voting station in Moscow (TASS/ Kyodo)

to an "executive body as a system of public power."[10] As a result, executive power is exercised under the general command of the president. Combined with the authority of the president to remove the prime minister from office, we can conclude that presidential authority has been strengthened.

The presidential term of office has been changed from 12 years consisting of two *consecutive* terms to 12 years consisting of *a total of* two terms, which clarified the prohibition on being elected three times. However, during the deliberation process in the Lower House, a "presidential terms reset provision" that excludes incumbent or former presidents from the scope of this stipulation was introduced while amending the Constitution, thereby enabling President Putin and Deputy Chairman of the Security Council Medvedev to run in the next presidential election under the new system. In addition, the system guaranteeing the status of the president was strengthened, including immunity from arrest after leaving the presidency and status as a senator (Upper House member) for life.[11] In summary, while the authority of the Federal Assembly was partially expanded, the authority of the president was also substantially strengthened, thus maintaining Russia's strong presidential system, or so-called "super-presidentialism."

The recent amendments to the Constitution were implemented ahead of the expiration of President Putin's term of office in 2024 and in the context of growing interest in the Post-Putin issue, and the aforementioned system changes have further increased the uncertainty in Russian politics. Regarding the prospects for Russian politics from 2024 onwards, under the current system, the following scenarios can be anticipated: (i) a new Putin administration, his fifth term in total, will be inaugurated as a result of Putin running in the next presidential election (this scenario includes Putin resigning partway through his term of office); (ii) Putin will be entitled to a lifetime seat as a senator, a position that also comes with immunity from prosecution; and (iii) Putin will take up a position as the head of another institution, for example, as the prime minister or the chairman of the State Council.

Whereas it is important to pay attention to the moves of core members of the current regime—not only President Putin and Deputy Chairman of the Security Council Medvedev, who are both able to run in the next presidential election, but also powerful local governors—anticipating a scenario in which an unknown figure assumes the position of supreme power is also necessary, as was the case with Putin in the mid-1990s. If the next president inherits the core policies implemented since 2000, important elements of management of the administration will undoubtably be the ability to manage federal–regional relations, relations with the *siloviki* (officials of the military or security agencies), and strong leadership on the public stage, including summit diplomacy and dialogue with Russian citizens.

(2) Inauguration of the New Mishustin Cabinet and Transformation of the Administrative Core

In January 2020, a new cabinet led by Mikhail Mishustin was inaugurated, replacing former prime minister Medvedev. Prime Minister Mishustin was a 54-year-old Moscow-born expert in economics and taxation who served as the head of the Federal Taxation Service from 2010.[12] In the new cabinet, 14 ministers including the deputy prime ministers, the minister of economic development, and the minister of digital development, communications and mass media were newly appointed, while the heads of the national defense, internal affairs, foreign affairs, and intelligence ministries/agencies were retained in their posts.[13] Appointment of *siloviki*, who have supported the Putin administration over many years since 2000, has been characterized by ossification and increasingly elderly appointees.

Along with the resignation *en masse* of the cabinet, the post of deputy chairman of the Security Council was created for Medvedev, allowing him to continue to remain at the core of power. Along with the establishment of the new deputy chairman post, the security legislation was also partially amended. Under the new Security Council regulation, the deputy chairman is granted certain authority, including the power to supervise the implementation of presidential decrees, etc., and power to issue orders in the national security domain.[14] Furthermore, a secretariat consisting of five top officials (one head of the secretariat and four aides) was established under the deputy chairman, which supports the activities of Medvedev. After his appointment, Deputy Chairman Medvedev showed his diplomatic presence by holding meetings on economic and security cooperation with the leader of Kyrgyzstan in February and the leader of Kazakhstan in March. In addition, he is still responsible for practical matters in domestic affairs to some extent, even after resigning as prime minister. For example, he presided over the cabinet-level meetings on COVID-19 countermeasures.[15]

Subsequently, in July 2020, the Interdepartmental Commission of the Security Council on Protecting National Interests in the Arctic (hereinafter, "Security Council Arctic Commission") was established with Deputy Chairman Medvedev as its chair and cabinet-level ministers, including the defense minister and foreign minister, as members.[16] The current Putin administration is advancing policies—and the building of the implementation structures for those policies—in order to accelerate the development of resources and energy as a matter of importance for national security, beginning with the Northern Sea Route and Arctic LNG 2 project. For example, in February 2019, the Ministry for Development of the Russian Far East was reorganized into the Ministry for the Development of the Russian Far East and Arctic, and in October 2020, a policy document titled *Strategy for Developing the Russian Arctic Zone and Ensuring National Security until 2035* was approved.[17]

Meanwhile, the State Commission for Arctic Development (hereinafter, "State Commission"), chaired by Yury Trutnev, deputy prime minister and presidential plenipotentiary envoy to the Far Eastern Federal District, and comprised of regional governors and vice-ministers, has been established in the federal government led by the prime minister.[18] The division of roles between the Security Council Arctic Commission and the State Commission is a problem, but given the ranks of the commission members and the fact that Deputy Prime Minister Trutnev has been appointed vice-chair of the Security Council Arctic Commission, it is likely that the Security Council Arctic Commission led by Medvedev exercises leadership in the execution of policy. In the Security Council, in which most of the members are *siloviki* forces, it has yet to be seen whether Deputy Chairman Medvedev, who has served as both president and prime minister, will continue to play the role of propping up the administration or search for ways to expand his political influence. Therefore, we cannot take our eyes off the political trends in the Kremlin when considering the Post-Putin issue.

Furthermore, in the nationwide local elections held on September 13, 2020, the elections for governors of federal subjects of Russia, Duma elections, local government Duma elections, and State Duma (Lower House) by-elections were held, during which measures to prevent the spread of COVID-19 were taken, including the establishment of two to three days for voting.[19] In the elections for governors of federal subjects of Russia, 18 incumbents and acting governors won (United Russia party: 12; independent: 5; Liberal Democratic Party: 1). In the Duma elections, as well, United Russia came out on top,[20] while new political parties also made strides. New People gained seats in Novosibirsk, Kaluga, Ryazan, and Kostroma oblasts. For Truth gained seats in Ryazan oblast, and Green Alternative gained seats in the Komi Republic and Chelyabinsk oblast.[21] As these political parties gained seats in the Dumas of the federal subjects of Russia, they can participate in the Lower House election planned to be held in September 2021 without collecting signatures, in accordance with federal law.[22] With the decline of the administration's approval ratings, the prolonged protests in Khabarovsk, and other problems, a tough election campaign for the Putin administration was anticipated. Despite this, the United Russia party put up a solid battle.

(3) The Putin Administration Faces the Need for COVID-19 Countermeasures: Foreign Emergency Aid and Domestic Explosion of Infections

In late March 2020, the COVID-19 situation rapidly worsened in Russia. President Putin responded by giving a televised address to the people calling for their cooperation with infection countermeasures and outlined emergency measures in accordance with Article 80 of the Constitution, which stipulates the wide-ranging authority of the president. These measures included designating the five days from March 30 to April 3 as non-working days with full pay. However, in the early stages of the pandemic at the beginning of 2020, because the number of people confirmed to be infected in Russia was small compared to China and Western countries, the administration's efforts focused on providing emergency assistance to foreign countries such as Italy, Serbia, and the United States. For example, after the telephone conversation between Prime Minister Giuseppe Conte of Italy and President Putin on March 21,[23] a transport operation by the Russian Aerospace Forces was commenced on the following day, March 22 (see Section 3 for details). The operation was named "From Russia With Love," and scenes of IL-76 transport aircraft loaded with medical supplies and personnel landing one after another at Pratica di Mare Air Base on the outskirts of Rome were actively publicized through social media and other mediums.[24] This had the impact of dispatching Russian military aircraft to a major member country of the North Atlantic Treaty Organization (NATO), and demonstrated to Russia and the world the high mobility of overseas operations by the Russian military and Russia's governing style characterized by rapid decision-making and policy implementation.

On the other hand, from late March 2020 onwards, the number of confirmed cases of infection increased rapidly in Russia, exceeding a cumulative total of three million people as of December, the fourth highest number in the world.[25] Because social policy including public health is basically under the jurisdiction of the federal government (cabinet), and because the authority of the federal government regarding emergency situations was strengthened by the April 1 revision of the Federal Law on the Protection of the Population and Territories from Emergency Situations of Natural and Technogenic Character, Prime Minister Mishustin, Deputy Prime Minister Tatiana Golikova, and Mayor of Moscow Sergey Sobyanin have played the central role in developing the COVID-19 countermeasures. On the other hand, the direct involvement of the Kremlin, including President Putin and Deputy Chairman of the Security Council Medvedev, among others, has been seen at critical stages of the pandemic. Given that executive power is divided between the president and the federal government (cabinet) led by the prime minister, the general coordination mechanism for dealing with the situation—as well as federal–regional relations, which have a centrifugal nature—will undoubtedly be the focus of Russia's long-term COVID-19 countermeasures.

The surge of COVID-19 infections in Russia had significant impact on the political situation, as it happened to coincide with the timing of the establishment of the political calendar for the amendments to the Constitution after the annual address to the Federal Assembly by the president in January 2020 and the inauguration of the new cabinet. The all-Russian vote on amendments to the Constitution planned for April 22 and the military parade to commemorate the 75th anniversary of victory over Nazi Germany in World War II planned for May 9 were postponed, and a number of cabinet ministers and top government officials, including Prime Minister Mishustin and Presidential Press Secretary Dmitry Peskov, were infected. The economy slumped due to a historical fall in crude oil prices, and the administration's approval rating hit a record low of 59% for the two consecutive months of April and May.[26] Due to these and other factors, the Putin administration was forced to greatly revise its scenario for 2020, which had been based on amending or revising the Constitution and commemorating the 75th anniversary of the victory in the war.

In this context, on August 11, the world's first COVID-19 vaccine, Sputnik V, received a registration certificate from the Ministry of Health,[27] and the safety and effectiveness of this Russian-produced vaccine was promoted domestically and overseas. For example, images were released of Sergei Shoigu, defense minister, receiving the vaccine in September.[28] Moreover, on October 13, a second domestically produced vaccine, EpiVacCorona, received a registration certificate, and it has been reported that distribution of this vaccine commenced in January 2021.[29] Russian-produced vaccines are planned to be supplied to more than 10 countries, including India, Brazil, and Saudi Arabia.[30] Russia is seen to be starting full-scale "vaccine diplomacy" through frameworks on which it places diplomatic importance, such as the Shanghai Cooperation Organization (SCO) and BRICS.

Furthermore, in July 2020, *On the National Development Goals of the Russian Federation through 2030* (hereinafter, "July Decree"), a policy document stipulating the basic policy for Russia's long-term social and economic policies, was approved by a presidential decree.[31] This document examines the outcomes of the previous version, *On National Goals and Strategic Objectives of the Russian Federation through to 2024* (hereinafter, "May Decree"),[32] which was approved in May 2018, and aims for a course correction given the present social and economic situations. It quantifies the priority goals of social and economic policy based on five pillars, including preservation of the population, the health and welfare of the people, a comfortable and safe environment, and digital transformation. At the time of the inauguration of his administration in 2018, President Putin issued the May Decree to strongly promote the "modernization" of the economic structure, a long-standing issue, with a strong sense of crisis over lagging economic development. Nonetheless, the prolonged economic sanctions on Russia imposed by Western countries, combined with lockdowns due to the coronavirus catastrophe and the historical slump in crude oil prices, have made the road to achieving the goals set out by the July Decree steep. Even in the three-year federal budget law for 2021–2023 approved in December 2020, national defense expenditure is expected to remain at three trillion rubles for the single fiscal year of 2021 (2.7% of GDP) and maintained in the 2% to 3% range of GDP in the 2022 and 2023 planned budgets,[33] trending toward restraint.

2. Foreign Policies:
The Strategic Environment Surrounding Russia

(1) Approval of the *Basic Principles of State Policy of the Russian Federation on Nuclear Deterrence* and Arms Control

Since the annexation of Crimea in March 2014, a pattern of opposition has become entrenched in relations between Russia and the West over issues such as the unstable situation in eastern Ukraine and economic sanctions. In recent years, the wavering of the arms control and disarmament regime has become the focus. With the expiration of the INF Treaty in August 2019 and the declaration by the United States in May 2020 that it would withdraw from the Open Skies Treaty, the symbols of the arms control and disarmament regime constructed from the end of the Cold War period to the post-Cold War period are being lost.

In the U.S.-Russia Strategic Security Dialogue held in Vienna on June 22, 2020 with the participation of Russian deputy foreign minister Sergei Ryabkov and Marshall Billingslea, the U.S. special presidential envoy for arms control, agreement was reached to establish a working group on strategic stability issues.[34] The main themes of the working group meeting held at the end of July were reported to be space, nuclear doctrine and warheads, and transparency and inspections.[35] In a series of negotiations, the delegation of the United States strongly called for the participation of China in the arms control regime, and also raised issues with subjecting new strategic weapons such as the hypersonic glide vehicle to new treaty restrictions and flaws in the current inspection system.

In 1979, during the Cold War, then senator Joseph Biden of the United States made a visit to Moscow for talks on arms control. President Biden has been involved in diplomacy with Russia for many years since the Cold War period, first as the Senate Foreign Relations Committee chairman and then as vice-president during the Barack Obama administration. The new Biden administration has presented a policy agenda that places importance on multilateral cooperation and alliances,[36] and diplomacy with Russia concerning the problem of extending the New START treaty became their first policy issue. The process rapidly progressed, and it was announced that agreement on extending the treaty was reached in a telephone conversation between the leaders of the United States and Russia on January 26, 2021.[37] Although the expiration of the treaty has been avoided, there is an urgent need to construct a multilateral arms control regime that puts the brakes on the arms race from a long-term perspective.

Regarding all other aspects of U.S.-Russia relations, if the Biden administration strongly deploys value-based diplomacy that emphasizes human rights and democracy, it will undoubtedly be difficult to build substantial relations with the Putin administration, as it has been strengthening its conservative tendencies after the 2020 amendments to the Constitution.

In this context, on June 2, 2020, the *Basic Principles of State Policy of the Russian Federation on Nuclear Deterrence* were approved by a presidential decree.[38] This document is thought to be the successor document to the non-disclosed document *Principles of State Policy in the Sphere of Nuclear Deterrence Until 2020*[39] approved together with the Military Doctrine on February 5, 2010. The timing of the approval of the document by the president and the document's disclosure may be related to the stalling of the U.S.-Russia arms control and disarmament regime.

This document comprises four chapters: (I) General Provisions; (II) Essence of nuclear deterrence; (III) Conditions for the use of nuclear weapons; and (IV) Tasks and functions of federal government authorities, other government bodies and organizations for implementing state policy on nuclear deterrence. It states that the legal foundation of these Basic Principles is the Federal Constitution and international treaties on defense and arms control ratified by the federation (paragraph 6), but it also states that these Basic Principles may be further specified depending on the external and internal factors that influence defense implementation (paragraph 8).

The conditions for the use of nuclear weapons presented in (III) mainly anticipate four scenarios.[40] Firstly, Russia reserves the right to use nuclear weapons in response to the use of nuclear and other types of weapons of mass destruction against it and/or its allies (paragraph 17). The second scenario is the use of nuclear weapons in the event of aggression against the Russian Federation with the use of conventional weapons when the very existence of the state is in jeopardy (paragraph 19(b) and 19(g)). The third scenario is the use of nuclear weapons in the event of the arrival of reliable data on a launch of ballistic missiles attacking the territory of the Russian Federation and/or its allies (paragraph 19(a)), the so-called launch on warning. The fourth scenario is the use of nuclear weapons in the event of an attack by an adversary against critical governmental or military sites of the Russian Federation, disruption of which would undermine nuclear forces response actions (paragraph 19(v)).

Furthermore, the division of duties is clearly laid out in (IV). The chapter stipulates that the president is the supreme commander of nuclear deterrence policy, and that the federal government led by the prime minister implements measures to carry out the economic policy aimed at maintaining and developing nuclear deterrence assets and shapes and exercises the foreign and information policy in the area of nuclear deterrence, while the Security Council chaired by the president shapes the basic principles of military policy in the area of nuclear deterrence and coordinates the activities of the related bodies. In addition, the defense minister, acting through the chief of the General Staff, directly plans and carries out organizational and military measures in the area of nuclear deterrence.

What caught the attention of the strategy community inside and outside Russia were the third and fourth scenarios, which had not been stated previously in other key policy documents such as the Military Doctrine, as well as the affirmation of the escalate to de-escalate (E2DE) policy.[41] Regarding E2DE, the (I) General Provisions chapter in this document states as one state policy for nuclear deterrence that "in the event of a military conflict, this Policy provides for the prevention of an escalation of military actions and their termination on conditions that are acceptable for the Russian Federation and/or its allies," but as discussed above, this point was not included in the conditions for the use of nuclear weapons presented in (III). This lack of consistency within the policy document and the remaining ambiguity in its interpretation has not settled the debate concerning Russia's nuclear deterrence policy, particularly the E2DE policy which is frequently raised.[42] The nuclear forces have occupied a particularly vital position in the national security policy of modern Russia since the fall of the Soviet Union, and so the release of this document has had a large impact. On the other hand, Russia's policy documents originally formed a hierarchical structure with the National Security Strategy at the top. The Russian Security Council is working toward revising the strategy,[43] and consistency among policy documents, including the Military Doctrine which the Putin administration is also planning to revise, will attract attention.

(2) The Poisoning of Alexey Navalny and Russia-Europe Relations

The attempted murder by poisoning of Russian opposition leader Navalny had a major impact on relations between Russia and the West due to concerns about democracy and political plurality in Russia and the use of chemical weapons prohibited under international treaties. In mid-August 2020, Navalny was visiting Novosibirsk and Tomsk in Siberia to engage in political activities for the nationwide local elections (held on September 13). His "smart vote strategy," whose primary goal was to prevent the ruling bloc from winning elections, had some degree of success in the 2019 nationwide local elections, and the main purpose of his visit to the cities in Siberia was to roll out the strategy.[44] On the morning of August 20, a civilian aircraft bound for Moscow that had flown out of Tomsk Airport made an emergency landing at nearby Omsk Airport when Navalny suddenly became ill. Navalny was taken to an emergency hospital near the airport, but he remained in a coma, and on August 22, he was transported to Berlin, Germany for treatment.

The German government determined that Navalny had been attacked using a chemical nerve agent from the Novichok family,[45] and in response to this, the European Union (EU), NATO and the G7 each issued their own statements. The G7 Foreign Ministers' Statement, dated September 9, 2020, called on the Russian government to bring the perpetrators to justice under the Chemical Weapons Convention, and stated that the Navalny incident "is another grave blow against democracy and political plurality in Russia."[46]

Amidst the deepening opposition between Russia and Western countries since the annexation of Crimea in March 2014, German chancellor Angela Merkel has maintained a certain level of economic relations with Russia, most notably the construction of the gas pipeline Nord Stream 2, which directly connects Russia and Germany. On the other hand, against the backdrop of Europe's concerns about increasing its dependence on Russian-produced energy resources, in December 2019, U.S. president Donald Trump signed a bill imposing sanctions on companies that participate in the installation of Nord Stream 2.[47] Chancellor Merkel strongly opposed this, and there have frequently been other gaps in perception among Western countries with regards to economic relations with Russia after the annexation. In response to the Navalny incident, the United States announced further strengthening of sanctions in relation to Nord Stream 2, and further diplomatic maneuvering with Germany is predicted.

(3) Japan-Russia Relations at a Time of Transition

With the transition from the Abe Shinzo administration to the Suga Yoshihide administration in September 2020, attention in Russia has turned to the direction of Japan's policy toward Russia. Under the second Abe administration inaugurated in December 2012, active diplomacy toward Russia was developed with Japan's National Security Strategy approved in December 2013 as the basis of policy. Regarding Japan-Russia relations, the National Security Strategy mentions that "under the increasingly severe security environment in East Asia, it is critical for Japan to advance cooperation with Russia in all areas, including security and energy, thereby enhancing bilateral relations as a whole, in order to ensure its security,"[48] advancing Japan's approach to Russia on the security front.

Under the second Abe administration, there was a deepening of Japan-Russia defense and security cooperation, beginning with the Summit Meeting in April 2013. In the joint statement issued as a result of the meeting, the two leaders welcomed the launch of the Japan-Russia 2+2 Foreign and Defense Ministerial Consultation and the memorandum between the Ministry of Foreign Affairs of Japan and the Apparat of the Security Council of the Russian Federation, which was signed under the Democratic Party of Japan administration, and

Japan's MSDF destroyer *Harusame* carrying out tactical maneuvers with Russian Navy ships (Japan Joint Staff official website)

agreed to hold regular consultations based on the memorandum.[49] Under the second Abe administration, the Japan-Russia 2+2 Ministerial Meeting was held a total of four times, and consultations between the foreign affairs and defense authorities, unit-to-unit exchanges between the Self-Defense Forces and the Russian military, and joint training were continuously conducted. Exchanges between Japan's Maritime Self-Defense Force (MSDF) and the Russian Navy were particularly active. In addition to the regular holding of joint Japan-Russia Search and Rescue Exercises (SAREX), most recently, in January 2020, the second Joint Exercise in Counter Piracy activities was held in the Gulf of Aden with the participation of Japan's MSDF destroyer *Harusame*, the Russian Navy frigate *Yaroslav Mudryi*, and other ships.[50]

Furthermore, with the establishment of the National Security Council (NSC) in Japan in December 2013, the National Security Secretariat (NSS) was established in the Cabinet Secretariat the following month, January 2014, which functioned as the counterpart to the Apparat of the Security Council in the Russian Federation. Consultations on security began to be regularly held between Yachi Shotaro, the first secretary general of the NSS, and Nikolai Patrushev, secretary of the Security Council. As relations between Russia and Western countries rapidly deteriorated due to the Ukraine conflict and annexation of Crimea at the beginning of 2014, Secretary General Yachi visited Moscow twice in rapid succession, on March 14 and May 5 of the same year, to hold consultations with Secretary Patrushev.[51] During Secretary General Yachi's term of office, consultations were held eight times. This diplomatic channel was inherited by his successor as Secretary General Kitamura Shigeru. On September 17, 2019, shortly after Secretary General Kitamura took up the post, Secretary Patrushev visited Japan to pay a courtesy call on Prime Minister Abe and hold an exchange of views with Secretary General Kitamura regarding all aspects of Japan-Russia relations and the security policies of the two countries.[52] Moreover, in January 2020, as the process of making amendments to the Constitution began in earnest in Russia, Secretary General Kitamura visited Moscow to hold consultations with Secretary Patrushev and pay a courtesy call to President Putin at his presidential residence.[53]

With the institutionalization of the 2+2 Ministerial Meeting between Japan and Russia and NSC diplomacy, diplomatic channels between Japan and Russia diversified during the second Abe administration. Many actors are involved in the foreign policies and military security policies of the Putin administration, including the Presidential Administration, Defense Ministry, Ministry of Foreign Affairs, SVR and FSB. However, it is likely that the Security

Secretary General Kitamura of the National Security Secretariat paying a courtesy call on President Putin (TASS/Kyodo)

Council and meeting body comprised of the heads of each department, as well as the Apparat of the Security Council which supports it, play a core role in the policy mechanism. Under the 2020 Security Council reforms, previous prime minister Medvedev took up the position of deputy chairman of the Security Council.

Going forward, it will be necessary to carefully monitor what kinds of diplomatic channels Russia uses for what purposes in its policies toward Japan, including the personnel policies and reorganization of the governing structure by the administration core. Furthermore, as mentioned in Section 1, new conservative provisions concerning territory and historical perceptions were established by the amendments to the Constitution of the Russian Federation in July 2020. As Japan-Russia relations enter a new phase with the inauguration of the Suga administration in September 2020, there is a need to adequately evaluate the impact that Russia's domestic political developments regarding the amendments to the Constitution and the Post-Putin issue have on Japan-Russia relations.

3. Response to COVID-19 and Capability Improvement Efforts of the Russian Military

(1) Response to COVID-19 and the Role of the Russian Military

The spread of COVID-19 has also been serious in Russia, and the Russian military has been busy with preventing the disease's outbreak and spread. According to a report regularly published by the Defense Ministry on the status of COVID-19 infections within the Defense Ministry and military, the total number of people who had been infected by the novel coronavirus and subsequently recovered as of December 24, 2020 was 22,979 soldiers and 3,312 civil servants. Furthermore, 4,228 soldiers and 571 civil servants had tested positive and were receiving treatment as of December 24.[54] Defense Minister Shoigu has maintained that the status of novel coronavirus infections within the military is not having any substantial impact on the Russian military.[55]

Countermeasures to prevent the spread of COVID-19 have been taken since March 2020. On March 12, an operational headquarters headed by Ruslan Tsalikov, first deputy defense minister, was established in the Defense Ministry, which decided to strengthen the inspection structures in each Russian military unit, each military educational institution, and various organizations in the

Defense Ministry. In addition, other countermeasures that were taken include the suspension of military delegations to and from foreign countries, the cancellation of large-scale events by military units, the implementation of military conscription according to plan with strict COVID-19 countermeasures in effect, the establishment of special sections for responding to COVID-19 in 32 military hospitals, and various measures pertaining to strengthening the posture of the nuclear, chemical and biological protection troops in order to enhance quarantine and disinfection operations.[56]

On March 25, Defense Minister Shoigu, in a report on the current situation of the Russian military to the Federation Council of Federal Assembly of the Russian Federation, revealed that the Defense Ministry was constructing 16 multifunctional medical centers for the response to COVID-19 in 15 regions of Russia.[57] The construction of the multifunctional medical centers proceeded in two stages, with the first eight centers constructed by April 30, 2020, and the remaining eight centers constructed by May 15. The reserve fund of the Russian government contributed 8.8 billion rubles to the construction, and approximately 12,000 staff in the construction section of Defense Ministry worked around the clock. Russia's engineer troops were also mobilized in the construction.[58] According to Timur Ivanov, deputy defense minister, who was in charge of the construction of the centers, the centers were equipped with cutting-edge medical equipment and the 16 facilities contained a total of 1,600 hospital beds. In addition, treatment in the centers is provided by approximately 2,300 medical staff who have received pre-training at the Military-Medical Academy. Moreover, the centers accept not only military workers, but also COVID-19 patients from among the general public.[59] As of December 24, the centers had treated a total of 13,325 patients, 4,442 of whom were members of the general public. Also, as of December 24, 30 multifunctional medical centers had ultimately been constructed, including centers constructed to strengthen the COVID-19 countermeasures of the federal subjects of Russia.[60]

The quarantine and disinfection operations by the nuclear, chemical and biological protection troops to prevent the spread of COVID-19 have also been strengthened. As of December 24, for the various units stationed in Moscow, they have carried out the disinfection of facilities with a total area of approximately 1,026,000 square meters, including approximately 38,000 pieces of equipment and the buildings of each unit, military educational institution, and national defense industry. In each military district and the Northern Fleet, disinfection of approximately 1,900 facilities has been carried out, covering a total area of approximately 200,000 square meters.[61]

The Russian military has not only responded to the novel coronavirus domestically as mentioned above; it has also provided support to foreign countries for responding to the novel coronavirus, including testing and treatment support for medical staff in partner countries, as well as disinfection operations for military and civilian facilities. In March 2020, in response to a request from the Italian government, the Russian Defense Ministry dispatched to Italy an expert team comprising Russian military physicians with abundant experience in infectious diseases and prevention of epidemics and experts from the nuclear, chemical and biological protection troops. This team carried out support activities at 83 locations in Lombardy. The same kind of support was provided to Serbia, with teams dispatched by Russia working in 28 cities in Serbia.[62] Moreover, Russia dispatched medical expert teams to Kyrgyzstan in July 2020 and to Kazakhstan in August of the same year to support the COVID-19 countermeasures of those two countries.[63] Behind this support for Italy, Russia's desire to gain an opportunity to improve deteriorating relations with Western countries can be observed.[64] Furthermore, behind the support for the two Central Asian countries and Serbia, Russia likely aimed to increase its influence by further strengthening its relations with allies and partners. These dispatches were carried out with the cooperation of the Aerospace Forces' long-range aero-transport forces, the Main Military-Medical Directorate in the Defense Ministry, and the nuclear, chemical and biological protection troops, and their activities were constantly monitored and controlled by the operational headquarters within the Defense Ministry.[65]

The Russian military demonstrated its high capabilities through its response to COVID-19. The following three points in particular are worth noting from the perspective of improving the operation executing capabilities of the Russian military. The first is the growing role of the engineer troops. It is notable that the engineer troops demonstrated a high level of capability in completing the construction of the multifunctional medical centers in regions throughout Russia in a short period. Defense Minister Shoigu has also recognized the growing importance of deploying the engineer troops to solve a variety of problems that arise in the execution of special operations by the Russian military and in the process of conducting exercises.[66]

The second is the growing role of the nuclear, chemical and biological protection troops. The high level of capability demonstrated by these units both in Russia and in foreign countries in preventing the spread of COVID-19 is notable. The role of these troops is becoming increasingly important, especially as there are particular concerns about terrorism using nuclear materials, chemical weapons, or biological weapons. In 2020, the nuclear, chemical and biological protection troops participated in a greater number of exercises. In August of the same year, in Sakhalin in the Eastern Military District, the anti-terrorist troops from this military district conducted a joint exercise with the nuclear, chemical and biological protection troops.[67]

The third is the growing role of the long-range aero-transport forces. In February 2020, when the COVID-19 situation became more serious in Wuhan, Hubei Province, China, the Aerospace Forces, under the instructions of President Putin, sent two IL-76 transport aircraft to bring home 144 Russian citizens who had been staying in that province.[68] In addition to this, they demonstrated a high level of capability regarding the transportation of personnel and equipment when providing the aforementioned support to foreign countries.

(2) Ongoing Military Reform and the Strengthening of the Military Posture

In the May 2020 meeting of the Defense Ministry Board, Defense Minister Shoigu expressed the perception that Russia continued to face the most serious military threat in the western strategic front. In order to respond to this threat, he pointed out that it was necessary to steadily execute the various measures from 2019 to 2025 stipulated in the activity plan of Western Military District. Thanks to 28 organizational measures executed in 2020, including the formation of a new motorized sniper division, missile brigade, and artillery brigade, in order to establish the combat-readiness of the units commensurate with the introduction of the latest armaments, Defense Minister Shoigu presented the outlook that overall possession of the latest armaments for the Western Military District would increase to 65% with the introduction of approximately 2,000 of the latest armaments. Moreover, he pointed out that there were approximately 320 exercises in the Western Military District in 2020, 10 of which were large-scale exercises.[69]

Coinciding with reinforcement of the military posture of the Western Military District, moves to strengthen the posture of the Northern Fleet (Northern Joint Strategic Command), which is responsible for the Arctic region, have become more notable. In June 2020, President Putin issued the Ukaz on military-administrative division of the Russian Federation, which divided Russia's military districts into the Western, Southern, Central, and Eastern military districts and the Northern Fleet from January 1, 2021.[70] Because of this, the Northern Fleet gained jurisdiction over the regions of the Komi Republic, Arkhangelsk oblast, Murmansk oblast, and Nenets autonomous district, which previously belonged to the Western Military District. Under a December 2020 presidential decree, the Northern Fleet was designated a Joint Strategic Command that executes the tasks of a military district.[71] Efforts are also being made to strengthen the Northern Fleet in terms of equipment. During 2020, six battle ships and more than 180 new pieces of equipment were introduced, including two nuclear submarines and a new model of landing ship. Likewise, many exercises for the improvement of operational capability have been conducted. In June 2020, exercises were performed in the Barents Sea and Norwegian Sea, and from August to September, the Arctic group of troops carried out a long-distance ocean navigation to Crest Bay in the Bering Sea. Along the way, they conducted tactical exercises for the protection of important industrial facilities on Taymyr Peninsula, Chukchi Peninsula, and Yakutia.[72]

The Russian military continues to make progress in its equipment upgrades. At the end of June 2020, a meeting of the Defense Ministry Board was held to consider the outcomes of the military reforms in the first half of 2020. According to the report by Defense Minister Shoigu at this meeting, 776 major pieces of the latest armaments were introduced to the Russian military in the first half of 2020. This number includes 58 airplanes and helicopters, more than 140 battle armored vehicles, 510 multipurpose vehicles, one strategic nuclear ballistic missile submarine (Borei-A class), and two replenishment ships. As a result, overall possession of the latest armaments by the Russian military rose to 68.5%, with the prospect of reaching 72% by the end of 2020.[73] A total of 1,200 small and large-scale exercises were conducted as planned in the winter training season, without being interrupted by the impact of the spread of COVID-19.[74]

During the summer training season that began on June 1, 15,500 exercises of a variety of types had been planned, and they were conducted as planned. The largest of these exercises was the large-scale exercises Kavkaz 2020 carried out from September 21 to September 26, 2020, primarily in the Southern Military District. Kavkaz 2020 was one of the strategic exercises that are performed by a different military district every year. It was a large-scale exercise that mobilized approximately 80,000 troops (including air defense troops), a maximum of 250 tanks, and a maximum of 450 infantry battle vehicles and armored transport vehicles. The related tactical exercises were conducted not only at the seven training ranges of the Southern Military District, the Black Sea, and the Caspian Sea, but also in Armenia, South Ossetia, and Abkhazia. The major stages of the exercises took the form of multilateral exercises, with the participation of military units from Armenia, Belarus, China, Myanmar, and Pakistan. Moreover, units of the Iranian military participated in the exercises of the Caspian Flotilla in the Caspian Sea.[75] The exercises were carried out in two stages: in the first stage, they considered the problem of how to best coordinate the multinational units in a fight against terrorist forces supported by a hypothetical enemy and how to repel an air attack by the hypothetical enemy. In the second stage, they worked to solve the issues arising when directly commanding multinational units

Figure 5.1. Large-scale exercises Kavkaz 2020 centered on the Southern Military District

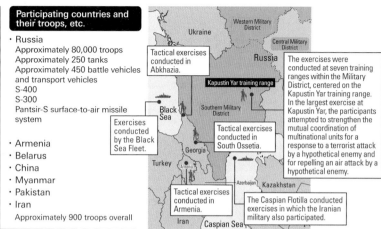

Participating countries and their troops, etc.

· Russia
Approximately 80,000 troops
Approximately 250 tanks
Approximately 450 battle vehicles and transport vehicles
S-400
S-300
Pantsir-S surface-to-air missile system

· Armenia
· Belarus
· China
· Myanmar
· Pakistan
· Iran
Approximately 900 troops overall

Sources: Compiled by the author based on *Krasnaia Zvezda*, September 28, October 12 and October 14, 2020.

in the process of executing actual combat operations. Although Kavkaz 2020 anticipated a scenario of a fight with terrorist forces supported by a hypothetical enemy, the fact that the stopping of an air attack was the important issue, and that the participating air defense troops deployed the S-400 and S-300 surface-to-air missile systems and the surface-to-air missile system Pantsir-S for anti-cruise missile defense, suggests that defense against an air attack by a state possessing high-tech weapons was the key issue in the exercises.[76]

Moves to strengthen the military posture of the Eastern Military District have also continued to make progress. In August 2020, Defense Minister Shoigu visited Kamchatka krai and Khabarovsk krai in the Eastern Military District and Irkutsk oblast in eastern Siberia to inspect the development of military facilities and the current condition of the national defense industries. In Kamchatka krai, Defense Minister Shoigu visited Vilyuchinsk Base, a major base for the strategic nuclear ballistic missile submarines of the Pacific Fleet, and inspected the construction of new facilities for the Borei-A class and Yasen-M class strategic nuclear ballistic missile submarines, which Russia plans to introduce to the Pacific Fleet going forward. Defense Minister Shoigu confirmed that the construction work was progressing as planned and gave instructions for the work to be completed by the end of 2020.[77] Furthermore, moves to improve the capabilities of units deployed in the Northern Territories and Kuril Islands have continued. For example, deployment of the surface-to-air missile S-300 V4 was newly announced,[78] and deployment of the flagship tank T-72B3 was reported.[79]

In Khabarovsk krai, Defense Minister Shoigu inspected the Amur Shipbuilding Company and Komsomolsk-na-Amure Aircraft Company. The Amur Shipbuilding Company is currently building four small missile ships (Project 22800) and two corvettes (Project 20380), but Defense Minister Shoigu announced that the Defense Ministry was prepared to conclude contracts for the building of a further six of the same model of corvette.[80] The Komsomolsk-na-Amure Aircraft Company is a branch office of Aircraft Building Company Sukhoi, and it is producing the multipurpose fighter Su-35 and the state-of-the-art fifth generation fighter Su-57. Iliya Tarasenko, general director of Company Sukhoi, explained in a report to Defense Minister Shoigu that delivery of the Su-35 and Su-35S aircraft to the Aerospace Forces in 2020 was progressing as planned. In response to this, Defense Minister Shoigu announced that the Defense Ministry was planning additional procurement of the Su-35S aircraft, the total value of which was on the scale of 70 billion rubles. Moreover, General Director Tarasenko mentioned a contract that requires the company to manufacture 76 Su-57s by 2028, stating that the company was currently advancing preparations for an assembly-line production facility for Su-57 manufacturing that was expected to be completed by the end of the year.[81]

In Irkutsk oblast, Defense Minister Shoigu visited the Irkutsk Aircraft Building Company Irkut. The Irkut company manufactures and repairs the multipurpose fighter Su-30SM and the battle training aircraft Yak-130. At this company, Defense Minister Shoigu announced that the Defense Ministry had decided to conclude additional contracts for 21 Su-30SM fighters and 25 Yak-130 aircraft (with a total value on the scale of 100 billion rubles).[82]

Russia is also aiming to strengthen the capabilities of the Eastern Military District units through tactical exercises. Exercises to improve coastal defense and the deployment capability to far-sea areas stood out in particular. In June 2020, two coastal defense exercises were carried out in Kamchatka. These were an exercise using a Ka-29 combat/transport helicopter to attack the maritime targets of a hypothetical enemy on the coast, and an exercise using the surface-to-air missile system Pantsir-S to repel the air attack of a hypothetical enemy.[83] In September 2020, an exercise to stop a landing by a hypothetical enemy was conducted in the Northern Territories and Kuril Islands.[84] Moreover, in the same month, the air regiment of the Pacific Fleet located in Primorsky krai participated in an exercise to defend Russian ships from the sky in open-sea areas, and aircraft belonging to this regiment were deployed to the Sea of Okhotsk and the Sea of Japan.[85]

(3) Strengthening of Military Cooperation and Arms Exports Aimed at Expansion

Russia is continuing to strengthen military cooperation through the Collective Security Treaty Organization (CSTO). In March 2020, a meeting was held by the CSTO Joint Staff concerning the strengthening of mutual collaboration between the Crisis Reaction Center established within the Joint Staff and each of the CSTO member countries. At the meeting, they considered the best approach to mutual collaboration between the military command institutions of each member country and the Crisis Reaction Center in the event of a crisis situation, and discussed in particular future directions for the development of a communications system to expand the possibilities of the mutual cooperation system in the area of information. They also confirmed that an education program for training the human resources essential to the Crisis Reaction Center would be offered at the Russian Military Academy of the General Staff. Furthermore, prior to this meeting, there were moves to expand the number of countries participating in the multilateral exercises carried out by the CSTO. Specifically, it was agreed that Serbia and Uzbekistan would participate as observers in the joint exercise

Nerushimoe Bratstvo (Unbreakable Brotherhood) 2020 and the joint exercise Rubezh (Border) 2020, respectively.[86]

In addition, a joint meeting of defense ministers of the three frameworks of the CSTO, the Commonwealth of Independent States (CIS), and the SCO was held in September 2020 in Moscow, and was attended by the defense ministers of 12 countries. Russia hoped to use this meeting as a foundation for promoting international military cooperation. The actual outcomes obtained at this meeting are as follows. Firstly, the defense ministers of all of the countries agreed to expand cooperation in the fight against terrorism. Secondly, they exchanged the experiences of each country in dealing with the spread of COVID-19 and discussed the problem of mutual support for the building of infectious disease response capabilities. Thirdly, a statement was incorporated into the joint statement of the meeting which said that it would be unacceptable to allow the collapse of the treaty-based system in the area of arms control, including control of nuclear weapons. Furthermore, there were outcomes in the individual frameworks of the CSTO and the CIS. In the CSTO, it was decided that the working group on electronic warfare of Defense Ministers' Council would be established. In the CIS, the activity plan of Defense Ministers' Council for 2021 was approved, and based on it, the budget for the development of a joint air defense system was decided.[87]

Russia has continued to strengthen military cooperation with China. Approximately 100 soldiers from China's People's Liberation Army (PLA) participated in the aforementioned large-scale exercises Kavkaz 2020.[88] Moreover, on December 22, 2020, the militaries of China and Russia carried out a joint air patrol from the East China Sea to the Sea of Japan, which was the second such patrol after the patrol carried out in July 2019. A formation including two of Russia's Tu-95MS strategic bombers and four of China's H-6K strategic bombers flew from the East China Sea over the Sea of Japan. According to the Russian Defense Ministry, the objectives of this flight were to deepen and develop the comprehensive partnership of China and Russia, further improve the level of mutual collaboration between the two militaries, improve the joint operation executing capability of the two militaries, and strengthen global strategic stability.[89]

Russia has been strengthening military cooperation with its CSTO allies across the board, but some problems have been occurring that are difficult for Russia to respond to, such as the intensification of the Nagorno-Karabakh conflict and the political turmoil in Kyrgyzstan. Military cooperation between Russia and Armenia has been strengthened; for example, Armenia participated in Kavkaz 2020 and related tactical exercises were conducted in the country. However, in the Nagorno-Karabakh conflict, which was reignited in September 2020, Russia's response was limited to leading the parties to a ceasefire agreement and dispatching peacekeeping units, rather than militarily supporting its ally Armenia. This might have negative implications on the credibility of the CSTO as a collective defense system. Behind this response by Russia is the recognition that good relations with Azerbaijan are also important for the stability of the Caucasus region. Regarding the political turmoil that occurred in October 2020 in Kyrgyzstan, where Russia is attempting to strengthen military cooperation including counter-terrorism cooperation, Russia has taken a wait-and-see stance without deploying any forces. This is due to the fact that Russia thinks that Kyrgyzstan, which is strongly dependent on Russia economically and militarily, will be forced to adopt a pro-Russia policy direction regardless of which forces are in charge of the administration.[90] Military cooperation with Belarus, which has formed the Union State with Russia, is one of the most important issues for Russia to manage its relations with allied countries. Belarus participated in Kavkaz 2020, and in August 2020, the joint exercise Slavyanskoe Bratstvo (Slavic Brotherhood) 2020 was carried out in Belarus by the airborne units of both Russia and Belarus.[91]

There have also been moves to diversify partner countries in military cooperation. One of those partner countries is Pakistan, which also participated in Kavkaz 2020. On September 5, 2020, Valery Gerasimov, chief of the General Staff met Nadeem Raza, chairman of Joint Chiefs of Staff Committee of Pakistan Armed Forces, and they agreed to strengthen joint exercises between their two militaries and strengthen the hotline between the chief of the General Staff and the chairman of Joint Chiefs of Staff Committee.[92] The strengthening of military cooperation between the two countries is likely against the backdrop of the Russian military leadership's perception that military cooperation with Pakistan, which is adjacent to Afghanistan, is essential in order to suppress the threats that the destabilization of Afghanistan and spread of Islamic extremist forces pose to Central Asia overall.

In 2020, Russia's arms exports to African countries showed a new trend. In April 2020, Russia's arms export company Rosoboronexport revealed that it had concluded a contract to supply assault ships to a certain country in the Sub-Saharan Africa region. It stated that this was the first time in 20 years of the arms trade with African countries that finished Russian-made navy equipment would be exported to this region. Russia has been attempting to take the opportunity presented by this kind of trade to build a foothold for exports to Africa and subsequently expand its export market. In the past 20 years, Russia has been the largest supplier of arms to African countries, and it has been indicated that Russia accounts for 49% of total arms exports to African countries.[93] Going forward, it will be necessary to closely monitor Russia's moves regarding arms exports to this region.

NOTES

1)   For the text and previous Japanese translations of the 1993 Constitution (before and after the amendments), the following literature was referenced unless otherwise noted: E.Iu. Barkhatova, *Kommentarii k Konstitutsii Rossiiskoi Federatsii novaia redaktsiia s popravkami 3-e izdanie* (Moskva: Prospekt, 2021); *Kommentarii k Konstitutsii Rossiiskoi Federatsii 2-e izdanie* (Moskva: Prospekt, 2020); Ueno Toshihiko, "Roshia ni okeru 2020 nen no kenpo shusei wo meguru shomondai" [Issues regarding the 2020 constitutional amendments in Russia], *Russia & NIS Business Monthly* 65, no. 5 (2020): 80–105; Mizoguchi Shuhei, "Roshia renpo" [Russian Federation], in *Shin kaisetsu sekai kenposhu dai-gohan* [Constitutions of Nations, 5th Edition], eds. Shiyake Masanori and Tsujimura Miyoko (Tokyo: Sanseido, 2020), 281–341; Shibuya Kenjiro, "Roshia" [Russia],

in *Shinpan sekai kenposhu dai-nihan* [New edition of the constitutions of nations, 2nd Edition], ed. Takahashi Kazuyuki (Tokyo: Iwanami Shoten, 2012), 457–517. The text of the Constitution in the footnotes is the text after the amendments unless otherwise noted.

2) Rasporiazhenie Prezidenta RF ot 15.01.2020g., no. 5-rp, "O rabochei gruppe po podgotovke predlozhenii o vnesenii popravok v Konstitutsiiu Rossiiskoi Federatsii," *Sobranie zakonodatel'stva Rossiiskoi Federatsii (SZRF)*, January 20, 2020, no. 3, art. 251.

3) Hasegawa Takeyuki, "Russian Presidential Power in the Putin Era and the Recent Discussion on Constitutional Revisions," *Briefing Memo*, National Institute for Defense Studies (NIDS) (January 2020).

4) Stat'i 135 i 136, Konstitutsii RF.

5) Punkt 87, Strategii natsional'noi bezopasnosti RF, Ukaz Prezidenta RF ot 31.12.2015g., no. 683, *SZRF*, January 4, 2016, no. 1 (chast' II), art. 212.

6) *Rossiiskaia gazeta*, July 2, 2013.

7) «a», «b», «b^1», «d» stat'i 83, «a^1» stat'i 103, chast' 1 stat'i 110, i chasti 3 i 4 stat'i 112, Konstitutsii RF.

8) «d^1» stat'i 83, Konstitutsii RF.

9) Stat'ia 1, Federal'nyi konstitutsionnyi zakon ot 17.12.1997g., no. 2-FKZ (red. ot 28.12. 2016g.), "O Pravitel'stve Rossiiskoi Federatsii," *SZRF*, December 22, 1997, no. 51, art. 5712.

10) Stat'ia 1, Federal'nyi konstitutsionnyi zakon ot 06.11.2020g., no. 4-FKZ, "O Pravitel'stve Rossiiskoi Federatsii," *SZRF*, November 9, 2020, no. 45, art. 7061.

11) Stat'i 81, 92^1, i «b» chasti 2 stat'i 95, Konstitutsii RF.

12) *Kommersant*, January 15, 2020.

13) *RBK*, January 21, 2020.

14) «zh» i «o», Punkta 23, "Polozhenie o Sovete Bezopasnosti Rossiiskoi Federatsii," Ukaz Prezidenta RF ot 07.13.2020g., no. 175, "O nekotorykh voprosakh Soveta Bezopasnosti Rossiiskoi Federatsii," *SZRF*, March 9, 2020, no. 10, art. 1323.

15) Hasegawa Takeyuki, "Dai niji puuchin seiken ni okeru anzen hosho hosei no henyo: Anzen hosho kaigi fukugicho secchi to sono hoteki shomondai wo chushin to shite" [The development of the Russian security legislation under the second Putin administration: The institutional reform of the Security Council], *Russian Eurasian Society*, no. 1052 (2020): 21–35.

16) Ukaz Prezidenta RF ot 25.08.2020g., no. 526, "Mezhvedomstvennoi komissii Soveta Bezopasnosti Rossiiskoi Federatsii po voprosam obespecheniia natsional'nykh interesov Rossiiskoi Federatsii v Arktike," *SZRF*, August 31, 2020, no. 35, art. 5549.

17) Ukaz Prezidenta RF ot 26.10.2020g., no. 645, "O Strategii razvitiia Arkticheskoi zony

Rossiiskoi Federatsii i obespecheniia natsional'noi bezopasnosti na period do 2035 goda," *SZRF*, November 2, 2020, no. 44, art. 6970.

18) Pravitel'stvo RF, "O Gosudarstvennoi komissii po voprosam razvitiia Arktiki" (March 23, 2015).

19) TASS, September 13, 2020.

20) *Kommersant*, "Itogi vyborov."

21) *Vzgliad*, September 15, 2020; *Vedomosti*, September 14, 2020.

22) *Kommersant*, September 14, 2020.

23) Prezident Rossii, "Telefonnyi razgovor s prem'er-ministrom Italii Dzhuzeppe Konte" (March 21, 2020).

24) *Telekanal* (Zvezda), March 23, 2020.

25) Johns Hopkins University, "COVID-19 Dashboard by the Center for Systems Science and Engineering (CSSE) at Johns Hopkins University (JHU)," JHU website; Stopkoronavirs. RF website.

26) Levada-Tsentr, Odobrenie deiatel'nosti Vladimira Putina.

27) Minzdrav Rossii, "Minzdrav Rossii zaregistriroval pervuiu v mire vaktsinu ot COVID-19" (August 11, 2020).

28) *Rossiiskaia gazeta*, September 4, 2020.

29) RIA Novosti, October 14, 2020; *Izvestia*, October 26, 2020.

30) *Wall Street Journal*, September 20, 2020.

31) Ukaz Prezidenta RF ot 21.07.2020g., no. 474, "O natsional'nykh tseliakh razvitiia Rossiiskoi Federatsii na period do 2030 goda," *SZRF*, July 27, 2020, no. 30, art. 4884.

32) Ukaz Prezidenta RF ot 07.05.2018g., no. 204, "O natsional'nykh tseliakh i strategicheskikh zadachakh razvitiia Rossiiskoi Federatsii na period do 2024 goda," *SZRF*, May 14, 2018, no. 20, art. 2817.

33) Interfax, September 30, 2020.

34) *Gazeta.ru*, June 23, 2020.

35) Kingston Reif and Shannon Bugos, "U.S.-Russian Arms Control Working Groups Meet," Arms Control Association (August 5, 2020).

36) Joe Biden for President, "The Power of America's Example: The Biden Plan for Leading the Democratic World to Meet the Challenges of the 21st Century," Biden-Harris Campaign website.

37) Prezident Rossii, "Telefonnyi razgovor s Prezidentom SShA Dzhozefom Baidenom" (January 26, 2021).

38) Ukaz Prezidenta RF ot 02.06.2020g., no. 355, "Ob Osnovakh gosudarstvennoi politiki Rossiiskoi Federatsii v oblasti iadernogo sderzhivaniia," *SZRF*, June 8, 2020, no. 23, art.

3623.

39) Prezident Rossii, "Utverzhdena Voennaia doktrina Rossiiskoi Federatsii" (February 2, 2010); *Vedomosti*, June 2, 2020.

40) Shannon Bugos, "Russia Releases Nuclear Deterrence Policy," *Arms Control Today* 50, no. 6 (2020): 41–42.

41) Paul Dibb, "Russia's New Strategy for Nuclear War," *Strategist*, Australian Strategic Policy Institute (June 19, 2020).

42) Koizumi Yu, "'*Kakuyokushi no bunya ni okeru roshia renpo kokka seisaku no kiso' ni miru roshia no kaku senryaku*" [The nuclear strategy of Russia as seen in the Basic Principles of State Policy of the Russian Federation on Nuclear Deterrence], Japan Institute of International Affairs (August 24, 2020).

43) *Rossiiskaia gazeta*, February 10, 2020.

44) *Meduza*, August 20, 2020.

45) *New York Times*, September 2, 2020.

46) [Japan] Ministry of Foreign Affairs, "G7 Foreign Ministers' Statement" (September 9, 2020).

47) [U.S.] Congressional Research Service, *Russia's Nord Stream 2 Pipeline: Running in Place*, by Paul Belkin, Michael Ratner, and Cory Welt, IF11138 (September 28, 2020).

48) [Japan] Cabinet Secretariat, "National Security Strategy," English edition (December 17, 2013).

49) [Japan] Ministry of Foreign Affairs, "Nichiro paatonaashippu no hatten ni kansuru nihonkoku sori daijin to roshia renpo daitoryo no kyodo seimei" [Joint Declaration by the Prime Minister of Japan and the President of the Russian Federation Concerning Developing the Japan-Russia Partnership] (April 29, 2013).

50) [Japan] Joint Staff, "Roshia kaigun tono kaizoku taisho kyodo kunren no jisshi ni tsuite" [About the holding of a joint exercise in counter piracy activities with the Russian Navy], (January 22, 2020).

51) Sovet Bezopasnosti RF, "Sekretar' Soveta Bezopasnosti Rossiiskoi Federatsii N. P. Patrushev vstretilsia s General'nym sekretarem Soveta natsional'noi bezopasnosti Iaponii S. Iati" (March 14, 2014); Sovet Bezopasnosti RF, "O vstreche Sekretaria Soveta Bezopasnosti Rossiiskoi Federatsii N. P. Patrusheva so spetsial'nym poslannikom Prem'er-ministra Iaponii S.Abe" (May 6, 2014).

52) [Japan] Ministry of Foreign Affairs, "Patorushefu roshia renpo anzen hosho kaigi shoki ni yoru Abe sori daijin hyokei" [Courtesy call on Prime Minister Abe by Nikolai Patrushev, Secretary of the Security Council of the Russian Federation], (September 17, 2019).

53) Prezident Rossii, "Vstrecha s General'nym sekretarem Soveta natsional'noi bezopasnosti

Iaponii Sigeru Kitamuroi" (January 16, 2020).

54) Ministerstvo oborony RF, "Informatsionnyi biulleten' Ministerstva oborony Rossiiskoi Federatsii po nedopushcheniiu rasprostraneniia novo koronavirusnoi infektsii," accessed December 24, 2020.

55) *Krasnaia Zvezda*, July 1, 2020.

56) *Krasnaia Zvezda*, March 23, 2020.

57) *Krasnaia Zvezda*, March 27, 2020.

58) *Krasnaia Zvezda*, May 6 and July 1, 2020.

59) *Krasnaia Zvezda*, May 6, 2020.

60) Ministerstvo oborony RF, "Informatsionnyi biulleten' Ministerstva oborony Rossiiskoi Federatsii po nedopushcheniiu rasprostraneniia novo koronavirusnoi infektsii," accessed December 24, 2020.

61) Ibid.

62) *Krasnaia Zvezda*, May 6, 2020.

63) *Krasnaia Zvezda*, August 5 and August 24, 2020.

64) Marlene Laruelle and Madeline McCann, "Post-Soviet State Responses to COVID-19: Making or Breaking Authoritarianism," PONARS Eurasia (March 2020).

65) Ibid.

66) *Krasnaia Zvezda*, May 22, 2020.

67) Ministerstvo oborony RF, "V armeiskom korpuse VVO na Sakhaline sostoialas' sovmestnaia trenirovka podrazdelenii antiterrora i RXB zashchity" (August 10, 2020).

68) *Krasnaia Zvezda*, February 7, 2020.

69) *Krasnaia Zvezda*, May 22, 2020.

70) Ukaz Prezidenta RF ot 05.06.2020g., no. 374, "O voenno-administrativnom delenii Rossiiskoi Federatsii," *SZRF*, June 8, 2020, no. 3, art. 3629.

71) Ukaz Prezidenta RF ot 21.12.2020g., no. 803, "O Severnom flote," *SZRF*, December 28, 2020, no. 52 (chast' I), art. 8795.

72) *Rossiiskaia Gazeta*, June 6 and June 7, 2020.

73) *Krasnaia Zvezda*, May 6 and July 1, 2020.

74) *Krasnaia Zvezda*, May 27, 2020.

75) *Krasnaia Zvezda*, September 28, 2020.

76) Roger McDermott, "Russia's Armed Forces Test UAV Swarm Tactics in Kavkaz 2020," *Eurasia Daily Monitor* 17, issue 136 (September 30, 2020).

77) *Krasnaia Zvezda*, August 12, 2020.

78) Ministerstvo oborony RF, "Noveishaia zenitnaia raketnaia sistema S-300V4 VVO v ramkakh ucheniia vpervye budet perebazirovana na Kurily" (October 26, 2020).

79) *Izvestiia*, October 28, 2020.

80) *Krasnaia Zvezda*, August 14, 2020.

81) *Krasnaia Zvezda*, August 14, 2020.

82) *Krasnaia Zvezda*, August 14, 2020.

83) *Rossiiskaia Gazeta*, June 5 and June 25, 2020.

84) *Krasnaia Zvezda*, September 11 and September 30, 2020.

85) *Krasnaia Zvezda*, September 14, 2020.

86) *Krasnaia Zvezda*, March 4, 2020.

87) *Krasnaia Zvezda*, September 7, 2020.

88) *Krasnaia Zvezda*, September 14, 2020.

89) *Rossiiskaia Gazeta*, December 22, 2020; *Krasnaia Zvezda*, December 23, 2020.

90) Kate Mallinson, "Kyrgyzstan's Protracted Political and Economic Crisis," *Expert Comment*, Chatham House (October 26, 2020).

91) *Krasnaia Zvezda*, September 23, 2020.

92) *Krasnaia Zvezda*, September 7, 2020.

93) *Nezavisimaia Gazeta*, November 12, 2020.

Chapter 6

The United States

National Security during the COVID-19 Crisis

KIKUCHI Shigeo

Members of the
Massachusetts
National Guard
providing security
support near
the U.S. Capitol
Building on the day
of the presidential
inauguration on
January 20, 2021
(Massachusetts
National Guard
photo by Capt.
Aaron Smith)

Summary

In 2020, important security policy developments were seen in the United States, most notably with regard to policies toward China, even as novel coronavirus disease (COVID-19) infections continued to spread. There has been an increasing emphasis on the threat of China's penetration into the United States, and a growing recognition that the state and local levels of government are targeted by Chinese influence operations. In response, specific measures were put in place from 2019 to 2020. First, the State Department began to require prior notification for Chinese government officials to contact U.S. state, local, and municipal government personnel. It also designated 15 Chinese state-run media entities as "foreign missions" under the Foreign Missions Act of 1982 and required them to abide by terms and conditions set by the State Department. Furthermore, in response to growing concerns in the United States about human rights violations in the Xinjiang Uygur Autonomous Region (XUAR) of China, the Uyghur Human Rights Policy Act of 2020 was enacted in June 2020, calling for sanctions against those complicit in human rights violations. In July, the U.S. government imposed sanctions on some Chinese officials by freezing their assets and denying them entry into the country, and also imposed export restrictions on Chinese companies and others allegedly involved in human rights violations.

On the other hand, as each service of the U.S. military develops its own operational concepts for China and Russia, the Department of Defense (DOD) has begun to develop a joint concept to encompass those operational concepts and give them a certain direction. In addition, although the impact of the spread of COVID-19 infections was seen in 2020, there was active deployment of strategic bombers and aircraft carriers in the Western Pacific.

The U.S. presidential election was held on November 3, 2020, and former vice president Joseph Biden was reported to be the winner on November 7. However, President Donald Trump claimed that large-scale election fraud had occurred and filed dozens of lawsuits in various battleground states. Furthermore, on January 6, 2021, an incident arose in which supporters of President Trump stormed the U.S. Capitol Building, where a Joint Session of Congress was being held to certify the electoral votes cast on December 14, 2020.

1. Unfolding Strategy toward China

(1) The "China Threat" in the Trump Administration

On January 21, 2020, the first case of COVID-19 in the United States was confirmed in Washington State. On January 31, the U.S. government declared a public health emergency and, beginning February 2, suspended entry into the country by foreign nationals who had stayed anywhere in China, with the exception of Hong Kong and Macao, within 14 days prior to entering the United States. However, the number of infections in the United States began to increase rapidly in March. On March 28, the United States surpassed China in the number of reported cases, becoming the country with the most infections in the world. This was followed by a second wave that peaked in July. In October, as the winter season approached, the number of patients increased rapidly, far exceeding the first and second waves. The number of people infected was 19,893,181 and the number of deaths was 344,497 in the United States as of December 31, 2020.

Despite this situation, there were important developments in U.S. security policy in 2020. One development was U.S. policy toward China. In his speech to the Silicon Valley Leadership Group on January 13, 2020, as well as in his speech to state governors at the National Governors Association meeting on February 8, Secretary of State Mike Pompeo called attention to the diversion of technology from U.S. companies operating in China for use in China's military modernization and China's growing influence at the state and local levels. In addition, on May 20, the White House submitted its "United States Strategic Approach to the People's Republic of China" report to Congress, pursuant to the FY2019 National Defense Authorization Act's requirement to submit a "whole-of-government strategy" with regard to China.

Furthermore, from June to July 2020, Robert O'Brien, assistant to the president for national security affairs (June 24); Christopher Wray, director of the Federal Bureau of Investigation (FBI) (July 7); Attorney General William Barr (July 16); and Secretary of State Pompeo (July 23) gave a series of speeches

Table 6.1. Selected speeches on China by Trump administration officials in 2020

Date	Speaker	Host/venue	Speech title
January 13	Pompeo	Silicon Valley Leadership Group, San Francisco, California	Silicon Valley and National Security
February 6	Barr	China Initiative Conference, Washington, DC	
February 8	Pompeo	National Governors Association, Washington, DC	U.S. States and the China Competition
June 19	Pompeo	Virtual Copenhagen Democracy Summit	Europe and the China Challenge
June 24	O'Brien	Phoenix, Arizona	Chinese Communist Party's Ideology and Global Ambitions
July 7	Wray	Hudson Institute, Washington, DC	Threat Posed by the Chinese Government and the Chinese Communist Party to the Economic and National Security of the United States
July 16	Barr	Ford Presidential Museum, Grand Rapids, Michigan	
July 23	Pompeo	Nixon Presidential Library and Museum, Yorba Linda, California	Communist China and the Free World's Future
September 23	Pompeo	Wisconsin State Capitol, Madison, Wisconsin	State Legislatures and the China Challenge
December 9	Pompeo	Georgia Institute of Technology, Atlanta, Georgia	Chinese Communist Party on the American Campus

Sources: Compiled by the author based on U.S. Department of State, Department of Justice, Federal Bureau of Investigation, and White House websites.

designed to expose the threat posed by China (Table 6.1). The four speeches were organized as a set, presumably orchestrated by Secretary Pompeo. Rather than setting a new direction, they were made to clarify what they consider to be the China threat, to highlight the measures that Donald Trump's administration had been developing in response, and to draw attention to the matter and seek understanding in the United States and abroad.

Several common themes permeate these speeches. The first is the positioning of the threat posed by China as ideologically based. Addressing the issue of ideology in his speech, National Security Advisor O'Brien explained that failure to understand China was because "we did not pay heed to the CCP's

Secretary of State Pompeo delivers his policy speech on China at the Nixon Presidential Library and Museum on July 23, 2020 (UPI/Newscom/Kyodo News Images)

[Chinese Communist Party] ideology," and described the CCP as a "Marxist-Leninist organization" and "the last 'ruling communist party that never split with Stalin.'" He asserted that "individuals do not have inherent value under Marxism-Leninism" and they "exist to serve the state," and that this way of thinking "remain[s] as fundamental to the Chinese Communist Party." He added that based on this way of thinking, the CCP "seeks total control over the people's lives," including economic control, political control, physical control, and thought control. Additionally, Secretary of State Pompeo made statements in his speech that: "the CCP regime is a Marxist-Leninist regime"; "it's this ideology that informs his [General Secretary Xi's] decades-long desire for global hegemony of Chinese communism"; and that "America can no longer ignore the fundamental political and ideological differences between our countries."

At the same time, these speeches make a clear distinction between the CCP, which happens to be ruling China and the Chinese people, as seen in the statement by National Security Advisor O'Brien that the "Chinese Communist Party does not equal China or her people." To the latter, the United States' "long history of friendship" and "deep respect and admiration" (O'Brien) are emphasized throughout the speeches.

The second theme is that these speeches position CCP-led activities in China and abroad as ideology-based "propaganda." National Security Advisor O'Brien asserted that "propaganda plays a central political role for the CCP," quoting the work of an Australian journalist who said that for "Lenin, Stalin, Mao and Xi," "words" are "bullets" that are for "defining, isolating, and destroying opponents." O'Brien also noted that propaganda activities are not confined to China; rather, the CCP is using corporate acquisitions and other methods to "eliminate 'unfriendly' Chinese language media outlets worldwide" and is also spreading "subtle pro-Beijing propaganda" through the radio stations it has acquired in the United States.

The third theme, which is clearly demonstrated by the second theme, is the emphasis that the threat of China has penetrated into the United States and is coming closer to the American people. Secretary of State Pompeo said that when "we opened our arms to Chinese citizens…China sent propagandists into our press conferences, our research centers, our high-schools, our colleges, and even into our PTA meetings." In addition, Attorney General Barr stated, "All too often, for the sake of short-term profits, American companies have succumbed to that [China's] influence—even at the expense of freedom and openness in the United States." Citing U.S. films such as *World War Z* (2013) and *Doctor Strange* (2016) as examples, Barr commented that "Hollywood now regularly censors its own movies to appease the Chinese Communist Party, the world's most powerful violator of human rights."

FBI Director Wray also cited "malign foreign influence" as a tool that "China and the Chinese Communist Party use to manipulate Americans." He stated that if, for example, the Chinese authorities learn that a U.S. official is planning to visit Taiwan, they may threaten to revoke permission for U.S. companies in the official's constituency to operate factories in China, or they may approach close associates of the official "to act on China's behalf as middlemen" and have them persuade the official to cancel the visit. Director Wray also warned that these "co-opted middlemen" may not reveal to the official in question that they are "Chinese Communist Party pawns," and that they might "not even realize they're being used as pawns."

As indicated by the fact that two of the four people, who delivered the aforementioned speeches in June and July were the attorney general and the director of the FBI, the fourth theme is that policy toward China has also been positioned as a law enforcement and counterintelligence issue that entails concrete actions within the United States. In particular, at the Department of Justice, under the leadership of then attorney general Jeff Sessions, the China Initiative, chaired by the assistant attorney general for national security, was established in November 2018 to strengthen prosecution of cases related to the theft of trade secrets allegedly involving China. FBI Director Wray's speech emphasized the threat that economic espionage by China poses to U.S. companies and the economy. He raised the example of a Chinese scientist participating in China's Thousand Talents Program, an overseas high-level recruitment program, who stole advanced technical information from the U.S. company that formerly employed him and provided it to China. He also cited the example of a Chinese-American businessman who set up a company to "digest" and "absorb" U.S. technology and provide it to Chinese state-owned enterprises, and then headhunted engineers from a U.S. company to have them provide proprietary technical information. According to Director Wray, the number of economic espionage cases involving China has increased 14-fold in the past 10 years.

In his speech, Secretary of State Pompeo said that since the presidency of Richard Nixon in the United States, it had been presumed to be "inevitable" that China would become freer as it became more prosperous, and that the freer it became, the less of a threat it would pose to the international community. However, he asserted that that "age of inevitability is over." Secretary Pompeo's choice of the Nixon Presidential Library and Museum as the venue for this statement may have been intended to underscore that the Trump administration's review of policy toward China constituted a fundamental shift since the establishment of diplomatic relations between the United States and China.

(2) Countering China's Influence Operations

China's influence operations in the United States had been an issue even before the speeches by Secretary of State Pompeo and the others. Congress included a provision in the National Defense Authorization Act for Fiscal Year 2020, enacted in December 2019, to establish the Foreign Malign Influence

Response Center within the Office of the Director of National Intelligence (ODNI). The mission of the center is "analyzing and integrating all intelligence possessed or acquired by the United States Government" regarding "any hostile effort" undertaken by Russia, Iran, North Korea, or China, with the objective of influencing, through overt or covert means, U.S. government policies or public opinion in the United States. It provides to employees and officers of the Federal Government in policy-making positions and Congress "comprehensive assessments, and indications and warnings," and makes recommendations on countermeasures upon request. The act also included a provision stipulating that the ODNI's National Counterintelligence and Security Center (NCSC) submit an "annual report on the influence operations and campaigns in the United States by the Communist Party of China," including those conducted by the United Front Work Department that is in charge of foreign operations in the CCP.

This particular vulnerability to Chinese influence operations in the United States was recognized to be at the state and local levels. On September 25, 2018, Director of National Intelligence Dan Coats referred to Chinese influence operations in the United States in a speech at The Citadel, stating that "the Chinese government uses all the capabilities at their disposal, to influence US policies, spread propaganda, manipulate media, pressure individuals, including students, critical of Chinese policies." He additionally stated that China: "is also targeting US, state, and local governments and officials. It is trying to exploit any divisions between federal and local levels of policies." He added that China "uses investments and other incentives to expand its influence." Vice President Mike Pence also referred to China's influence operations targeting U.S. states and localities in his China speech at the Hudson Institute on October 4, 2018, citing U.S. Intelligence Community assessments. Furthermore, Secretary of State Pompeo, in his speeches to the National Governors Association on February 8, 2020 and to the Wisconsin State Senate Chamber on September 23, stated that China has started influence operations against localities below the state government level, which it perceives as "weak link[s]," and warned against being approached by Chinese diplomats and others under the guise of "cooperation or friendship."

Against the backdrop of this growing sense of crisis, the U.S. government has taken measures to limit the Chinese government's influence, especially at the state, local, and municipal government levels. On the *Federal Register* dated October 21, 2019, the State Department designated that "all official meetings" planned with "representatives of state, local, and municipal governments in the United States and its territories" involving members of Chinese foreign missions in the United States (including its representatives temporarily working in the United States, and accompanying Chinese dependents and members of their households) as a "benefit" to be provided through the State Department and required such members of the Chinese missions to submit prior notification to the department, if they plan such official meetings or visits. Furthermore, in the *Federal Register* dated July 6, 2020, the State Department expanded the scope of those requiring advance notice. It came to require any personnel of the Chinese government "temporarily visiting" the United States to submit advance notification of engagement with "any personnel" (including elected and appointed officials, representatives, and employees) of state, local, and municipal governments. Furthermore, the State Department announced on the *Federal Register* of September 21, 2020 that it would require the Chinese foreign missions in the United States to obtain advance approval from the department to "host a cultural event" with more than 50 people in attendance, outside the physical boundaries of the mission.

The U.S. government's stance against China's influence operations was demonstrated in its treatment of the Chinese media. The State Department announced, during the press conference on February 18, 2020, that it had designated five Chinese state-run media organizations as "foreign missions" under the Foreign Missions Act of 1982. Subsequently, the State Department announced that it had designated "the representative offices and operations in the United States" of four Chinese state-run media organizations on June 22, and six on October 21, as "foreign missions." In each of above determinations on designation of "foreign mission," the State Department requested the Chinese media entities to comply with the terms and conditions specified by the department.

The Foreign Missions Act, cited in the determinations, defined as "foreign mission," "any mission to or agency or entity in the United States," which is (i) involved in the diplomatic, consular, or other activities, or (ii) "substantially owned or effectively controlled by" a foreign government.[1] The State Department claimed these Chinese media entities came under (ii). During the February 18 press conference, State Department officials explained that these Chinese state-run media entities "work 100 percent for the Chinese Government and the Chinese Communist Party," and the designation merely recognized the fact that they are "part of the PRC [People's Republic of China] party state propaganda news apparatus." At that time, the officials explained that the purpose of this was to ask the Chinese media entities which had been designated as foreign missions to report on two points: first, basic information on individuals working for these entities in the United States, current state of personnel and update on personnel changes; and second, the status of real estate holdings in the United States. On the other hand, the officials stated, "We're not in any way, shape, or form constraining any of the journalistic activities these entities engage in." In fact, if we read the actual public notices, these media entities are exempted from the requirement for Chinese government officials to give prior notice when contacting state, local, and municipal government personnel.

On February 19, the day after the February 18 press conference at which the State Department announced the designation of five Chinese state-run media entities as foreign missions, the Chinese Ministry of Foreign Affairs announced that it had revoked the press credentials of three Beijing-based reporters from the *Wall Street Journal* because of an article by a university professor that appeared in the newspaper on February 3 (the *Wall Street Journal* stated that the three journalists were ordered to leave the country within five days). On March 2, the State Department disclosed that it had asked the five Chinese state-run media entities that it designated as foreign missions on February 18 to set "personnel caps" on the number of Chinese citizens able to work for them in the United States, reducing the number to a total of 100 people at the five entities. At a press conference on March 22, State Department officials explained in regard to the "personnel caps" at the five companies that "the caps aren't placed on individuals; they're only on the entities," and that it was up to each entity to decide who would stay and who would leave the country in order to stay within the personnel cap. The officials also stated that this was in reaction to "a very longstanding negative trend in the treatment of the press" in China, and "not linked to any one particular incident," such as the deportation of the *Wall Street Journal* reporters.

The State Department's designation of a total of 15 Chinese state-run media entities as foreign missions was, in fact, not for the purpose of obtaining information on their personnel and real estate holdings in the United States, which a State Department official stated would be requested from Chinese media entities at the February 18, 2020 press conference. At a June 22, 2020 press conference when a second designation was announced, David Stilwell, assistant secretary of state for East Asian and Pacific affairs, stated that the CCP "has always tightly controlled China's state news agencies," but that its "control has actually tightened in recent years." He also pointed out that "the word they [China's state news agencies] were putting out was in fact aligned with what the Communist Party wanted," adding, "That's not journalism." Stilwell said that designating the media entities as foreign missions indicated formal recognition of "the China party state's effective control over so-called media entities, including those that operate here in the United States," and that this would lead to "increasing the transparency of these and other PRC government propaganda activities in the United States." The State Department also gave a similar explanation when it announced the designation of foreign missions on October 21. Thus, arguably, the series of designations of Chinese state-run media entities as foreign missions was actually aimed at labeling them as "CCP propaganda outlets."

The State Department has taken the same measures against Confucius

Institutes as it has against the 15 Chinese state-run media entities. Confucius Institutes are overseen by the Office of Chinese Language Council International (Hanban), a subordinate organization of the Chinese Ministry of Education, and are established within cooperating universities and other educational institutions overseas for purposes including overseas Chinese language education, promoting understanding of Chinese language and culture, enhancing educational and cultural exchanges and cooperation, and promoting friendly relations. According to the Hanban website, 541 Institutes have been established worldwide (confirmed on December 31, 2020).[2] In addition to university-level Confucius Institutes, Confucius Classrooms have been established at secondary education institutions.

Since the first Confucius Institute was established in the United States in 2004, more than 100 Confucius Institutes and more than 500 Confucius Classrooms have been established.[3] This has led to concerns about the presence of Confucius Institutes on U.S. college campuses. In June 2014, the American Association of University Professors issued a statement on Confucius Institutes, stating that most agreements establishing Confucius Institutes include "unacceptable concessions to the political aims and practices of the government of China." The statement also observed that Confucius Institutes "advance a state agenda in the recruitment and control of academic staff, in the choice of curriculum, and in the restriction of debate," asserting that "allowing any third-party control of academic matters is inconsistent with principles of academic freedom, shared governance, and the institutional autonomy of colleges and universities."[4] In addition, in a report released in April 2017, the National Association of Scholars cited a statement by Li Changchun, a CCP Politburo Standing Committee member, who stated that Confucius Institutes are "an important part of China's overseas propaganda set-up," and recommended that U.S. universities with Confucius Institutes and Classrooms close them and sever ties with Hanban.[5]

Furthermore, the report titled *China's Impact on the U.S. Education System* released by the Senate Homeland Security and Government Affairs Committee on February 27, 2019, noted, "The Chinese government controls nearly every aspect of Confucius Institutes at U.S. schools." It also pointed out that Confucius Institute directors and faculty members "pledge to protect Chinese national interests," and that "Confucius Institute funding comes with strings that can compromise academic freedom." It also pointed out that the State Department and the Department of Education were not fully aware of these conditions.[6]

In response to deepening concerns over the presence of Confucius Institutes in U.S. universities, on August 13, 2020, Secretary of State Pompeo announced the State Department's designation of the Confucius Institute U.S. Center (CIUS) as a foreign mission, saying that it is the "de facto headquarters of the Confucius Institute network" in the United States. Furthermore, in the August 24 *Federal Register*, the State Department announced that the CIUS would have to comply with the terms and conditions specified by the Department related to the CIUS' activities in the United States, requiring (i) a report detailing all financial and other support the CIUS had provided or would provide to Confucius Institutes, Confucius Classrooms, or other educational institutions in the United States in calendar years 2018, 2019, 2020, (ii) a list of all PRC citizens referred or assigned by CIUS to a Confucius Institute or Confucius Classroom in the United States since 2016 (as well as biannual updates thereafter), (iii) provision of 60 days' notice to the State Department prior to dispersing funds, personnel, or other resources in support of new Confucius Institutes or other educational organizations in the United States, and (iv) courtesy copies of curriculum materials that CIUS had provided to individual Confucius Institutes or other U.S.-based educational institutions for use in calendar years 2016–2020.

In the August 13 statement on the designation of the CIUS as a foreign mission, Secretary of State Pompeo expressed that these measures "recogniz[ed] CIUS for what it is: an entity advancing Beijing's global propaganda and malign influence campaign on U.S. campuses and K-12 classrooms" and that the Institutes were "funded by the PRC and part of the Chinese Communist Party's global influence and propaganda apparatus." The statement also explained the "goals" of the designation as allowing school officials to "make informed choices about whether these CCP-backed programs should be allowed to continue." In light of this explanation, the designation of the CIUS as a foreign mission seems to have been aimed at highlighting the fact that Confucius Institutes, including the CIUS, are Chinese propaganda organizations and surveillance agencies aimed at Chinese students in the United States. A letter to the governing boards of American institutions of higher education and affiliates dated August 18 from Under Secretary of State Keith Krach and a joint letter to state commissioners of education dated October 9 from Secretary of State Pompeo and Secretary of Education Betsy Devos, pointed out that Confucius Institutes and Confucius Classrooms at U.S. campuses, while they are run on the curricula approved by the Chinese government and taught by teachers trained by the Chinese government, were in fact "an important element of the PRC's global influence campaign." The letters, likely with the same goals as the designation, also emphasized the disadvantages of accepting Confucius Institutes and Confucius Classrooms, such as the possible interference by the Chinese into academic freedom at universities, using financial incentives as lever.

(3) Sanctions on Human Rights Violations in China

Another characteristic of the development of policy toward China in 2020 was the strengthening of sanctions against China, particularly in response to growing concerns in the United States over human rights violations in the XUAR. The Congressional-Executive Commission on China (CECC), composed of Republican and Democratic Party members of the House and Senate as well as members appointed by the executive branch, stated in its 2018 Annual Report released on October 10, 2018: "Since Chen Quanguo's appointment as XUAR Party Secretary in August 2016, reports have documented the escalation of rights abuses against local ethnic minority populations."

As an example of this, the 2018 Annual Report raised "the extrajudicial detention of 1 million or more individuals in 'political reeducation' centers or camps." Reasons for detention include "frequency of prayer, expression of 'politically incorrect' views, history of travel abroad, and connections with people outside of China." The report also pointed out that at the reeducation centers, which promote "transformation through education," detainees were forced to chant "Thank the Party! Thank the Motherland! Thank President Xi!" and that there was "torture" including the use of interrogation chairs as well as "medical neglect and maltreatment, solitary confinement, [and] sleep deprivation." The 2019 Annual Report, released on January 8, 2020, similarly mentioned Chinese media reports that the XUAR People's Congress had amended its regulations on "vocational training centers." The report also said that in 2019, Chinese authorities had "expanded a system of extrajudicial mass internment camps" and detained 1.5 million people.

Furthermore, the 2018 Annual Report mentioned that in the XUAR, the Chinese government has established "data-driven surveillance," facilitated by iris and body scanners, voice pattern analyzers, DNA sequencers, and facial recognition cameras in neighborhoods, on roads, and in train stations. The report pointed out that Chinese companies such as Hikvision and Dahua Technology were awarded upwards of $1.2 billion in government contracts to build the surveillance systems.

Congress has also expressed strong concerns about this "unprecedented repression of ethnic minorities in the Xinjiang Uyghur Autonomous Region" (2018 Annual Report). On August 28, 2018, 17 Republican and Democratic Party members of the House and Senate, led by Senator Marco Rubio, chairman of the CECC, jointly sent a letter to the secretary of state and secretary of the treasury that states that the Chinese government is "creating a high-tech police state in the XUAR" that constitutes a "gross violation of privacy and international human rights," and that they were thus calling for sanctions against the Chinese government and CCP officials who "oversee these repressive policies" in the region, including XUAR Party Secretary Chen Quanguo, that would hold them accountable under the Global Magnitsky Human Rights Accountability Act.[7] On December 12 of the following year, a group of members of Congress, led by Senator Rubio, sent another letter to the secretaries of state, treasury, and commerce calling for sanctions to be imposed on XUAR Party Secretary Chen and others, this time signed by 48 members of Congress.[8] The Global Magnitsky Act authorizes the president to impose sanctions, including ineligibility for or revocation of visas to enter the United States and blocking of property, on "foreign person[s]" who are "responsible for extrajudicial killings, torture, or other gross violations of internationally recognized human rights." In response to this act, Executive Order 13818 (December 20, 2017) granted the secretary of the treasury the authority to designate sanctions targets.

Furthermore, in 2019, bills calling for stronger measures related to the human rights situation in the XUAR, including sanctions and investigations, were introduced in the House and Senate and passed in their respective floors. In 2020, based on these bills, Senator Rubio introduced the Uyghur Human Rights Policy Act of 2020, which was passed in the Senate by unanimous consent and in the House by 413-1. It was signed into law by President Trump on June 17. The act requires the president to identify persons who are "responsible" for "torture," "cruel, inhuman, or degrading treatment or punishment," "prolonged detention without charges and trial," and other such acts against Uyghurs, Kazakhs, and others in the XUAR, and report to Congress within 180 days after the enactment of the act. It also calls for the imposition of sanctions such as asset blocking and denial or revocation of U.S. visas against such persons.

Despite repeated calls from Congress, it was not until 2020 that the Department of the Treasury imposed sanctions under the Global Magnitsky Act in relation to the human rights situation in the XUAR. On July 9, 2020, the Department of the Treasury designated four people—XUAR Party Secretary Chen Quanguo; Zhu Hailun, a former deputy party secretary of the XUAR; Wang Mingshan, director and party secretary of the Xinjiang Public Security Bureau (XPSB); and Huo Liujun, former party secretary of the XPSB—as well as the XPSB as subject to asset blocking under the Global Magnitsky Act. On the same day as the Treasury Department's announcement, Secretary of State Pompeo announced that Chen Quanguo, Zhu Hailun, and Wang Mingshan would be subject to denial of entry to the United States. Then, on July 31, the Treasury Department announced that it had additionally designated the

Xinjiang Production and Construction Corps and two of its executives as targets of sanctions, including asset blocking, under the Global Magnitsky Act. The press release stated that the Xinjiang Production and Construction Corps is a "paramilitary organization in the XUAR that is subordinate to the Chinese Communist Party" that has "helped implement" the "comprehensive surveillance, detention, and indoctrination program targeting Uyghurs and members of other ethnic minority groups" advanced by XUAR Party Secretary Chen. Congressman James McGovern, chair of the CECC, and Senator Rubio issued a statement on July 10 regarding the imposition of sanctions under the Global Magnitsky Act, saying that they welcomed the "long overdue" sanctions, and called for more action from the government regarding the situation in the XUAR, "one of the worst human rights situations in the world."

In addition, steps were also taken in terms of trade control, to impose sanctions related to the human rights situation in the XUAR. On October 7, 2019, the U.S. Bureau of Industry and Security (BIS) of the Department of Commerce announced that it would add the XPSB, 19 organizations under the XPSB, and eight businesses (including Hikvision and Dahua Technology which were mentioned in the CECC Annual Report), to the "Entity List" on the ground of being implicated in human rights violations and abuses targeting Uyghurs and other predominantly Muslim ethnic minorities in the XUAR. Furthermore, on May 22, 2020, China's Ministry of Public Security's Institute of Forensic Science and eight Chinese companies were added to the Entity List.

The Entity List identifies entities for which there is reasonable cause to believe have been, are, or may become "involved in activities that are contrary to the national security or foreign policy interests of the United States" based on the Export Administration Regulations (EAR) administered by the BIS. When exporting to those on the Entity List, even in cases of exporting items that would not normally require a license for export, such as low-technology consumer goods, one is specifically required to submit license applications, which in principle are not granted.[9] The scope of the EAR is extremely broad, and with the exception of items under the jurisdiction of other government departments and agencies, it includes "all items in the United States," "all U.S. origin items," and "foreign-made commodities that incorporate controlled U.S.-origin commodities, foreign-made commodities that are 'bundled' with controlled U.S.-origin software, foreign-made software that is commingled with controlled U.S.-origin software, and foreign-made technology that is commingled with controlled U.S.-origin technology."[10]

While the sanctions under the EAR relate to exports to China, imports from China have also been addressed in relation to the XUAR. In its "Global Supply Chains, Forced Labor, and the Xinjiang Uyghur Autonomous Region" report released in March 2020, the CECC pointed out that Uyghurs, ethnic Kazakhs, and Kyrgyz in the XUAR are forced to work in factories located in mass internment camps or in factories outside the camps in the XUAR, and that the products produced there are entering the international supply chain. The report listed textiles, cotton, electronics, food products, shoes, tea, and handicrafts as categories that contain products from forced labor, and it named 20 companies "suspected of directly employing forced labor or sourcing from suppliers that are suspected of using forced labor."

The "Xinjiang Supply Chain Business Advisory" jointly issued on July 1 by the Departments of State, Treasury, Commerce, and Homeland Security also reflected such concerns. The advisory refers to the mass detentions, abuse, and forced labor of Uyghurs in the XUAR, and warns U.S. companies of several patterns concerning "reputational, economic, and, in certain instances, legal, risks" that may arise from "supply chain links" to human rights abuses in the case of doing business with Chinese companies that are located in the XUAR or have involvement with the XUAR.

Currently, although the Trump administration's strengthening criticism of China over "human rights abuses" in the XUAR reflects the growing recognition in the United States that such abuses are a problem in and of themselves, it also seems to include the objective of using the human rights issue as a springboard to put pressure on China.

In his speech on July 23, 2020, Secretary of State Pompeo stressed the importance of "in-person diplomacy," appealing directly to the "Chinese people" who are "dynamic, freedom-loving people who are completely distinct from the Chinese Communist Party," and mentioned meetings he had with "Uyghurs and ethnic Kazakhs who escaped Xinjiang's concentration camps," "Hong Kong's democracy leaders," and "Tiananmen Square survivors." He pointed out that the "CCP fears the Chinese people's honest opinions more than any foe, and save for losing their own grip on power, they have reason—no reason to." Pompeo's logic recognized that engaging directly with "dynamic, freedom-loving people" and eliciting "the Chinese people's honest opinions," which "the CCP fears...more than any other foe," will strike the internal vulnerabilities of China's current regime.

In concluding his speech, Secretary of State Pompeo asserted that "securing our freedoms from the Chinese Communist Party is the mission of our time" and that "America is perfectly positioned to lead" it because of the "founding principles" of the Declaration of Independence of 1776 that all people have "inalienable rights." By positioning the United States as "a beacon of freedom for people all around the world, including people inside of China," he emphasized that these internationalist declarations are also directed at China's domestic human rights situation.

Furthermore, on July 8, 2019, when Secretary of State Pompeo announced the establishment of the Commission on Inalienable Rights, composed of human rights specialists, philosophers, and outside experts on activism, he explained the Commission's significance by linking it to how, "with the indispensable support of President Ronald Reagan, a human rights revolution toppled the totalitarian regimes of the former Soviet Union." This was a reference to how the Reagan administration placed multifaceted pressure on the Soviet Union not only to strengthen its own military power, but also to pursue the Soviet Union's human rights issues.[11] The Trump administration's pursuit of China's human rights issues seems to show aspects of a cold war strategy modeled on the New Cold War pursued by the Reagan administration.

2. Implementing the 2018 National Defense Strategy

(1) Defense Capabilities in the Age of Great Power Competition

During the Trump administration, the National Defense Strategy (NDS), a summary of which was released in January 2018, was used as "a clear roadmap for the Department of Defense to address the re-emergence of long-term strategic competition from near-peer competitors: China, then Russia" (Secretary of Defense Mark Esper, Senate Armed Services Committee, March 4, 2020). The NDS provides direction for the development of operational concepts with China and Russia as "pacing threats," and force development based on these concepts.

One of these DOD efforts is the development of an operational concept that encompasses the entire U.S. military. Up until this point, each of the armed services had separately developed concepts premised on conflict with China and Russia, including the Army's Multi-Domain Operations (MDO), the Air Force's Multi-Domain Command and Control (MDC2), the Navy's Distributed Maritime Operations (DMO), and the Marine Corps' Expeditionary Advanced Base Operations (EABO).[12] In a September 2019 article, Thomas Greenwood and Pat Savage stated that "each of the service concepts focuses on a different aspect of multidomain operations," and "each has adopted different assumptions about war against a major power, which makes integration difficult." Thus, the two pointed out that "the bottom-up effort [of each initiative of the armed services] should be complemented by a more robust top-down approach."[13]

The Joint Warfighting Concept (JWC), which Secretary of Defense Esper pushed to develop since taking office in July 2019, is an attempt at such a "top-down approach." On March 4, 2020, Secretary of Defense Esper described the JWC at a Senate Armed Services Committee hearing. While acknowledging elements of a bottom-up approach by saying, "This concept builds on the recent experimentation conducted by the Services," he noted that the JWC will "enable our transition to All-Domain Operations by aligning our personnel, equipment, training, and doctrine." This was an acknowledgement of the need to provide a certain direction to the efforts of each of the armed services from above.

As Secretary Esper testified, at the core of the JWC is what is called All-Domain Operations or Joint All-Domain Operations (JADO). The Air Force released a doctrine publication on JADO in March 2020 and has been updating it since then. According to *Annex 3-99*, dated October 8, 2020, JADO is "[c] omprised of air, land, maritime, cyberspace, and space domains, plus the EMS [electromagnetic spectrum]," and encompasses "[a]ctions by the joint force in multiple domains integrated in planning and synchronized in execution, at speed and scale needed to gain advantage and accomplish the mission." The emphasis in JADO is on "convergence across domains." This convergence signifies "synchronization and integration of kinetic and non-kinetic capabilities to create lethal and nonlethal effects." The doctrine explains that to achieve this, it is necessary to "align" the various operations in special operations, tactical air, global strike, global mobility, cyberspace, space, and information environment, which have hitherto been planned and conducted according to "disparate planning timelines," so as to create "desired effects."[14]

The concept of "convergence" in JADO was initially proposed in the Army's MDO concept to mean "rapid and continuous integration of capabilities in all domains, the EMS, and information environment." Lieutenant General Eric J. Wesley, director of the Futures and Concepts Center (FCC) and deputy commanding general of the Army Futures Command (AFC), stated on July 22, 2020 that the Army is playing "the lead role in facilitating its [the JWC/JADO's] development," and that the inclusion of the concept of "convergence" in JADO can be seen as an indication of the influence of the MDO concept that the Army has been developing.[15]

The problem is how one can achieve "rapid and continuous integration of capabilities in all domains." Although the U.S. military has been able to achieve cross-domain convergence through "episodic synchronization of domain-federated solutions," it does not yet have the capability to achieve "rapid and continuous integration of capabilities in all domains." The Air Force's MDC2, one of the three focus areas identified by General David Goldfein, chief of staff of the Air Force, who retired in August 2020, is an effort to achieve it. MDC2 was designed to "integrate real-time information from a variety of sources—some non-traditional—and evaluate that information as fast as systems can process it,"[16] on the premise that the Air Force has capabilities in the three domains of aviation, space, and cyberspace. In 2019, MDC2 developed into a joint concept, with its name changed to Joint All-Domain Command and Control (JADC2).[17] JADC2 is based on the recognition that the incompatibility between the tactical networks established by each of the military services would be a barrier to the execution of operations in future conflicts where decisions would need to be made within hours, minutes, or potentially seconds, and will enable faster decision-making through sharing of information obtained from sensors of each of the military services on a cloud-like environment.

The Air Force is in charge of leading DOD efforts to develop JADC2, in part because it originated from the Air Force's MDC2 concept. In November 2019, the Navy reportedly reached an informal agreement with the Air Force on building a JADC2 network to enable sharing of targeting information between the two services' ships and aircraft, and there are reports that work between the two services has begun. In a speech on December 5, 2019, Admiral Michael Gilday, chief of naval operations, disclosed that the Navy and the Air Force were working together on JADC2, which he said was the "first, biggest challenge" for the Navy, given the current lack of an "adequate net" connecting various weapons and platforms. In addition, on September 29, 2020, General Charles Q. Brown, chief of staff of the Air Force, and General James McConville, chief of staff of the Army, signed an agreement to develop Combined Joint All-Domain Command and Control (CJADC2) between the Army and Air Force for a two-year period through the end of FY2022. The addition of the "C" meaning "combined" to JADC2 has been interpreted as being aimed at incorporating allies in the future.[18]

As the centerpiece of JADC2, the Air Force is developing the Advanced Battle Management System (ABMS), which is positioned as a network to fill the gaps in interoperability and information sharing among air, land, sea, space, and cyberspace domains. Originally, the ABMS was started as a replacement for the E-8 Joint Surveillance Target Attack Radar System (JSTARS) and the E-3 Airborne Warning and Control System (AWACS). However, rather than procuring it as a complete platform like JSTARS and AWACS, which are based on large passenger aircraft, it is envisioned as a distributed system using cloud technology. The development of ABMS will also focus on an open and modular system, with the aim of gradually improving its capabilities by successively introducing technologies when it becomes possible.

Three "Onramp" exercises of the ABMS were conducted during FY2020. The first exercise was conducted on December 16 to 18, 2019, in which a sensor "mesh network" that included low-orbit satellites was used to transmit information on aerial target drones simulating a cruise missile attack on the U.S. homeland to an Aegis destroyer, F-35 and F-22 aircraft of the Air Force, F-35 aircraft of the Navy, and an Army unit equipped with a High Mobility Artillery Rocket System (HIMARS). The second exercise was conducted in the United States from August 31 to September 3, 2020, in which the coordinates provided by Air Force assets enabled the Army's howitzer to fire a hyper velocity projectile (HVP) to actually shoot down a target drone that simulated a cruise missile. Furthermore, the third exercise was conducted as part of the Valiant Shield exercise, which took place from September 14 to 25 of the same year. The exercise tested the options to link the Army's Multi-Domain Task Force (MDTF), carrier strike groups (CSG), and Air Force units at the Multidomain Operations Center – Forward (MDOC-F).

On the other hand, in the Army, the AFC is working on Project Convergence (PC). As symbolized by its designation PC is an effort to achieve convergence, a central idea of the MDO/JADO concepts, as well as to incorporate the Army into CJADC2, which is being built with the Air Force. The project aims to gain the ability to "rapidly and continuously converge effects across all domains" in order to "overmatch our adversaries in competition and conflict." To that end, it aims to reduce the time required for decision-making by delivering data and cloud technologies to the tactical command, with work planned to proceed on an annual cycle that will include a large-scale annual exercise beginning in FY2020. The first large-scale exercise associated with the PC, Project Convergence 2020 (PC20), focused on "close combat" by brigade combat teams, combat aviation brigades, and others, and was held at the Yuma Proving Ground in Arizona from August 11 to September 18, 2020. In PC20, targeting information acquired by low-earth orbit satellites, the MQ-1C Grey Eagle unmanned aircraft system, and ground sensors was transmitted to Joint Base Lewis-McChord in Washington State, where it was processed and sent to the howitzer unit at the Yuma Proving Ground for firing. The exercise reportedly took less than 20 seconds from target detection to firing. According to officials related to PC20, obtaining information from the satellite's sensors and using it in the attack "seemed really simple and happened super-fast," but it had taken several weeks of work to connect systems and networks, which were not normally connected, in advance. PC21 is planned to be held in 2021, and it will include participation by the Navy, Air Force, Marines, and the Intelligence Community, and incorporate elements of the JWC.

(2) "Dynamic Force Employment" in the Indo-Pacific

In 2020, there were restrictions on movement related to U.S. military force deployment due to the spread of COVID-19. On March 11, the DOD ordered a 60-day suspension of movement by all DOD personnel and their family members traveling to, from, and through Centers for Disease Control and Prevention (CDC) Travel Health Notices Level 3 (COVID-19) designated locations, effective March 13. On March 13, the DOD ordered the suspension of domestic movement by DOD personnel and their family members from March 16 to May 11. On March 25, it ordered suspension of overseas travel by DOD personnel and their family members for 60 days effective the same date. Furthermore, on April 20, the DOD extended the period of the suspension of domestic and overseas movement by about one month until June 30. Later, on May 22, the DOD transitioned from a deadline-based approach to a conditions-based phased approach in which restrictions are relaxed according to local conditions.

The spread of infection also affected a variety of exercises. Large-Scale Exercise 2020, originally scheduled for summer 2020 to test operational concepts being developed by the Navy and Marine Corps, such as Littoral Operations in a Contested Environment (LOCE), DMO, and EABO, was postponed to 2021. The Defender-Europe 20 exercise, which began in January 2020, was designed to test the Army's ability to send troops and equipment on a large-scale to Europe. It was planned to move 20,000 troops and 20,000 pieces of equipment from the Continental U.S. (CONUS) to Europe, the largest such movement in 25 years, and to conduct an exercise in May in conjunction with this. However, as of March 13, the movement of troops and equipment to Europe was suspended, and it was decided to hold the exercise with troops that had already been moved to Europe and pre-positioned stocks (6,000 troops and 12,000 pieces of equipment).

The Pacific Air Forces also cancelled Red Flag-Alaska 20-1 (scheduled for April 30 to May 15) and 20-2 (scheduled for June 11 to 26), two of the three Red Flag-Alaska exercises normally held in Alaska each year. The exercise was later resumed, with 20-3 being held from August 1 to 14 and 21-1 being held from October 8 to 23. In addition, the Rim of the Pacific Exercise (RIMPAC), which is conducted every other year, was reduced in scale and duration in 2020. The previous RIMPAC, held in 2018, included a shore portion, and according to U.S. sources, 45 surface ships, five submarines, over 200 aircraft, and over 25,000 personnel from 26 countries participated over a month-long period from June 28 to August 2. In contrast, the 2020 exercise, which took place over a two-week period from August 17 to 31, was limited to at-sea activities, with participation by only 10 countries, 22 surface ships, one submarine, several aircraft, and 5,300 personnel. Also in 2020, the annual Balikatan exercise with the Armed Forces of the Philippines was suspended.

Perhaps the most attention-garnering impact of COVID-19 on military operations was the suspension of the deployment of the aircraft carrier USS *Theodore Roosevelt*. She departed San Diego on January 17, 2020 for deployment to the Indo-Pacific. On March 5, 2020, it made a port call in Da Nang, Vietnam, to commemorate the 25th anniversary of the normalization of diplomatic relations between the United States and Vietnam. However, on March 8, after receiving notification from the Vietnamese government that there were COVID-19 cases at a local hotel where some crew members of *Theodore Roosevelt* were staying, 39 crew members who had stayed or visited the hotel were quarantined aboard the ship and the rest of the itinerary was canceled (the 39 crew members were subsequently released after a two-week quarantine). *Theodore Roosevelt* then departed from Da Nang on March 9. Then, on March 24, while the ship was underway in the Philippine Sea, COVID-19 cases were confirmed on board, prompting the ship to move up its schedule and arrive in Guam on March 27, where it took measures such as moving the infected sailors ashore, quarantining the crew, and disinfecting the ship. This halted the ship's deployment for over two months. In the end, 1,200 of the 4,800 crew members were infected with COVID-19. It is estimated that the virus was brought on board during the port call in Da Nang and then spread on the ship without being identified. As of November 4, over 200 Navy ships out of the 296 deployable ships had at least one COVID-19 case. However, as of the end of 2020, ever since the outbreak of the *Theodore Roosevelt* case, which happened early in the COVID-19 pandemic, there have been no outbreaks on U.S. Navy ships on a comparable scale due to aggressive measures taken within the service, including swift isolation of infected people, contact tracing, and thorough infection prevention measures.

However, despite constraints posed by the COVID-19 pandemic, the deployment of U.S. forces in the Indo-Pacific continued in 2020. The concept of "dynamic force employment" (DFE), put forth in the 2018 NDS was emphasized for this. The NDS made clear that the DOD intends to change the way it deploys its forces, setting forth DFE, which would "more flexibly use ready forces to shape proactively the strategic environment." It is intended to achieve "strategic predictability" and "operational unpredictability," meaning, not allowing adversaries to predict the specific disposition of U.S. forces deployed and the mode of their operations, while clearly demonstrating the U.S. military's commitment to the security of the region in question.

Table 6.2. Deployment of CONUS-based bombers to the Western Pacific after discontinuation of the Continuous Bomber Presence (CBP) in April 2020

Period	Bombers deployed	Actions during Western Pacific deployment
April 22	B-1B 1 aircraft 28BW	A B-1B flew a "30-hour sortie" from Ellsworth AFB, South Dakota, and integrated with USAF F-16s, JASDF F-2s and JASDF F-15s for bilateral training in Draughon Range near Misawa AB, Japan. Returned to Ellsworth.
April 29	B-1B 2 aircraft 28BW	Two B-1Bs flew a "32-hour round-trip sortie" from Ellsworth AFB to conduct operations over the South China Sea. Returned to Ellsworth.
May 1 – end of May	B-1B 4 aircraft 7BW	Four B-1Bs deployed to Andersen AFB, Guam from Dyess AFB, Texas with 200 airmen and C-130. They conducted training in the East China Sea, Hawaii, the South China Sea, Alaska, and the Sea of Japan, before returning to Dyess on May 31.
June 17	B-52H 2 aircraft 2BW	On June 14, three B-52Hs moved from Barksdale AFB, Louisiana to Eielson AFB, Alaska. A B-52H integrated with USAF F-22s and Royal Canadian Air Force CF-18s for training in support of NORAD. On June 16, two B-52Hs left Eielson, and conducted bilateral training on June 17 with JASDF F-2s, JASDF F-15s, and USN E/A-18s over the Sea of Japan.
July 4	B-52H 1 aircraft 2BW	A B-52H took off from Barksdale AFB and conducted a maritime integration exercise with two CSGs (USS *Nimitz* and *Ronald Reagan*) in the South China Sea, before arriving at Andersen AFB on July 4.
July 17 – August 18	B-1B 2 aircraft 28BW	On July 17, two B-1Bs deployed from Ellsworth AFB to Andersen AFB, with 170 airmen, after conducting bilateral training with JASDF F-15Js over the Sea of Japan. On July 21, they conducted a maritime integration operation with the *Ronald Reagan* CSG in the Philippine Sea and flew over the South China Sea. On July 27, a B-1B conducted bilateral training with JASDF F-2s in the vicinity of Japan. On August 7, a B-1B, launched from Andersen AFB, and conducted bilateral training with JASDF F-2s and F-15s in the vicinity of Japan.
August 17 – 18	B-1B 2 aircraft 7BW	On August 17, two B-1Bs deployed from Dyess AFB to the Sea of Japan. They trained with another pair of B-1Bs, already deployed to Andersen AFB from 28BW in Ellsworth, Kadena-based F-15Cs, Iwakuni-based F-35Bs, the *Ronald Reagan* CSG, and JASDF F-15s. Upon completion of the training, the four B-1Bs returned to CONUS bases. In addition, two B-2s of the 509th Bomb Wing, then deployed to Diego Garcia from Whiteman AFB, Missouri, conducted a simultaneous mission in the Indian Ocean.
September 10 –	B-1B 4 aircraft 28BW	On September 10, four B-1B and 200 airmen, flew from Ellsworth AFB to Andersen AFB. Before arriving at Andersen, they conducted bilateral training with JASDF fighters. On September 23 - 25, the four B-1Bs participated in the Valiant Shield exercise, integrated with F-22s, Navy air and surface assets. On September 30, two B-1Bs conducted training with JASDF fighters in the vicinity of Japan.
October 20 – November 22	B-1B 4 aircraft 7BW	On October 20, four B-1Bs and 200 airmen arrived at Andersen AFB from Dyess AFB. Before arriving at Andersen, the B-1Bs conducted bilateral training with JASDF F-2s and F-15s. A B-1B flew from Andersen AFB to Misawa AB on October 28, followed by two more B-1Bs on October 29. On November 8, two B-1Bs took off from Andersen AFB and flew over the South China Sea, before returning to Andersen. On November 12 and 13, a B-1B conducted a joint interoperability exercise with the USAF, USN, and USMC. On November 12, a B-1B of 28BW, deployed from Ellsworth AFB, participated in the exercise.
December 5 –	B-1B Multiple aircraft 28BW	On December 5, B-1Bs flew from Ellsworth AFB to Andersen AFB. On December 10, a B-1B launched from Andersen, and conducted stand-off weapons training and rapid response training with two F-22s (94th Fighter Squadron, Joint Base Langley-Eustis).

Sources: Compiled by the author based on Department of Defense websites.

Notes: Air Base (AB); Air Force Base (AFB); Continental United States (CONUS); Carrier Strike Group (CSG); Japan Air Self Defense Force (JASDF); North American Aerospace Defense Command (NORAD); United States Air Force (USAF); United States Navy (USN); United States Marine Corps (USMC); 2nd Bomb Wing, Barksdale AFB, Louisiana (2BW); 7th Bombs Wing, Dyess AFB, Texas (7BW); and 28th Bomb Wing, Ellsworth AFB, South Dakota (28BW).

A recent manifestation of DFE was a change in the way bombers are deployed to the Western Pacific. Since 2004, the U.S. Air Force had maintained a Continuous Bomber Presence (CBP) in which bombers were deployed from CONUS bases to Andersen Air Force Base (AFB) in Guam on a six-month rotation. The CBP was terminated on April 17, 2020, when B-52 bombers of the 5th Bomb Wing (Minot AFB, North Dakota) returned after completing their deployment to Guam. As the word "continuous" in its name implied, the CBP was intended to maintain an uninterrupted bomber presence in the Western Pacific. It was relatively regular in nature, mainly involving alternating six-month deployment by two remaining wings in the U.S. Air Force that operate B-52 aircraft, namely the 5th Bomb Wing and the 2nd Bomb Wing (Barksdale AFB, Louisiana).[19]

Some have expressed concern that the abrupt end of CBP signals diminishing U.S. commitment to the Indo-Pacific.[20] However, a U.S. Air Force official explained the end of the CBP: "In line with the National Defense Strategy, the United States has transitioned to an approach that enables strategic bombers to operate forward in the Indo-Pacific region from a broader array of overseas locations, when required, and with greater operational resilience, while these bombers are permanently based in the United States." He further added that "U.S. strategic bombers will continue to operate in the Indo-Pacific, to include Guam, at the timing and tempo of our choosing."[21]

After the end of the CBP, Western Pacific deployment of CONUS-based bombers has been continued as Bomber Task Force (BTF) missions. While B-52Hs bore the bulk of the burden in CBP missions, BTF missions are primarily

A B-1B bomber, Navy ships, and Navy and Air Force aircraft participate in the Valiant Shield exercise on September 25, 2020 (U.S. Navy photo by Petty Officer 3rd Class Erica Bechard)

conducted by B-1Bs, which can carry and launch state-of-the-art Long-Range Anti-Ship Missiles (LRASM) (Table 6.2). This makes them, in the words of a U.S. Air Force official, "perfectly suited for the Pacific theater," and the move can also be seen as a check on China's rapidly growing naval power. In BTF deployments in May, July to August, September, October to November, and December, B-1Bs were forward-deployed for about a month at Andersen AFB in Guam with a contingent of about 200 personnel. During month-long deployment at Andersen, B-1Bs conducted training at various locations throughout the Western Pacific. Otherwise, bombers conducted round-trip sorties, flying directly in the vicinity of Japan, conducting bilateral training, and then returning to the CONUS without landing (deployments in April, July, and August). In the August 17–18 deployment, B-1Bs flying from Dyess AFB, Texas, trained with B-1Bs already deployed at Andersen AFB and B-2 bombers that had been deployed from the CONUS to Diego Garcia and flown in the vicinity of Japan. Furthermore, in the June 17 deployment of B-52Hs in the vicinity of Japan, a pair of B-52Hs departed from their CONUS base to Alaska, where one B-52H split off and headed for Japan. In this way, deployment patterns are becoming more varied and complex, and these deployments are carried out on short notice, with no advance public notification of the duration. These factors are thought to have increased what the NDS calls "operational unpredictability."

Surely, the deployment of Navy ships in the Western Pacific was also affected by the spread of COVID-19, as in the case of *Theodore Roosevelt*. That being said, 2020 saw multiple instances of dual carrier operations by two CSGs in the Western Pacific, which had not occurred since the November 2018 deployment of USS *Ronald Reagan* and USS *John C. Stennis* to the Philippine Sea. *Theodore Roosevelt*, which departed San Diego in January for deployment to the Indo-Pacific, left Guam on June 4 and resumed deployment in the Western Pacific after a two-month interruption. *Ronald Reagan*, forward-deployed at Yokosuka, left for Indo-Pacific deployment on May 21 after completing annual repairs. Furthermore, USS *Nimitz* departed San Diego on June 8 to relieve USS *Harry S. Truman*, which had been deployed in the Middle East, and reached the Seventh

Table 6.3. Dual carrier operations in the South China Sea and the Philippine Sea in 2020

Period	CSGs	Area	Actions during dual carrier operations
June 21–23	Theodore Roosevelt, Nimitz	Philippine Sea	On June 21, the *Theodore Roosevelt* and *Nimitz* CSGs conducted dual carrier flight operations in the Philippine Sea. They conducted air defense drills, sea surveillance, replenishments at sea, and a long range strikes exercise. On June 23, the two CSGs conducted dual carrier and airwing operations, after which the *Nimitz* CSG called at Guam and the *Roosevelt* CSG left for San Diego.
June 28	Nimitz, Ronald Reagan	Philippine Sea	On June 28, the *Nimitz* and *Ronald Reagan* CSGs conducted dual carrier operations in the Philippine Sea.
July 4–6	Nimitz, Ronald Reagan	South China Sea	The two CSGs formed the *Nimitz* and *Ronald Reagan* Carrier Strike Force and conducted high-end integrated exercises that included air defense exercises, tactical maneuvering drills, simulated long-range maritime strike scenarios, and coordinated air and surface exercises.
July 17	Nimitz, Ronald Reagan	South China Sea	The *Nimitz* and *Ronald Reagan* CSGs conducted high-end dual carrier exercises in the South China Sea, after which the *Nimitz* CSG moved to the Indian Ocean.

Sources: Compiled by the author based on Department of the Navy websites.
Note: Carrier Strike Group (CSG).

Fleet's area of operation (west of the International Date Line) on June 17. From June to July 2020, dual carrier operations by these CSGs took place multiple times in the South China Sea and the Philippine Sea (Table 6.3).

There were also instances of integrated training by bombers and CSGs deployed in the Western Pacific. When the *Nimitz* and *Ronald Reagan* CSGs were deployed in the South China Sea from July 4 to 6, a B-52H flew in from Barksdale AFB to conduct a maritime integration exercise with the two CSGs on July 4. The exercise was reportedly conducted under the assumption of a contested and degraded communications environment, with Air Force bombers, Navy aircraft, and Navy ships operating on shared networks to accomplish integrated missions. Additionally, the *Ronald Reagan* CSG forward-deployed in Yokosuka conducted a series of dual carrier operations with the *Nimitz* CSG in the South China Sea and the Philippine Sea, followed by a trilateral exercise with the Royal Australian Navy and Japan's Maritime Self-Defense Force (MSDF) in the Philippine Sea from July 19 to 23, training in the South China

Sea on August 14, and a bilateral training with JDS *Ikazuchi* in the Philippine Sea on August 15.

3. The 2020 Election and the Presidential Transition

(1) President Trump's Post-Election Legal Challenges

As a result of the presidential election held on November 3, 2020, former vice president Joseph Biden and Senator Kamala Harris received 81.28 million votes, winning the election over incumbent President Trump and Vice President Pence, who received 74.22 million votes (hereinafter, the date and time in this section are Eastern Standard Time). In this election, former vice president Biden not only received 306 electoral votes versus the 232 electoral votes received by President Trump, a victory by a margin of 74 electoral votes, but also beat Trump in the popular vote by seven million votes. In the 2016 election, President Trump won the Electoral College by 74 electors' votes over former secretary of state Hillary Clinton, even though he had received 2.86 million fewer votes than her in the popular vote. Former vice president Biden also won by more than 10,000 votes in each of the swing states, which made his victory clear. This was the first time in 28 years that an incumbent president has lost an election for a second term since President George H.W. Bush was defeated by Arkansas Governor Bill Clinton in the 1992 election.

During this election, in response to the spread of COVID-19, states relaxed the eligibility requirements for mail-in voting and extended the deadline for receiving mail-in ballots, and the number of voters who chose mail-in voting increased significantly. On the other hand, ever since President Trump claimed at a press conference on April 7, 2020, that mail-in voting is "corrupt" and "a very dangerous thing for this country" due to what he depicted to be cheating committed via mail-in voting, he continued to attack mail-in voting as an institution, repeatedly claiming that forces opposed to him would use mail-in voting to commit voter fraud.

The background for President Trump making this claim was that it was estimated that Democratic Party supporters were far more inclined to choose mail-in voting over in-person voting. Therefore, disputes arose in states like Pennsylvania as Democrats tried to make it easier for voters to vote by mail by setting a longer period for accepting mail-in ballots, while Republicans tried to set the period as short as possible, and at the same time tried to stop election officials from conducting "pre-canvassing": preparatory work done by poll workers before the election day, such as preparing mailed-in ballots to be ready for scanning and checking for incomplete identification information filled out on the declaration envelopes that contained the ballots.[22] This was a move coordinated with President Trump, who repeatedly called for a halt to the vote counting process immediately after the general election. It was a strategy aimed at invalidating as many mail-in votes as possible by prematurely terminating the vote counting process, as delays in the counting process are far more pronounced for mail-in votes than for in-person votes.[23]

Furthermore, the issue of voter fraud came to be mentioned in connection with the refusal to commit to a "peaceful transfer of power," in which the losing incumbent admits defeat and proceeds with a transfer of power. In an interview on July 19, 2020, President Trump claimed that there would be voter fraud through mail-in voting and refused to answer a question about whether he would accept the election results if he lost. In addition, during a press conference at the White House on September 23, when asked if he would commit to a "peaceful transition of power," President Trump strongly insisted on the existence of voter fraud and said that there would be a peaceful "continuation" of power, in other words, his own victory, if fraudulently cast votes were excluded.

This was not the first time that President Trump alleged voter fraud. During his 2016 election campaign he frequently claimed that there would be massive voter fraud in the upcoming election, but once his own victory was confirmed, he reversed his assessment and called it "a very open and successful presidential election" in a November 10, 2016 tweet. However, when attention was drawn to former secretary of state Clinton's lead in the popular vote, President Trump began to contend that voter fraud occurred on a scale of millions of votes, tweeting on November 27: "In addition to winning the Electoral College in a landslide, I won the popular vote if you deduct the millions of people who voted illegally." Even after his inauguration as president, he continued to insist on the existence of voter fraud, tweeting on January 25, 2017: "I will be asking for a major investigation into VOTER FRAUD." On May 11, 2017, he established a bipartisan commission headed by Vice President Pence to investigate fraud in the 2016 election. However, this commission was disbanded by the president himself in January 2018 without uncovering any piece of evidence for the existence of fraud.

While the presidential election in the United States takes the form of an indirect election, in which voters choose electors on election day and those electors then cast votes to choose the president thereafter, the entire process consists of multiple steps. Following the general election (which took place on November 3 for the 2020 election), each state compiles the results of the count, corrects any errors in the count if they occur, and in some states, audits the count by verifying samples of the votes cast. Based on this confirmation work, the county and then the state boards of canvassers certify the votes. The governors of each state then compile the names of electors chosen by voters as well as the number of votes each received into certificates of ascertainment, which are mailed to the archivist of the United States with the signature of each state's secretary of state, who serves as the state's chief election official. The process up to this point is the "ascertainment" of the voting results in each state.

The electors chosen in this way then meet in their state capital and cast their electoral votes, official votes for the president and vice president in each state, on the first Monday after the second Wednesday in December (December 14 for the 2020 election). According to federal law, if a state makes a "final determination" of any controversy or contest concerning the appointment of the electors "by judicial or other methods or procedures" six days before that date (December 8 in the 2020 election), that determination is "conclusive," and it is necessary to follow the "conclusive" determination when counting the electoral votes.

For this reason, the six days prior to the casting of electoral votes is called the "Safe Harbor" deadline, meaning that the results of the popular vote in any state cannot be overturned if its ascertainment is made by the deadline. The electors then mail certificates with the results of the electoral vote to the president of the Senate, who is the vice president. At 1:00 p.m. on January 6 of the following year, a Joint Session of both houses of Congress is held with the vice president as the presiding officer. The vice president opens the certificates of the electoral votes sent from each state. Four "tellers"—two appointed beforehand from both the Senate and House of Representatives—read the certificates and count the votes. The presiding officer then declares who has won a majority of the electoral votes and has been elected president and vice president. This procedure is commonly referred to as the "certification" by Congress, of the results of the electoral vote.

During this presidential election, President Trump claimed victory in a speech in the early hours of the morning after election day, and at the same time said that there was "a major fraud in our nation" and that he would take the case to the U.S. Supreme Court. In other words, it was at this stage that Trump began to send the message he would later repeat: that if he lost the vote, it must be because of fraud. Following this, the Trump campaign, the president's allies, and President Trump himself filed dozens of lawsuits, mostly in swing states, and pressured Republican officials in various states to cooperate in overturning the election results in their respective states.

Among the lawsuits filed by President Trump's side, the one filed in Pennsylvania, a key state in the entire presidential election, with 20 electors, received a great deal of attention.[24] In the case of *Donald J. Trump for President, Inc. v. Boockvar*, the Trump campaign sued Pennsylvania Secretary of the Commonwealth Kathy Boockvar and seven county boards of elections, claiming that the canvassing and tabulation of the 682,479 ballots cast by mail in Allegheny and Philadelphia counties, which include large cities, was conducted "without review by the political parties and candidates" (such as only allowing observers dispatched from each party to observe the canvassing and tabulation far from the areas where the work was being done). Furthermore, the lawsuit claimed that "Democratic-heavy counties" started pre-canvass work of reviewing received mail-in ballots for deficiencies before election day, while such work was not done before election day in "Republican-heavy counties," and this thus gave an advantage to voters in the former counties over the latter counties because the work was done without state-wide uniform guidelines. The Trump campaign then sought to prohibit the certification of commonwealth-wide ballot results, or to certify Pennsylvania's ballot results by excluding the roughly 680,000 mail-in ballots (the latter request was later dropped). In response, the U.S. District Court for the Middle District of Pennsylvania dismissed the suit in a November 21 ruling. The Trump campaign then appealed, but on November 27, the U.S. Court of Appeals for the Third Circuit dismissed the case.

Trump allies led by Republican Representative Mike Kelly also filed a lawsuit (*Kelly v. Pennsylvania*) on November 21, just before the deadline to ascertain the results of the vote in Pennsylvania. The plaintiffs claimed that the Pennsylvania Election Code amendment enacted October 31, 2019, that allows "no-excuse" mail-in voting by all eligible voters, violates Article VII, Section 14 of the Pennsylvania Constitution, which sets forth the conditions under which mail-in voting is allowed. The lawsuit sought to prohibit the certification of the results of the state's elections based on the amendment, to exclude the results of mail-in ballots from certification, or to invalidate the election itself, and to have the electors chosen by the Pennsylvania General Assembly. In response, on November 28, the Pennsylvania Supreme Court dismissed the lawsuit on the grounds that the plaintiffs failed to act with "due diligence" in not seeking legal relief soon after the October 2019 enactment of the Pennsylvania Election Code amendment and in not filing suit until the ascertainment of election results in Pennsylvania was imminent. The plaintiffs then appealed to the U.S. Supreme Court, which on December 8 issued a one-sentence ruling stating, "The application for injunctive relief...is denied," without any explanation or mention of any dissenting opinions. Similar lawsuits aimed at invalidating votes statewide were also filed by the Trump campaign, Trump allies, or President

Trump personally in Arizona, Georgia, Michigan, and Wisconsin.

In addition to the legal challenges, President Trump used blatant political pressure on state officials of Georgia, pushing what had been considered a "Red" state into "Republican civil war."[25] In the 2020 election, not only did former vice president Biden win by a narrow margin, but the incumbent Republican candidates also failed to win a majority of votes in both the regular and special elections for Georgia's two Senate seats, leading to a runoff election. Moreover, this runoff election would determine whether Republicans could maintain their majority in the Senate (the Democrats won both Senate seats in the January 5 runoff election, and thus gained majority party status, with the tie-breaking vote held by the vice president, who is also president of the Senate). Within the Republican Party, many came to believe that voter fraud, which they claimed existed, was responsible for the outcome of these elections, and began to criticize the state's election officials, including Republican Georgia secretary of state, Brad Raffensperger. Amidst this, there was mounting pressure on Georgia election officials within the Republican Party, especially from supporters of President Trump.[26]

After votes were cast on election day, the state of Georgia conducted a full manual recount from November 11 to 19 in order to meet the November 20 deadline for ascertainment of election resultss.[27] Against this backdrop, President Trump repeated his claim that there was widespread voter fraud through mail-in voting in Georgia, including identity fraud, and demanded that the signatures on the declaration envelopes used to mail the ballots be audited. He also claimed that without such voter fraud, he would have won the election in Georgia. During this period, Secretary of State Raffensperger admitted that he and others were pressured to invalidate mail-in ballots by Senator Lindsay Graham (R-South Carolina) and other Republicans who supported President Trump, and even received death threats and other severe intimidation aimed at overturning the election results. In a November 16 interview with the *Washington Post*, Raffensperger stated, "Other than getting you angry, it's also very disillusioning," "particularly when it [threats] comes from people on my side of the aisle."[28]

In response to these attacks alleging fraud in Georgia's election, Raffensperger and Gabriel Sterling, Georgia voting system implementation manager, addressed the theories about evidence of voter fraud one by one and showed that they were wrong. They also asserted that although Georgia election officials were investigating every accusation of voter fraud, they had not found any evidence that fraud occurred on a broad enough scale to affect the outcome of the election.

As for the signature audit demanded by President Trump, for the 2020 election in Georgia, signature matching was conducted twice. First, the signatures on the mail-in voting application forms were checked against the signatures in the voter registration database. Second, the signatures on the envelopes containing the mail-in ballots were checked before the envelopes were opened. After the envelopes were opened following the signature match, the ballots and envelopes were kept separate following the principle of voter secrecy stipulated in the Constitution of Georgia. Because of this, even if a problem were to be found during the signature audit, there would be no way to know which candidate the ballot was in support of. In other words, the system could not produce a situation such as the one alleged by President Trump in his November 19 tweet stating, "When the much more important signature match takes place, the State will flip Republican, and very quickly."[29] For this reason, Georgia Secretary of State Raffensperger rejected President Trump's demand for a signature audit, stating, "[T]here has been no evidence presented of any issues with the signature matching process," and, "[T]he signature verification process was—and always has been—public and that they [observers from both parties] could observe it." (A signature match audit was later conducted in Georgia with the cooperation of the Georgia Bureau of Investigation for a county that was criticized for not having done proper signature matching. However, no cases of fraudulent absentee ballots were found, according to a December 29, 2020 statement from Secretary of State Raffensperger.)

The results of the audit, which took place through to November 19, reaffirmed former vice president Biden's victory in Georgia. On November 20 the following day, Georgia Secretary of State Raffensperger and Governor Brian Kemp signed a certificate of ascertainment. After this, a recount was conducted at the request of the Trump campaign. On December 7, the day before the Safe Harbor deadline, Governor Kemp and

On December 1, 2020, Gabriel Sterling, Georgia voting system implementation manager, urges President Trump to stop inciting violence against Georgia election officials (TNS via ZUMA Wire/Kyodo Images)

Secretary of State Raffensperger conducted a second ascertainment based on the results of the recount and confirmed that there was no change to Biden's victory in Georgia. Although President Trump had once praised Raffensperger as "a fantastic Secretary of State for Georgia" in a November 26, 2018 tweet, at the White House on November 26, 2020, he attacked Raffensperger by calling him "an enemy of the people," a term that was also favored by Joseph Stalin. The background for this was that the recount was then in progress at the request of the Trump campaign, following the first ascertainment of the election results in Georgia.[30]

In early December, when Georgia ascertained its election results for the second time, the margin for President Trump to overturn the results of the vote became increasingly narrow. In addition, the results of 41 states were ascertained in time for the Safe Harbor deadline of December 8, and by this point, Biden had officially secured 270 electors. Furthermore, the Safe Harbor deadline of December 8 was also that date on which the United States Supreme Court ruled against the plaintiffs in the aforementioned case of *Kelly v. Pennsylvania*, which sought to invalidate the election in Pennsylvania and have the Pennsylvania General Assembly appoint electors.

It was in early December that President Trump began repeatedly demanding

Governor Kemp to call a special session of the Georgia General Assembly, aiming to have the state assembly appoint its own electors during the special session. On December 5, President Trump reportedly asked Governor Kemp to do this, with which the governor refused to comply (on the same day, President Trump mentioned the special session for the first time on Twitter). On December 6, the following day, in a jointly issued statement, Governor Kemp and Lieutenant Governor Geoff Duncan rejected President Trump's request to call a special session, stating that "convening of a special session of the General Assembly" in order to "select a separate slate of presidential electors is not an option that is allowed under state or federal law," and "any attempt... to retroactively change that process for the November 3rd election would be unconstitutional." In response, President Trump called fellow Republican Governor Kemp and other Georgia officials "RINO [Republican in name only]." He continued to press for a special session while attacking them with harsh rhetoric, including his December 7 tweet stating, "People are ANGRY!"; his December 12 tweet stating, "[T]wo RINO Republicans...allowed states that I won easily to be stolen...vote them out of office!"; his December 14 tweet stating, "What a fool Governor" and "Demand this clown [Georgia Governor Kemp] call a Special Session"; and his December 18 tweet stating, "So easy to do, why is he not doing it? It will give us the State. MUST ACT NOW!"

President Trump's attempt to overturn the election in Georgia did not end with his attempt at a special session. On January 2, 2021, in a telephone conversation with Georgia Secretary of State Raffensperger that lasted over an hour after 18 attempts by the president to contact him, Trump asked for Raffensperger's help, saying, "I just want to find 11,780 votes" to turn around his 11,779-vote loss to former vice president Biden in Georgia. In doing so, President Trump reiterated various conspiracy theories concerning election fraud in Georgia, saying that it was a "criminal offense" for Secretary of State Raffensperger to know about the fraud and not make it public, and that it would be a "big risk" for him to let it go. The statement was criticized as an "attempt at extortion" to make Secretary Raffensperger cooperate with President Trump by implying that without his cooperation, the president "might deploy the Justice Department to launch an investigation." The conversation between President Trump and Georgia Secretary of State Raffensperger was reported in the *Washington Post* on January 3, and the audio data was made available on the newspaper's website.[31]

In a new development in the legal challenges since the U.S. Supreme Court rejected the appeal by Representative Kelly and others in the *Kelly v. Pennsylvania* case, on December 7, Texas Attorney General Ken Paxton, an ally of President Trump, filed a lawsuit (*Texas v. Pennsylvania*). With the State of Texas as the plaintiff, the lawsuit sought to invalidate the election results in the states of Georgia, Michigan, Wisconsin, and Pennsylvania and to order the legislatures of those states to appoint electors. At the time the lawsuit was filed, most of the states had already finished ascertaining their results, and it was regarded as highly unlikely that the U.S. Supreme Court would disregard state jurisdiction and allow a lawsuit by a state unrelated to the four states in question to go forward. However, President Trump himself joined the lawsuit as an intervenor, saying it was "[t]he case that everyone has been waiting for" in a tweet on December 9. Additionally, from the Republican Party, 17 state attorneys general and 126 members of the U.S. House of Representatives participated in the lawsuit as *amici curiae* to the plaintiffs who submitted an *amicus brief* in support of the Texas lawsuit. In response, on December 11, the U.S. Supreme Court declined to hear the case on the grounds that Texas lacked standing.

According to the Democracy Docket website, of the lawsuits filed by the Trump campaign, allies of President Trump, and the president himself related to the outcome of the presidential election, 64 had been lost or withdrawn by the time he left office. Only one minor case filed in Pennsylvania had been allowed to go forward. This series of losses was due to the fact that President Trump's side never accused a specific person or organization of voter fraud with a concrete fact. When they stood before court, they only provided mere speculations in each case, such as: that voter fraud must have occurred due to the actions of election officials or that double voting must have occurred, citing issues with voter registration. In this respect, President Trump's public statements in the media and on Twitter differ greatly from the actions in court. In some cases, lawyers for the Trump campaign were forced to admit that the cases were not about voter fraud when questioned by judges. One example was when Rudolph Giuliani, a lawyer for the Trump campaign, stated, "This is not a fraud case" in response to the judge in the oral argument of the *Donald J. Trump for President, Inc. v. Boockvar* case on November 17.

Explaining the Trump campaign's conduct, Senator Ben Sasse (R-Nebraska) stated, "[W]hen Trump campaign lawyers have stood before courts under oath, they have repeatedly refused to actually allege grand fraud—because there are legal consequences for lying to judges."[32] Such conduct by the Trump campaign inevitably severely undermined the persuasiveness of its arguments in court. In its November 21 decision in the *Donald J. Trump for President, Inc. v. Boockvar* case, the U.S. District Court for the Middle District of Pennsylvania stated that because the Trump campaign has presented nothing but "strained legal arguments without merit and speculative accusations," they "cannot justify the disenfranchisement of a single voter." The Trump campaign later appealed. In its November 27 decision, regarding the Trump campaign's claim that the election was "unfair," the U.S. Court of Appeals for the Third Circuit stated that "its [the Trump campaign's] allegations are vague and conclusory." It also stated in regard to "specific allegations and then proof" necessary for claims in court, "We have neither here." These rulings were reported as a "harsh rebuke" by the judiciary to the Trump campaign for publicly alleging voter fraud but not presenting its claims and evidence in court.[33]

Contrary to President Trump's claims, a number of public organizations denied the existence of large-scale fraud in the 2020 election. On November 12, the Cybersecurity and Infrastructure Security Agency (CISA) of the Department of Homeland Security released a joint statement on the election saying, "There is no evidence that any voting system deleted or lost votes, changed votes, or was in any way compromised," and "the November 3rd election was the most secure in American history." The CISA is responsible for election security that entails protection of election infrastructure (including the IT infrastructure and systems used to register voters, count, audit, and display election results, and certify and validate election results, as well as voting systems and polling places) from external hacking and tampering. The November 12 statement was issued by the Election Infrastructure Government Coordinating Council Executive Committee, a consultative body of federal and state election officials, and the Election Infrastructure Sector Coordinating Council, a consultative body of private businesses that manufacture and sell equipment for voter registration, voting, and vote counting. The statement can be seen as a reflection of the consensus of public and private parties involved in election administration.

In addition, Attorney General Barr told the Associated Press on December 1 that "to date, we have not seen fraud on a scale that could have effected a different outcome in the election." Previously, Barr had authorized federal prosecutors and the FBI to "pursue substantial allegations of voting and vote tabulation irregularities" in a memorandum dated November 9. Moreover, the Organization for Security and Co-operation in Europe (OSCE), which dispatched election observers for the election, concluded in a report dated November 4 that "the number and scale of alleged and reported cases of fraud associated to absentee ballots remained negligible." Similarly, in a report dated November 6, the Organization of American States (OAS) noted, "The OAS observers...did not witness any of the aforementioned irregularities" as claimed by President Trump.

Mail-in voting was not something that was introduced for the first time in the 2020 election. It has also been implemented in past elections. Generally speaking, the margin for fraud to occur via mail-in voting is not great, which FBI Director Wray made clear when he told the Senate Homeland Security and Governmental Affairs Committee on September 24, 2020, that "we have not seen, historically, any kind of coordinated national voter fraud effort in a major election, whether it's by mail or—or otherwise." On the contrary, studies conducted by election experts up to this point have shown that the potential for voter fraud is extremely small.[34] According to a study conducted by the *Washington Post* with the help of the Electronic Registration Information

Center, of the 14.6 million mail-in ballots cast in the 2016 presidential election and 2018 midterm elections in three states, 372 ballots, or 0.0025% of the total, were identified by state election officials as possible cases of voter fraud (double voting or voting on behalf of deceased people). The Brennan Center for Justice at New York University Law School explains that multiple factors have made it more difficult for fraud to occur, including signature verification of mail-in ballots, tracking and control of ballots enabled by bar codes on ballot envelopes and verification by voters, installation of ballot drop boxes, harsh penalties for voter fraud (including up to five years in prison for each act of fraud), and the implementation of post-election audits.[35]

In addition, during the 2020 election, a conspiracy theory developed that Dominion Voting Systems, which delivers voting and tabulation equipment to U.S. states, is a "far-left company" set up at the direction of former Venezuelan president Hugo Chavez to manipulate the results of referendums in Venezuela, and that during the 2020 election, the company's vote counting equipment had incorporated an "algorithm" that flipped a certain percentage of votes cast for President Trump into votes for former vice president Biden. This is one of the conspiracy theories that Trump campaign lawyer Sidney Powell espoused at a press conference on November 16, 2020, and that President Trump repeatedly mentioned. (On January 8, Dominion filed a defamation lawsuit against Powell in the U.S. District Court for the District of Columbia.)

Protecting election infrastructure from external hacking has been a key mission of the CISA since its establishment, and for this it has been engaged in intensive efforts. One of them has been to update voting equipment. In the past, nine states had statewide or large-scale installations of voting equipment that only records the voter's intent electronically, without a verifiable paper trail. However, such voting equipment could not be used to verify voting results after the fact in the event of a hack or if the data was rewritten. Therefore, through a series of federal grants to state governments from FY2018 to FY2020 to improve election security, completely paperless voting equipment was retired in favor of voting equipment that always keeps paper trails, such as those that enable voters to fill out a paper ballot and then scan it, or to select a candidate on a touch screen and then print it out. As a result, in the 2020 election, the percentage of votes cast with paper audit trail, meaning they could be verified after the fact, increased to 92–95% from 80% in 2016. In other words, even if the voting results had been changed due to hacking, it would have been possible to find out whether 92–95% of the votes had been tampered with after the fact and correct the results. The manual audit of all votes cast in Georgia in the 2020 election, which was conducted in mid-November, was possible only because the state government had switched to a type of voting equipment that keeps paper trails in time for the 2020 presidential election.

Amidst this situation, to perpetrate voter fraud on a scale that could affect the outcome of the presidential election, it would have been necessary to override every single measure instituted to prevent voter fraud. This would have required massive, covert operations involving many parties. As Karl Rove, a senior advisor to former president George W. Bush and "the architect" of Bush's 2004 reelection, said in the November 4 issue of the *Wall Street Journal*, "[S]tealing hundreds of thousands of votes would require a *conspiracy on the scale of a James Bond movie*. That isn't going to happen" (emphasis added). Rove's statement was also made in light of the inherent difficulty of perpetrating such large-scale voter fraud. Due to these remarks and reports, it is only natural that the Trump campaign and President Trump's allies avoided making accusations about specific criminal acts of voter fraud by specific people that could overturn the election results in the courtroom, even though they claimed the existence of such fraud in public statements intended for the political campaign.

(2) The January 6 Attack on the U.S. Capitol Building

President Trump experienced a series of losses in court, and his attempts to overturn the election results in Georgia were unsuccessful. The electoral votes were cast in each state on December 14, and the victory of former vice president Biden and Senator Harris, who received 306 electoral votes, was confirmed. In response, Senate Republican leader Mitch McConnell, who had not previously recognized the election victory of former vice president Biden, formally recognized Biden and Senator Harris as the president-elect and vice president-elect of the United States and expressed his congratulations at the Senate session on December 15.

Amidst this, President Trump tried to find a way out of the situation at the Joint Session of Congress scheduled for January 6. During the Joint Session, where electoral votes are opened and counted state-by-state, the returns of any individual state can be challenged in writing with the signatures of at least one senator and one representative. In such cases, the Joint Session recesses and the House and Senate meet separately to consider the objection. If the objection is accepted by both houses, the votes of the state concerned are excluded from the tally.

In the 2020 election, as some House Republicans were planning to challenge the electoral vote returns at the Joint Session, Senate Majority Leader McConnell strongly urged Republican senators not to join such efforts. He made this warning because even if a member of the House of Representatives raises an objection, and if no Senator seconds it, the president of the Senate, meaning the vice president, can reject the objection on the spot to minimize confusion. Later, however, when Senator Josh Hawley (R-Missouri) announced his intention to file an objection, Republican senators, led by Senator Ted Cruz (R-Texas), moved to follow suit, raising the prospect that the objection would be considered by the House and Senate.

Amidst this, as symbolized by the hashtag "#PenceCard," there was an expectation which had no legal basis but was increasingly prevalent among President Trump's supporters that Vice President Pence, presiding over Joint Sessions as Senate president, could overturn the election results by invalidating the votes of some states. On December 27, Republican Congressman Louie Gohmert and others filed a lawsuit (*Gohmert v. Pence*) in the U.S. District Court for the Eastern District of Texas Tyler Division, alleging that the aforementioned provision of federal law governing the procedures and conditions for objections in a Joint Session of Congress is unconstitutional, and demanding that the vice president, in his role presiding over the Joint Session, be granted "the exclusive authority and sole discretion in determining which electoral votes to count for a given State." The request by Congressman Gohmert and others was meant to grant Vice President Pence the authority to nullify the results of elections at will, without regard to the provisions of the law. In response, on December 31, Vice President Pence filed a brief requesting that the plaintiffs' case be dismissed, and the Tyler Division dismissed the case by Congressman Gohmert and others on January 1. On the other hand, President Trump himself demanded that Vice President Pence overturn the election results by invalidating some votes in the Joint Session of Congress that he would preside over. In President Trump's January 5 tweet, he stated, "The Vice President has the power to reject fraudulently chosen electors," and in his January 4 speech in Georgia, he stated that "our great vice president comes through for us." In response, Vice President Pence reportedly told President Trump that the vice president does not have such authority. Finally, on the day of the Joint Session, Vice President Pence, in a letter to each member of Congress, argued that the role of the vice president in presiding over the Joint Session was "largely ceremonial" and that he did not have the "unilateral authority to decide presidential contests."

Meanwhile, as of December 19, plans had already been announced for a large-scale rally to be organized by a President Trump supporter group on January 6, the date of the Joint Session. In a tweet on December 19, President Trump called on his supporters to participate by writing: "Big protest in D.C. on January 6th. Be there, will be wild!" Subsequently, he repeatedly encouraged participation in the rally, sharing the details of said rally, such as the start time and location, and on January 3, he announced on Twitter that he himself would participate. It was also reported that at this time, the Trump campaign had asked groups supporting President Trump to organize large-scale protest rallies and mobilize supporters for "waving the flag and yelling the president's name and support," because "[a]t a moment's notice, we may need your help and support on the ground."[36] In other words, since neither legal means nor interventions in the state ascertainment processes had been successful, they opted for exerting direct pressure from outside these processes. The planned scale of the January 6 rally jumped from 5,000 to 30,000 people, and the venue was changed to the Ellipse, an area adjacent to the south side of the White House premises, in order to accommodate President Trump's attendance.

At the January 6 rally, President Trump appeared as scheduled and gave a speech for over an hour. During his speech, President Trump repeatedly claimed, "We won in a landslide" and the "election victory [was] stolen" by "radical left Democrats," and demanded that "Congress do the right thing and only count the electors who have been lawfully slated." This meant overturning the election results by declaring the electoral votes in the swing states won by former vice president Biden invalid because they were not by "electors who have been lawfully slated." President Trump also told participants, "We fight like Hell and if you don't fight like Hell, you're not going to have a country anymore," and "you'll never take back our country with weakness." He ended with an appeal of "let's walk down Pennsylvania Avenue," urging the participants to head to the U.S. Capitol Building to directly pressure Congress to agree with the objections.

President Trump's rhetoric was aimed more directly at Vice President Pence. He called for Vice President Pence to use his position as the presiding officer of the Joint Session to overturn the election results, repeatedly making statements such as: "I hope Mike is going to do the right thing," "if Mike Pence does the right thing, we win the election," and "Mike Pence is going to have to come through for us. If he doesn't, that will be a sad day for our country." President Trump's reference to the possibility that Vice President Pence might not do "the right thing" was presumably asking the vice president to reverse the intention he stated earlier on rejecting President Trump's request.

Furthermore, President Trump also tried to put pressure on Republican lawmakers attending the Joint Session, from the crowd of rally participants. He stated, "We're going to walk down to the Capitol, and we're going to cheer on our brave senators, and congressmen and women," but also said, "We're probably not going to be cheering so much for some of them." Additionally, referring to "our Republicans, the weak ones," he stated, "We're going to try and give them the kind of pride and boldness that they need to take back our country." The statement "give them the kind of pride and boldness," referring to Republican lawmakers who did not support the objection and whom President Trump called the "weak ones," can be interpreted as him urging the rally crowd to exert

On January 6, 2021, Vice President Pence presides over the Joint Session of Congress, where electoral votes are opened and counted (UPI/Newscom/Kyodo News Images)

direct pressure on Republican lawmakers to force them to support the objection. Donald Trump Jr., who took the stage before President Trump, was more direct, stating to Republican lawmakers: "You can be a hero, or you can be a zero. And the choice is yours. But we are all watching." He was thus demanding that they participate in the objection to the electoral votes, and threatened them by saying, "we are coming for you" if they did not comply.

Answering President Trump's call to "walk down Pennsylvania Avenue," the rally participants who proceeded down Pennsylvania Avenue joined other groups that had gathered around the U.S. Capitol Building before them. They then surrounded the building and stormed into the building, breaking through the barricades and smashing windows and doors. After overwhelming the U.S. Capitol Police inside, they occupied and vandalized the U.S. Capitol Building for about four hours. Some rioters said that they were responding to President Trump's call, saying, "Our president wants us here," and "We wait and take orders from our president."[37]

Some rally participants were reportedly having discussions in open online spaces, such as Internet forums and social media, about plans to storm the U.S. Capitol Building in conjunction with the January 6 rally and to detain lawmakers and disrupt deliberations in the Joint Session.[38] On the day of the attack, some rioters were also recorded clad in camouflage fatigues and tactical gear and carrying large zip ties (often used by the police to detain suspects), suggesting that the attack had been pre-planned.[39]

The Joint Session was convened at 1:05 p.m. on January 6, and despite interruption caused by the mob invading the Capitol Building, the prescribed proceedings were completed and the session was dissolved at 3:44 a.m. on January 7, after the declaration of the victory of former vice president Biden and Senator Harris. During the Joint Session, Congressman Paul Gosar (R-Arizona, 4th) and Senator Cruz, with the support of seven senators and 58 representatives, objected to the electoral votes in Arizona. In addition, Congressman Scott Perry (R-Pennsylvania, 10th) and Senator Hawley objected to the electoral votes in Pennsylvania with the support of 79 representatives. The objection to the Arizona results was defeated 93-6 in the Senate, and 303-121 in the House. The objection to the Pennsylvania results was defeated 92-7 in the Senate, and 282-138 in the House. Congress voted on the two objections only after the mob that had occupied the Capitol was removed. Some lawmakers who initially indicated support for the objections changed their positions, such as Senator Kelly Loeffler of Georgia, who said she could not "in good conscience" object to the certification of the electoral votes, citing the "violence, the lawlessness, and siege of the Halls of Congress."

In response to the attack on the U.S. Capitol Building, FBI Director Wray made it clear that the rioters who participated in the attack would be subject to criminal investigation, saying in a statement on January 7 that "we do not tolerate violent agitators and extremists who use the guise of First Amendment-protected activity to incite violence and wreak havoc." In addition, on January 12, Michael Sherwin, acting U.S. attorney for the District of Columbia, said that over 70 people had been charged in connection with the incident and that the number is expected to grow "geometrically." He also announced that a "strike force" had been formed to "build seditious and conspiracy charges." This was an acknowledgement that the attack on the Capitol Building was not a mere case of trespassing or destruction of property, but rather involved a conspiracy to overthrow the government. In other words, the incident was perceived as a violent attack on the constitutional system itself, which stipulates a peaceful transfer of power in accordance with the provisions of the Constitution and the law.

President-elect Biden denounced the attack on the Capitol Building, saying on January 7: "Don't dare call them protesters. They were…insurrectionists. Domestic terrorists." At a Senate session on the evening of January 6, Senator Graham stated: "[C]ount me out. Enough is enough." He also said at a press conference on January 7 that "the Capitol of the United States was taken over by domestic terrorists that are not Patriots," indicating his perception that the mob's actions were domestic terrorism. This incident served to confirm a point in the Department of Homeland Security's *Homeland Threat Assessment* report (October 2020) that notes, "[a]mong DVEs [domestic violent extremists], racially and ethnically motivated violent extremists—specifically white supremacist extremists (WSEs)—will remain the most persistent and lethal threat in the Homeland."

Even though the mob's attack on the Capitol Building was reported in real time, President Trump did not immediately condemn the mob. Instead, at 2:24 p.m. on January 6, just after the mob began to invade the Capitol, he tweeted, "Mike Pence didn't have the courage to do what should have been done to protect our Country and our Constitution." This prompted rioters to seek out Vice President Pence, exchanging messages on social media seeking Vice President Pence's whereabouts. A group of rioters who stormed the Capitol was seen chanting, "Hang Mike Pence!" Later, in a tweet at 2:38 p.m., President Trump stated, "Capitol Police and Law Enforcement…are truly on the side of our Country," and appealed to the mob to "Stay peaceful!" Furthermore, although he tweeted at 3:13 p.m., "I am asking for everyone at the U.S. Capitol to remain peaceful," telling them to stop the violence, at 6:01 p.m., he repeated his view that his "landslide election victory [was]…stripped away," and called the mob "great patriots who have been badly & unfairly treated for so long." In a video message to the mob occupying the Capitol Building posted that same day, he repeated his claim that a "landslide election" was "stolen from us," and urged the mob to go home while saying: "We love you. You're very special." Ultimately, it was in a video message shared on Twitter in the evening of January 7, the following day, that President Trump clearly condemned the attack on the Capitol Building, calling it "the heinous attack."

In essence, President Trump reacted in the same way as he had in the past, by avoiding direct criticism of his base, instead sympathizing with them when they committed violence. For example, on August 12, 2017, when a participant in a far-right rally in Charlottesville rammed his car into a group of counter-protesters, killing one of them, President Trump called those present, including the far-right group that attacked, "very fine people," and said, "there's blame on both sides."

Likewise, the fact that President Trump took more than a day to condemn the attack on the Capitol Building despite urging from those around him and criticism from the media and his former cabinet members constituted a deliberate attempt to avoid harming support for him among his broad base, including those who participated in the attack. The desire to arouse and maintain the loyalty of his base has permeated the series of actions President Trump took since the general election. In an article published shortly after the general election, Anne Applebaum argued that President Trump's lawsuits and extreme rhetoric were in fact intended to "create a misleading impression of electoral fraud so deep." She further noted, despite his repeated defeat in legal challenges and former vice president Biden's victory, confirmed on numerous occasions, continuing to "maintain the fiction that the election was stolen," was even more important for his efforts to mobilize his base.[40]

With Applebaum's point in mind, the fact that the Trump campaign, President Trump's allies, and the president himself continued legal battles for two months, with dozens of lawsuits filed one after another, can be seen as relentless campaigning to continue sending messages such as one President Trump tweeted on December 16, two days after the electoral votes: "Too soon to give up. Republican Party must finally learn to fight. People are angry!" They thereby sought to mobilize his base of supporters. From the outset, the Trump campaign reportedly did not expect the lawsuits to succeed, and instead believed that continuing the legal fight would enable them to keep the loyalty of his support base intact.[41] From this perspective, President Trump's rhetoric, such as his tweets mentioning "*our* election victory stolen by emboldened radical left Democrats" and the "election stolen from *you*" (emphasis added), was effective in brewing a shared feeling of "victimhood" among his supporters and strengthening the emotional connection they felt to President Trump. The effectiveness of President Trump's messaging to his supporters that the "election was stolen" is evidenced by the fact that 72% of Republican supporters said that they did not trust the results of the November 3 election in a poll conducted after election day. Applebaum's statement that "[p]aradoxically, Trump's loss may well increase the loyalty of his most ardent fans" also pointed to the existence of dynamics in which the stronger the sense of victimhood among President Trump's supporters, the stronger their ties to President Trump.[42] Additionally, the fact that participants responded to President Trump's call to "fight like hell" at the large-scale rally on January 6 by chanting, "Fight for Trump!," "We love Trump!," and "We love you," shows that his efforts to mobilize his supporters were working.

It is because of this huge base of supporters that President Trump has been able to have so much influence within the Republican Party. Of the Republican members of Congress who experienced the horror of the mob storming of the Capitol Building, only seven in the Senate and two in the House of Representatives reversed their original decision to join the objections. Overall, eight Senators and 139 Representatives signed either the Arizona or Pennsylvania objections,[43] a significant number compared to the single Senator and 31 Representatives who signed the objection in the Joint Session of Congress on January 6, 2005. In addition, only 10 Republican Representatives supported the impeachment of President Trump by the House of Representatives, led by Democratic Speaker Nancy Pelosi. There are moves within the Republican Party to maintain relations with President Trump even after he left office, with some Republicans backtracking on comments they made immediately after the January 6 riot, attributing the responsibility of the attack to President Trump. These developments have led some to suggest that the Republican Party is "still Donald Trump's party," a view that is rooted in the strength of President Trump's base.[44]

In a video message on January 7, President Trump said he would focus on a "smooth, orderly, and seamless transition of power." However, the transition had already been thrown into unprecedented chaos by the attack on the Capitol Building. In the United States, the transition is believed to be "inherently dangerous" because the time it takes for the new administration to consolidate after an administration change tends to invite provocations by adversaries who try to take advantage of the situation.[45] However, undeniably, there were more elements of confusion in the transition of power on the part of the outgoing administration, rather than the incoming one, to say the least, and the United States has experienced an unprecedented transition of power with dramatically increased difficulties. While the Biden administration is working to restore U.S. international leadership, there are still significant forces that do not accept the outcome of the 2020 presidential election. This will not only constrain the work of the current administration, which relies on having a paper-thin majority in the House and Senate, but could also lead to the recurrence of a crisis for democracy. This makes it now more important than ever to pay due attention to the developments of the domestic situation in the United States.

NOTES

1) 10 U.S.C. § 4302 (a)(3).

2) Confucius Institute (Hanban), "Constitution and By-Laws of the Confucius Institutes," Confucius Institute website.

3) U.S. Senate Permanent Subcommittee on Investigations, Committee on Homeland Security and Governmental Affairs, *China's Impact on the U.S. Education System* (2019), 5.

4) American Association of University Professors, "On Partnerships with Foreign Governments: The Case of Confucius Institutes" (June 2014).

5) Rachelle Peterson, *Outsourced to China: Confucius Institutes and Soft Power in American Higher Education* (New York: National Association of Scholars, 2017), 9, 10, 11.

6) Permanent Subcommittee on Investigations, *China's Impact*, 1, 5, 6, 7.

7) Marco Rubio et al., letter to Mike Pompeo and Steven T. Mnuchin, August 28, 2018.

8) Marco Rubio et al., letter to Mike Pompeo, Steven T. Mnuchin, Wilbur Ross, December 12, 2019.

9) Export Administration Regulations, Part 744, § 744.11; Export Administration Regulations, Supplement No. 4 to Part 744, 1.

10) Export Administration Regulations, Part 734, § 734.3.

11) Joseph Bosco, "To Confront China, Let Trump Be Reagan," *Hill*, August 7, 2019.

12) Kikuchi Shigeo, "Beirikugun maruchidomein sakusen (MDO) konseputo: '21 Seiki no shoheika rengo' to arata na tatakaikata no mosaku" [U.S. Army multi-domain operations concept: An army in search of novel ways of winning], *Boei Kenkyusho Kiyo* [NIDS Journal of Defense and Security] 22, no. 1 (November 2019): 15–58; Kikuchi Shigeo, "Enkaiiki sakusen ni kansuru beikaiheitai sakusen konseputo no tenkai: 'Zenpo kaigun kichi' no 'boei' to 'kaigun kaiheitai togo'" [Evolving Marine Corps concept for littoral operations: "Naval integration" for the "defense" of "advanced naval bases"], *Anzenhosho Senryaku Kenkyu* [Security & Strategy] 1, no. 1 (August 2020): 67–81.

13) Tom Greenwood and Pat Savage, "In Search of a 21st-Century Joint Warfighting Concept," *War on the Rocks*, September 12, 2019.

14) Curtis E. LeMay Center for Doctrine Development and Education, *Annex 3-99 Department of the Air Force Role in Joint All-Domain Operations* (October 8, 2020), 5, 16, 17.

15) Kimberly Underwood, "The Army Shapes Joint All-Domain Operations," *Signal*, August 1, 2020.

16) Chief of Staff of the Air Force, *Enhancing Multi-Domain Command and Control... Tying It All Together* (March 2017), 1, 2.

17) John A. Tirpak, "The Goldfein Years: Chief 21's Legacy Is His Vision for the Future; A Highly Connected Joint Force," *Air Force Magazine* 103, no. 7/8 (July/August 2020): 37.

18) Rachel S. Cohen, "USAF, Army Move Forward under New Command and Control Agreement," *Air Force Magazine*, October 19, 2020.

19) Kikuchi Shigeo and Arakaki Hiromu, "The United States: Addressing an Increasingly Harsh Strategic Environment," in *East Asian Strategic Review 2016*, English edition,

Chapter 6 The United States

ed. National Institute for Defense Studies (NIDS) (Tokyo: NIDS, 2016), 265.

20) Peter Layton, "Discontinued: America's Continuous Bomber Presence," *Interpreter*, May 6, 2020.

21) Joseph Trevithick, "The Air Force Abruptly Ends Its Continuous Bomber Presence on Guam after 16 Years," *Drive*, April 17, 2020.

22) Nick Corasaniti and Danny Hakim, "Facing Gap in Pennsylvania, Trump Camp Tries to Make Voting Harder," *New York Times*, November 3, 2020.

23) Matthew Yglesias, "Trump's Plan to Win by Invalidating Votes, Explained," *Vox*, November 1, 2020.

24) For the complaints, motions, and court opinions of individual legal challenge, see the Democracy Docket website (https://www.democracydocket.com/states).

25) Marc Caputo, "'One of the Nuttier Things I've Seen': MAGA Civil War Erupts in Georgia," *Politico*, December 3, 2020.

26) Rick Rojas and Richard Fausset, "Georgia Senators Ask Election Official to Resign in G.O.P. Squabble," *New York Times*, November 9, 2020.

27) Secretary of State, State of Georgia, "Risk-Limiting Audit Report, Georgia Presidential Contest, November 2020" (November 19, 2020).

28) Amy Gardner, "Ga. Secretary of State Says Fellow Republicans Are Pressuring Him to Find Ways to Exclude Ballots," *Washington Post*, November 16, 2020.

29) Ga. Const. of 1983 art. II, § 1; Jonathan Raymond, "Signature Matching Can't Be Done during Georgia's Audit: Here's Why," *11 Alive*, last updated December 4, 2020.

30) Andrew Higgins, "Trump Embraces 'Enemy of the People,' a Phrase with a Fraught History," *New York Times*, February 26, 2017; David Remnick, "Trump and the Enemies of the People," *New Yorker*, August 15, 2018.

31) Amy Gardner, "'I Just Want to Find 11,780 Votes': In Extraordinary Hour-Long Call, Trump Pressures Georgia Secretary of State to Recalculate the Vote in His Favor," *Washington Post*, January 3, 2021; Amy Gardner and Paulina Firozi, "Here's the Full Transcript and Audio of the Call between Trump and Raffensperger," *Washington Post*, January 5, 2021; Zeynep Tufekci, "This Isn't Just Political Theater," *Atlantic*, January 6, 2021.

32) Jon Ward (@jonward11), Twitter, November 19, 2020, 7:42 p.m., EST, https://twitter.com/jonward11/status/1329585966051446789.

33) Alan Feuer, "In Harsh Rebuke, Appeals Court Rejects Trump's Election Challenge in Pennsylvania," *New York Times*, November 27, 2020.

34) Max Feldman, "10 Voter Fraud Lies Debunked," Brennan Center for Justice (May 27, 2020); Lorraine C. Minnite, *The Politics of Voter Fraud* (Washington, DC: Project

Vote, 2010).

35) Wendy R. Weiser and Harold Ekeh, "The False Narrative of Vote-by-Mail Fraud," Brennan Center for Justice (April 10, 2020).

36) Will Steakin, John Santucci, and Katherine Faulders, "Trump Allies Helped Plan, Promote Rally That Led to Capitol Attack," ABC News, January 9, 2021.

37) Dan Barry, Mike McIntire, and Matthew Rosenberg, "'Our President Wants Us Here': The Mob That Stormed the Capitol," *New York Times*, January 9, 2021.

38) Sheera Frenkel, "The Storming of Capitol Hill Was Organized on Social Media," *New York Times*, January 6, 2021; Craig Timberg, Drew Harwell, and Marissa J. Lang, "Capitol Siege Was Planned Online. Trump Supporters Now Planning the Next One," *Washington Post*, January 9, 2021.

39) Alexander Mallin and Ivan Pereira, "Capitol Riot Suspects Who Allegedly Brought Zip Ties, Wore Tactical Gear Arrested," ABC News, January 11, 2021.

40) Anne Applebaum, "Trump Won't Accept Defeat. Ever.," *Atlantic*, November 7, 2020.

41) Colleen Long and Zeke Miller, "Fraud Claims Aimed in Part at Keeping Trump Base Loyal," AP News, November 9, 2020.

42) Applebaum, "Trump Won't Accept Defeat. Ever."

43) Harry Stevens et al., "How Members of Congress Voted on Counting the Electoral College Vote," *Washington Post*, January 7, 2021.

44) James Downie, "It's Still Donald Trump's Party," *Washington Post*, January 11, 2021.

45) Kurt M. Campbell and James B. Steinberg, *Difficult Transitions: Foreign Policy Troubles at the Outset of Presidential Power* (Washington, DC: Brookings Institution, 2008), 23, 24.

Chapter 6 The United States

Chapter 7

Japan

Toward a Post-COVID-19 Security Posture

TSUKAMOTO Katsuya

The Japan-
Australia-
India-U.S.
multilateral
exercise
Malabar 2020
(MSDF official
website)

Summary

On January 29, after the emerging pandemic situation in China had become apparent, the Ministry of Defense (MOD) and the Self-Defense Forces (SDF) began the dispatch of personnel to support the quarantine of Japanese nationals repatriated on charter flights from China. Since then, various support operations under the name of disaster relief have been carried out in each prefecture, employing the SDF's own unique infrastructure for these operations. The SDF personnel involved in such support operations have not experienced secondary infections, and accordingly, the preventive measures they have taken have received strong praise. Based on lessons in preventing secondary infection learned through their operations, the SDF is now providing support for education and training, primarily relaying this knowledge to local governments. Going forward, as long as the prevention of the spread of the novel coronavirus disease (COVID-19) remains a critical challenge, the MOD/SDF are expected to make further contributions utilizing their unique capabilities.

The year 2020 marked the 60th anniversary of the revision of the Japan-U.S. Security Treaty, which forms the cornerstone of Japan's security. Although there are no changes in the actual clauses of the revised treaty, bilateral defense cooperation has been substantially deepened through the establishment of the Guidelines for Japan-U.S. Defense Cooperation and successive revisions. Against this backdrop, the administration of newly inaugurated Prime Minister Suga Yoshihide is expected to continue emphasizing the role of the Japan-U.S. Alliance. At the same time, in order to further enhance response and deterrence under the Alliance, bilateral defense cooperation with the United States could expand into multi-layered security cooperation—including cooperation with other U.S. allies. In particular, trilateral Japan-U.S.-Australia cooperation, Japan-U.S.-Republic of Korea (ROK) cooperation, and Japan-U.S.-India cooperation have been prominently promoted since the 2000s. The expanding bilateral and trilateral security cooperation could be further developed into quadrilateral cooperation among Japan, the United States, Australia, and India.

In building a Multi-Domain Defense Force as outlined in the National Defense Program Guidelines (NDPG) issued in December 2018, various measures are being implemented to respond to the increasingly severe security environment under the concept of cross-domain operations, leveraging the new domains of space, cyberspace, and the electromagnetic spectrum as force multipliers. In these new domains, the SDF is enhancing its capacity, particularly by forming new units. While cross-domain operations differ considerably from traditional ways of warfare, farsighted policies would be indispensable to the development of operational capabilities that is sustainable.

1. Roles of the MOD/SDF in COVID-19 Countermeasures

(1) Support by the SDF

National defense authorities of various countries play a variety of roles in responding to COVID-19 infections. The reasons for this have been nationwide command and control systems and their ability to dispatch highly trained human resources in a short period of time.[1] So far, the defense authorities' main roles have been centered on providing transport support, medical staff, and infrastructure, to which Japan is no exception.

In response to the spread of COVID-19 infections in China, the MOD/SDF began by dispatching personnel to provide quarantine support for Japanese nationals returning to Japan by chartered aircraft on January 29, 2020. This was followed by disaster relief operations to tackle the spread of COVID-19 from January 31, including such missions as transporting Japanese nationals and others returning to Japan and providing support for their daily lives. Likewise, in response to the outbreak of infections aboard the *Diamond Princess* cruise ship docked at Yokohama Port, the MOD/SDF provided medical care, transport, and emergency support to the passengers and crew on board.

Furthermore, from March 28, the SDF implemented the following measures to strengthen border enforcement measures against COVID-19: (i) quarantine support at airports by SDF medical officers and others; (ii) transport support from airports to accommodation facilities for people returning to or entering Japan who stayed at accommodation facilities until the results of polymerase chain reaction (PCR) tests were obtained; and (iii) support for people returning to and entering Japan who stayed at accommodation facilities.[2] When the number of infection cases due to community spread in Japan increased after April, the SDF conducted disaster relief operations and other missions in response to requests from prefectural governors and others. This support can mainly be divided into the following categories: (i) medical support; (ii) life support assistance to patients with mild or no symptoms at accommodation facilities; (iii) transport support; and (iv) support for training and education.

First, medical support includes cooperation in collecting samples necessary for PCR tests and dispatching nurses and other personnel to local medical institutions. In terms of sample collection, in April 2020, about 70 medical staff members including doctors and nurses from the

SDF personnel providing training and education to local government officials (Joint Staff Office/10th Division, GSDF)

SDF Sendai Hospital provided support for PCR sample collection in Sendai City. SDF medical staff also provided sample collection support to the crew members of a cruise ship stopping in Nagasaki Prefecture.[3] In addition, the SDF dispatched nurses in support of medical institutions in Okinawa Prefecture from August 18 to 31 due to the community spread of infections in the prefecture and the resulting pressure on the medical system. This medical support was carried out in response to a request from the Okinawa Prefectural Government. The SDF dispatched a total of 31 staff members, including 15 nurses and Licensed Practical Nurses from the Ground Self-Defense Force (GSDF) Western Army, the 15th Brigade, and the SDF Naha Hospital, as well as 16 logistical support personnel.[4] Moreover, the SDF also provided support with their own unique equipment, such as erecting tents to enable open-air PCR tests and providing diagnoses with CT diagnosis vehicles.

In regard to life support assistance to patients with mild or no symptoms at accommodation facilities, the main focus has been providing meals and other support to such patients staying in private facilities rented by local governments. Specifically, about 60 members of the 1st Division provided support to a total of about 760 people in eight prefectures, including emergency support for patients staying at private hotels who tested positive without severe symptoms.[5]

As for transport support, in addition to transporting patients from hospitals to private accommodation facilities, the SDF has mainly provided air transportation to patients infected on remote islands scattered across Japan. A total of about 80 patients have been transported by air from remote islands in five prefectures. On April 3, patients were transported from Iki City to the Omura Air Base of the Maritime Self-Defense Force (MSDF) in response to a disaster relief request from Nagasaki Prefecture, marking the beginning of the SDF's air transport support during the COVID-19 pandemic.[6]

Finally, support for training and education has focused on infection prevention mainly for local government staff. Since the SDF's infection control and preventive measures have been acknowledged as highly effective, they are sharing their knowledge with local governments and other organizations. For example, based on the experience they gained by responding to the mass outbreak of infections aboard *Diamond Princess*, strengthening border enforcement measures, and working to prevent community spread of infections, they have made knowledge of infection prevention measures such as facility zoning and the formulation of waste disposal standards available on the MOD website and provided support for training and education on infection control measures to local government staff and others. As early as April 8, five members of the GSDF Middle Army Headquarters provided training on infection prevention and other matters to about 20 staff members of the Osaka Detention House. On April 13, the same training was provided to about 70 Osaka Prefectural Government staff and employees of private accommodation facilities. Such support activities have been conducted in 35 prefectures, through which about 2,300 personnel in total received the training (as of January 22, 2021).

One of the reasons why the SDF's infection preventive measures have been highly praised is that there have been no secondary infections among SDF personnel who have been involved in disaster relief operations related to COVID-19, including the approximately 2,700 personnel who participated in the operation for *Diamond Princess* (as of May 31, 2020).[7] This is a result of the SDF's regular exercises and training on countermeasures against biological weapons and infectious diseases, and it shows their high level of protection capabilities.

(2) Role of the SDF in Infection Control Measures

Infection control measures have much in common with countermeasures against biological weapons, and the MOD/SDF have built up specialized response capabilities that include dealing with unknown viruses. There have been strong concerns in the international community about the possibility that terrorists and countries of proliferation concern may acquire weapons of mass destruction, such as nuclear, biological, and chemical (NBC) weapons, and use them for terrorism. Biological weapons, especially, are called the "poor man's atomic bomb," and it has been pointed out that the probability and danger of their use exceeds that of nuclear weapons and chemical weapons.[8] For example, Aum Shinrikyo, which conducted the sarin gas attack on the Tokyo subway system in March 1995, developed and actually used biological weapons. From September to October 2001 in the United States, terrorist attacks occurred in which powdered anthrax spores were put into letters addressed to television stations, news media, and senators. All of these incidents demonstrate that biological weapons pose a present threat to Japan.

Furthermore, in addition to terrorist attacks that intentionally cause infectious disease outbreaks, naturally occurring pandemics have become a serious threat, notable examples of which include the severe acute respiratory syndrome (SARS) outbreak in southern China in 2002 and the novel influenza (H1N1) pandemic in 2009. It was necessary for the government to adopt a unified response to these infectious disease outbreaks.

One of the capabilities that the MOD/SDF have been developing in response to these threats is the NBC Countermeasure Medical Unit, which was established within the GSDF in March 2008. This unit is capable of providing temporary quarantine and emergency treatment for infected people in the event of a biological weapon attack, as well as identifying the weapon used. The unit is composed mainly of medical doctors, nurses, and medics, and is accordingly equipped with the Mobile Laboratory Unit and the Negative Pressure Air Dome Unit. When the MOD provided quarantine support for the novel influenza (H1N1) at Haneda Airport and Narita Airport from April to June 2009, the NBC Countermeasure

Medical Unit was also dispatched to take part in this mission.

The SDF has also been working to enhance its medical functions so as to execute a variety of missions in various situations in Japan and abroad. For example, two SDF medical facilities, the SDF Central Hospital and the National Defense Medical College Hospital, are designated medical institutions for Category 1 infectious diseases and are always ready to receive patients with infectious diseases.[9] Furthermore, the SDF Central Hospital has conducted exercises to admit patients with Category 1 infectious disease in order to strengthen coordination with related institutions. In July 2019, as part of the training on admitting infectious disease patients, the SDF Central Hospital conducted its first joint exercise with the Tokyo Metropolitan Government and other relevant institutions. The experience gained from these exercises was utilized in their response to the spread of COVID-19.[10] These capabilities therefore would be leveraged in the event of coronavirus resurgence, or in response to future pandemics caused by novel infectious diseases.

Moreover, the MOD has been utilizing the channels established through the existing defense exchanges and security dialogues to share information with its counterparts on preventing the spread of COVID-19. For example, former defense minister Kono Taro and Defense Minister Kishi Nobuo have been holding telephone talks and teleconference meetings during the COVID-19 crisis with their counterparts from 24 countries and organizations and on 38 occasions in total between April and December 2020. The MOD places importance on communicating with other countries precisely because of the pandemic situation. The MOD also takes the position that even if the spread of COVID-19 comes to an end, further cooperation with other states that share values and interests is necessary in order to maintain the free and open international order that has supported the world's peace and prosperity.[11] In this respect, Japan is distinguishing itself from China, which aims to shape its favorable international and regional order through its own contributions for COVID-19 countermeasures.

National defense authorities of various countries are employing their assets to respond to COVID-19, but there are concerns that doing so will reduce their capabilities and readiness for national defense, which is their primary mission.[12] In addition, if the response to the spread of COVID-19 is further prolonged and, consequently, infections spread to SDF personnel on a large scale, the SDF's readiness would be affected. Therefore, the SDF must take the utmost care to ensure that its future activities do not seriously affect its core missions, particularly national defense. However, the MOD/SDF possess unique capabilities that cannot be easily replaced, and thus will be expected to contribute as long as preventing the spread of COVID-19 remains a critical issue.

2. The Japan-U.S. Security Treaty Marks the 60th Anniversary of Its Signing

(1) An Alliance Based on Shared Values

The Japan-U.S. Security Treaty (the former Security Treaty) was concluded on September 8, 1951 at the same time as the San Francisco Peace Treaty, and the Alliance has been the cornerstone of Japan's security since the end of World War II and throughout the Cold War. The importance of the treaty has not changed in the 30 years since the end of the Cold War. The National Security Strategy issued in 2013 positions the Japan-U.S. Alliance as the "cornerstone of Japan's security." It points out, "For more than 60 years, the Japan-U.S. Alliance, with the Japan-U.S. security arrangements at its core, has played an indispensable role for peace and security in Japan as well as peace and stability in the Asia-Pacific region." It also states, "In recent years, the Alliance has also played a more critical role for peace, stability, and prosperity in the international community."

Echoing the National Security Strategy, the National Defense Program Guidelines for FY2019 and Beyond (hereinafter, "2018 NDPG") also recognizes that, "As inter-state competitions prominently emerge, it has become all the more important for Japan's national security to further strengthen relationship with the United States, with whom Japan shares universal values and strategic interests." Reflecting this recognition, Prime Minister Abe Shinzo stated on January 19,

2020, "Today, more than ever, the U.S.-Japan Security Treaty is a pillar that is indestructible, a pillar immovable, safeguarding peace in Asia, the Indo-Pacific, and in the world, while assuring prosperity therein." He also went on to call the Japan-U.S. Alliance "an Alliance of Hope."[13]

However, the path by which the Japan-U.S. Alliance evolved into an "Alliance of Hope" was not straightforward. Firstly, the former Japan-U.S. Security Treaty signed in 1951 was created with the main purpose of allowing the continuous stationing of U.S. troops in Japan in order to maintain security for Japan, which had no military. However, at this time, the former Japan-U.S. Security Treaty did not clarify the obligation of the United States to defend Japan, which led some to believe the nature of the treaty was to ensure the United States' commitment to defend Japan in exchange for the United States having continued access to bases in Japan.[14]

Nine years later, the Japan-U.S. Security Treaty (the new Security Treaty), which was revised on January 19, 1960, aimed to rectify this unilateral nature of the Alliance. Firstly, Article V of the new Security Treaty clearly stated the defense obligations of the United States to Japan. Secondly, the Kishi-Herter Exchange of Notes was signed, which made clear that the use of facilities and zones by the United States as stipulated in Article VI would be subject to prior consultation with Japan by the United States. As a result, U.S. military bases in Japan came to be operated under close coordination between the two countries, which institutionally strengthened bilateral security cooperation.[15]

Since 1960, there has been no change in the text of the new Security Treaty itself. However, defense cooperation based on the Japan-U.S. Alliance has been dramatically strengthened. In particular, the bilateral cooperation deepened with the Guidelines for Japan-U.S. Defense Cooperation agreed in 1978 and has been further developed in the process of two major revisions of the Guidelines.

The first set of Guidelines promoted Japan-U.S. defense cooperation concerning the defense of Japan as codified in Article V of the Japan-U.S. Security Treaty. These Guidelines led to regularly held meetings between top Japanese and U.S. defense officials, and joint Japan-U.S. exercises became more frequent in the 1980s.

The Guidelines were next revised in 1997 after the end of the Cold War. While the 1978 Guidelines promoted cooperation in the case of contingencies in Japan, there had been comparatively less progress in considering responses and cooperation for contingencies other than the defense of Japan. However, with the escalation of the North Korean nuclear and missile issues from 1993 to 1994, as well as the Taiwan Strait crisis in 1996 caused by China's military exercises aimed at putting pressure on Taiwan's presidential election, there was growing recognition of the need to expand responses and cooperation in so-called "situations in areas surrounding Japan." This led to a review of the Guidelines in 1997.

The Guidelines were revised again in 2015 primarily due to the changes in the international environment since the 1997 revision. In a remark on January 16, 2020 at the Center for Strategic and International Studies (CSIS), Defense Minister Kono pointed out that the need to respond to changes in the security environment amid increasing uncertainty in the international environment led to a major review of the Guidelines. Kono listed such changes as the ballistic missile launch by North Korea in 1998, the September 11, 2001 terrorist attacks in the United States, the use of force in Afghanistan and the Iraq War, and the incident involving the collision of a Chinese fishing boat with Japan Coast Guard patrol vessels in Japan's territorial waters near the Senkaku Islands in September 2010.[16]

The new Guidelines formulated in 2015 strengthen deterrence and response capabilities in all phases from peacetime to contingencies, and include cooperation for regional and global peace and security. The Guidelines also include cooperation in the new strategic domains of space and cyberspace and play a role in promoting closer operational cooperation and policy coordination between the Japanese and U.S. defense authorities. Furthermore, one of the major characteristics of the new Guidelines is the establishment of the Alliance Coordination Mechanism (ACM) to seamlessly and effectively address all situations, including those that affect Japan's peace and security. The ACM can be used during peacetime, for large-scale disasters in Japan, and for regional and global cooperation. It also enables whole-of-government coordination including all relevant U.S. and Japanese agencies.[17] The establishment of the ACM has enabled Japan and the

Chapter 7

Japan

Prime Minister Suga receives a courtesy call from U.S. secretary of state Pompeo on October 6, 2020 (Prime Minister's Office of Japan official website)

United States to cooperate more closely together in response to the Kumamoto earthquake in 2016 as well as North Korea's ballistic missile launches and nuclear tests in 2016 and 2017.

The Legislation for Peace and Security enacted in September 2015 also facilitated alliance cooperation. For example, as stipulated by Article 95-2 of the Self-Defense Forces Law, the SDF is now able to protect naval vessels, aircraft, and other weapons and equipment of the units of the U.S. Forces actually engaged in activities that contribute to the defense of Japan in cooperation with the SDF. The scope of the supplies and services that the SDF can provide to U.S. Forces was also expanded through the legislation. At the same time, the Japan-U.S. Acquisition and Cross-Servicing Agreement (ACSA) was revised in April 2017, which enabled smooth provision of supplies and services during not only Situations that Will Have an Important Influence for Japan and Survival-Threatening Situations, but also in multilateral exercises in which both the SDF and the U.S. Forces participate. Together with making ammunition an eligible supply for provision, the revised ACSA has further increased the effectiveness of Japan-U.S. security cooperation.

Reflecting this deepening of alliance cooperation, on January 15, 2020, Defense Minister Kono met with Secretary of Defense Mark Esper and welcomed that the Japan-U.S. Alliance had become even stronger. The ministers affirmed that Japan and the United States would continue to closely work together to reinforce the Alliance's deterrence and response capability.[18] In addition, on January 17, 2020, the United States and Japan made a joint statement on the 60th anniversary of the signing of the new Security Treaty, stating that the Japan-U.S. Alliance has "played and will continue to play an integral role in ensuring the peace and security of our two countries, while realizing our shared vision of a free and open Indo-Pacific including through regional security cooperation."[19]

However, the Japan-U.S. Alliance is not without pressing issues. Securing the stable U.S. military presence is essential for maintaining the Alliance. However, the United States is asking its allies to bear more of the burden for defense, requesting not only their increased defense spending, but also a higher share of the cost of stationing the U.S. Forces. Nevertheless, in light of Japan's tight fiscal situation, it will be indispensable for both Japan and the United States to share the burden in an acceptable manner while enhancing the deterrence and response capabilities of the Alliance.

The Japan-U.S. Alliance is expected to remain the cornerstone of Japan's security even after Japan inaugurated a new cabinet on September 16, 2020, and the United States will make a fresh start under the new administration led by President Joseph Biden. Prime Minister Suga Yoshihide stated at his inaugural press conference on September 16 that he intends to "deploy policies that place a well-functioning Japan-US Alliance as their linchpin"[20] in the diplomacy and security fields. In addition, during a telephone talk with President-elect Biden on November 12, Prime Minister Suga stated, "[T]he Japan-U.S. Alliance is indispensable for the peace and prosperity of both the region surrounding Japan, where the security environment is becoming increasingly severe, as well as the international community, and that we must [work] together to further strengthen the Alliance." He also expressed his "wish for Japan and the U.S. to work together to realize a 'Free and Open Indo-Pacific.'"[21] His successive statements indicate that the previous administration's emphasis on the Japan-U.S. Alliance will be inherited by the new administration.

(2) Deepening Security Cooperation Centered on the Japan-U.S. Alliance

The United States' alliance network, including the Japan-U.S. Alliance, has developed since the Cold War period in a "hub-and-spoke" form resembling a wheel extending radially centered on the United States. This form of network was effective when individual allies only needed to respond to their respective threats jointly with the United States and did not require much cooperation among the allies. However, with the end of the Cold War and the disappearance of the clear threat of the Soviet Union, the United States and other countries came to face diverging threats. For example, in the 1990s, the nuclear and missile issues of North Korea and the crisis over the Taiwan Strait intensified, while at the beginning of the 21st century, the need to respond to non-traditional threats such as international terrorist groups, guerrillas, and insurgents also arose. In order to respond to this diversification of threats, since the early 2000s, conscious attempts have been made to strengthen a web of security cooperation by extending cooperation among U.S. allies in addition to bilateral cooperation with the United States.[22]

Reflecting this security trend, Japan's National Security Strategy formulated in 2013 calls for strengthening the Japan-U.S. Alliance as well as building trust and developing cooperative relations with partners in and outside the Asia-Pacific region in order to improve the security environment surrounding Japan. The 2018 NDPG also states, "Japan will position the Japan-U.S. Alliance as its cornerstone and will work closely with the countries that share universal values and security interests," and articulates enhanced cooperation with other U.S. allies and partners. Moreover, in the Guidelines for Japan-U.S. Defense Cooperation, the Japanese and U.S. governments agreed to "promote and improve trilateral and multilateral security and defense cooperation" as part of "cooperation for regional and global peace and security."[23] In this line of effort, particular importance has been placed respectively on trilateral cooperation with Australia and the ROK, which are U.S. allies, and India, which is gaining influence as a regional power.

Firstly, Australia is a "Special Strategic Partner" for Japan in the Indo-Pacific region, not only because it is a fellow U.S. ally, but also because it shares fundamental values such as freedom, democracy, respect for fundamental human rights, and the rule of law, as well as strategic interests for security. Mutual cooperation between Australia and Japan has been strengthened with a focus on disaster relief and humanitarian assistance operations, as well as cooperation on capacity building support. The scope of the Japan-Australia ACSA in light of increased joint operations with the Australian Defence Force is a result of the expanding bilateral defense cooperation and exchanges. In particular, at the Japan-Australia Defense Ministers' meeting on October 19, 2020, the ministers instructed their officials to commence necessary coordination to create a framework to protect Australian Defence Force assets by the SDF personnel under Article 95-2 of the Self-Defense Forces Law. In addition, at the Japan-Australia Summit Meeting on November 17, Prime Minister Suga and Prime Minister Morrison reached an agreement in principle on the Japan-Australia Reciprocal Access Agreement, laying the foundation for further strengthening of strategic cooperation between the two countries.

In parallel with the deepening bilateral ties, trilateral security cooperation between Japan, the United States, and Australia has been strengthened rapidly since the inaugural director general-level meeting of the Trilateral Strategic Dialogue (TSD) in the early 2000s. The TSD was elevated in March 2006 when the first ministerial-level meeting was held by the foreign ministers of the three countries. As for consultations among their defense authorities, a director general-level meeting of the Japan-U.S.-Australia Security and Defense Cooperation Forum was held in April 2007 in Tokyo, and a Japan-U.S.-Australia Defense Ministers' meeting was held in Singapore in June 2007. These initiatives, it is argued, were aimed at having Japan and Australia jointly support the United States' global and regional role to maintain and strengthen the U.S. presence in the region based on the "hub-and-spoke" system.[24]

As high-level discussions between Japan, the United States, and Australia deepened, defense cooperation and exchanges also progressed. As a major trilateral military exchange, in November 2019, the MSDF hosted a Japan-U.S.-Australia trilateral exercise (a special mine warfare exercise) with U.S. and Australian minesweepers in the Hyuga-nada Sea. The Air Self-Defense Force (ASDF) conducted a trilateral humanitarian assistance and disaster relief (HA/DR) exercise known as Christmas Drop in the South Pacific including the Federated States of Micronesia, and cohosted a trilateral field and HA/DR exercise, Cope

North, from February to March 2020.[25] Furthermore, the GSDF also conducted a trilateral exercise known as Southern Jackaroo in Australia together with the U.S. and Australian forces from May to June 2019.[26] These exercises have contributed to improved mutual understanding and interoperability among the three countries. At the same time, the fields of cooperation are expanding beyond peacekeeping operations and non-traditional security areas to include traditional security areas such as anti-submarine warfare and amphibious assault operations.[27]

The ROK is also an ally of the United States, which makes Japan-ROK bilateral cooperation as well as Japan-U.S.-ROK trilateral cooperation all the more important in dealing with North Korea's nuclear and missile issues. However, Japan-ROK relations have deteriorated since the October 2018 judgment by the ROK Supreme Court ordering Japanese companies to pay compensation to the "former civilian workers from the Korean Peninsula." Reflecting the tense relationship, affinity for the ROK fell in public opinion in Japan, and the Cabinet Office's public opinion survey conducted in October 2019 found that the percentage of respondents who "feel affinity" toward the ROK decreased (39.4% to 26.7%) and the percentage of those who "do not feel affinity" increased (58.0% to 71.5%) compared to the same period in 2018.[28] Moreover, the relationship between the Japan and ROK defense authorities is also very strained namely due to the ROK's response to the flag of the MSDF at the international fleet review hosted by the ROK in October 2018 and the incident of an ROK naval vessel directing its fire-control radar at an MSDF patrol aircraft in December 2018.

In terms of Japan-U.S.-ROK trilateral cooperation, Japan's National Security Strategy states that "trilateral cooperation among Japan, the U.S. and the ROK is a key framework in realizing peace and stability in East Asia," and that it will be strengthened, including cooperation on the North Korean nuclear and missile issues. At the working level, the three countries have held director general-level and director-level talks within the framework of the Defense Trilateral Talks (DTT) as well as Trilateral Joint Chiefs of Staff Meetings. For high-level consultations as well, Japan-U.S.-ROK Defense Ministerial Meetings have been regularly held using the opportunities of the Asia Security Summit (Shangri-La Dialogue) and the ASEAN Defence Ministers' Meeting Plus (ADMM-Plus). Although the 2020 Shangri-La Dialogue was cancelled, it is noteworthy that the DTT plenary meeting of director-generals was held in May 2020 via videoconference to discuss regional security issues, including the situation in North Korea, despite the strained Japan-ROK bilateral relations.[29] These trilateral dialogues play an important role in information sharing, especially on North Korea's nuclear and missile issues, and contribute to strengthening deterrence by publicly demonstrating trilateral cooperation.

As for trilateral defense cooperation, the three countries have sustained efforts to strengthen operational cooperation despite some constraints in Japan-ROK and U.S.-ROK relations. For example, the Pacific Dragon exercise to detect and track ballistic missiles in the vicinity of Hawaii was held for the first time in June 2016 with participation by Aegis-equipped destroyers from Japan, the United States, and the ROK. The three countries also conducted ballistic missile information-sharing exercises in the waters surrounding Japan in November 2016, January 2017, March 2017, October 2017, and December 2017, through which trilateral information sharing has been facilitated.[30] The sensors and interceptors of missile defense systems require extremely high performance, and the resulting cost is generally high. It is thus difficult for a single country to have a large number of these sophisticated systems. Accordingly, it would be significantly more effective to enhance synergy of the assets held by the three countries through strengthening trilateral cooperation in missile defense.

Both information sharing on North Korea and cooperation in missile defense among the three countries necessitate a framework ensuring the smooth sharing of classified information. In December 2014, Japan, the United States, and the ROK concluded the Trilateral Information Sharing Arrangement, which enables the sharing of classified information between Japan and the ROK via the United States on the nuclear and missile threats posed by North Korea. However, for timelier and smoother information sharing among the three countries, it is also essential to directly share a wide range of classified information between Japan and ROK made possible by stably maintaining the Japan-ROK General Security of Military

Information Agreement (GSOMIA).

Finally, although not an ally of the United States, India is highly important to Japan. India is a major power with the world's second largest population and a strong economy, and centrally located along the sea lanes connecting East Asia with the Middle East and Africa. The two countries share fundamental values and have common interests in the peace, stability, and prosperity of Asia and the world. Consequently, bilateral cooperation has been promoted in the fields of training, exercises, defense equipment and technology from the perspective of strengthening strategic cooperation with India. In particular, the ACSA signed between the two countries on September 9, 2020 enables smooth provision of supplies such as food, water, fuel, and clothing, as well as services such as transportation, use of facilities, repairs, and maintenance when both the SDF and Indian Armed Forces participate in multilateral exercises and United Nations Peacekeeping Operations.

Trilateral meetings between Japan, the United States, and India have been held at the director-general level since 2011. Subsequently, the level of consultations has increased with the first foreign ministers' meeting held in New York in July 2015 and the first Japan-U.S.-India Summit Meeting held in November 2018. In addition, at the Japan-U.S.-India Summit Meeting held on the sidelines of the G20 Summit in Osaka in June 2019, the leaders shared recognition of the increasingly complex security environment and agreed to promote cooperation in various fields, including maritime security, space, and cyberspace.[31] Furthermore, in the field of service-to-service exchanges, trilateral exercises among the MSDF and U.S. and Indian navies have been conducted as the centerpiece to enhance trilateral cooperation. In 2017, the Japan-U.S.-India trilateral naval exercise Malabar was conducted to improve the tactical skills of the MSDF and strengthen cooperation with the U.S. and Indian navies. The Malabar 2019 exercise was hosted in the waters around Japan, which demonstrates deepening trilateral cooperation.[32]

What is important in these initiatives to expand the web of multi-layered networks centered on U.S. allies and partners is the ongoing effort to further develop the Japan-U.S.-Australia and Japan-U.S.-India trilateral frameworks into quadrilateral cooperation. On the diplomatic front, the Japan-Australia-India-U.S. Ministerial was held in New York on September 26, 2019. In addition, the second Japan-Australia-India-U.S. Foreign Ministers' Meeting was held on October 6, 2020, at which it was agreed that the Foreign Ministers' Meeting would be held regularly. These frameworks are attracting attention as the four countries seemingly move to hedge against an uncertain future, in light of the intensifying Sino-U.S. rivalry as well as China's unilateral and coercive actions in the South China Sea and beyond.

The Japan-Australia-India-U.S. cooperation at present constitutes consultation between diplomatic authorities. However, it may develop into consultation and cooperation between defense authorities in the future. In a press conference held after the Japan-U.S. Defense Ministers' Telephone Talk, Defense Minister Kishi said that quadrilateral cooperation among the defense authorities of Japan, the United States, Australia, and India is important in promoting a "Free and Open Indo-Pacific," and that it is also useful to have a forum for exchanging views on defense.[33] In addition, the four countries are moving forward with more substantial defense cooperation. For example, the MSDF and the navies of Australia, India, and the United States conducted the quadrilateral exercise Malabar 2020 in the Bay of Bengal from November 3 and in the northern Arabian Sea from November 17. Defense Minister Kishi stated that the MOD will promote further cooperation among the defense authorities of the four countries, including the Malabar exercise.[34]

It is true that these four states have not always been completely aligned in terms of their threat perceptions and policies toward China. They also take different stances on the United States-led international order, which led some to conclude that high-level cooperation is still premature.[35] However, if China continues to take actions that are of concern to the international community, including unilateral changes to the status quo, it is highly likely that cooperation among the defense authorities of the four countries will be facilitated by the China factor.

3. Challenges for Realizing a Multi-Domain Defense Force

(1) Efforts to Improve "Cross-Domain Operations" Capabilities

The 2018 NDPG released in December 2018 recognizes that the security environment faced by Japan is becoming increasingly severe. One of the main rationales behind this statement is the dire situation that China's military power is further increasing. At a web conference held by the CSIS on September 9, 2020, Defense Minister Kono pointed out that China's defense spending is four times that of Japan, that it is increasing its fighter jets and submarines every year, and that there is a big gap in capabilities between Japan and China.[36]

The 2018 NDPG also points out that China is broadly and rapidly strengthening its military capabilities in terms of both quality and quantity, centered on nuclear and missile capabilities and naval and air forces. In particular, the NDPG also goes on to state that China is aiming for predominance in the new domains by rapidly developing its capabilities in the cyberspace and electromagnetic spectrum domains, which enable disruption of the chain of command, and strengthening its capabilities in the space domain, such as the development and testing of anti-satellite weapons. In order to respond to these changes in the security environment surrounding Japan, including the qualitative and quantitative enhancement of China's military power, it will become even more important for Japan to secure superiority in the new domains.

Defense Minister Kono hands over the squadron flag at the inauguration of the Space Operations Squadron (Public Relations Office, Air Staff Office)

The SDF must first improve the quality and quantity of its capabilities in individual domains to cope with military power that excels in terms of both quality and quantity. However, in light of Japan's rapidly aging population and dwindling birthrate, as well as its tight fiscal situation, it is increasingly difficult for the SDF to keep up with the rapid increase in military power of neighboring countries simply by augmenting its existing defense capabilities. Therefore, the SDF aims for capabilities that can complement inferior capabilities in individual domains through cross-domain operations that organically fuse capabilities in all domains, including space, cyberspace, and the electromagnetic spectrum, and leverage them as force multipliers.

In addition, in the space, cyberspace, and electromagnetic spectrum domains, it is likely that potential adversaries will conduct activities to disrupt the SDF's operations from peacetime, and thus the ability to conduct constant and continuous surveillance and to respond flexibly at all stages from peacetime to contingencies is needed to prevent such disruption.

Against this backdrop, the importance of the space domain for modern warfare is increasing, including the use of satellites for such functions as information gathering, communication, and positioning. At the same time, threats to the stable use of space are also growing. In addition to rapidly increasing space debris, the development of killer satellites that approach satellites to disturb, attack, and capture them is reportedly underway. Therefore, it is necessary for the SDF to develop a Space Situational Awareness (SSA) system to monitor space and accurately assess the situation.

The Space Operations Squadron, which plays the central role in enhancing SSA, was established within the ASDF on May 18, 2020. The squadron was launched at Fuchu Air Base with about 20 members and is planned to conduct operations to ensure the stable use of space, including operation of the SSA system.[37] Furthermore, from FY2021, the ASDF will establish a new unit in charge of command and control in the space domain, and plans to form the new Space Operations Group (provisional name) with this unit and the Space Operations Squadron as its subordinate units.[38] Against this backdrop, Prime Minister Abe stated that "[e]volution into the 'Air and Space Self-Defense Force' is no longer a pipe dream" at a MOD/SDF Senior Officials' Meeting on September 17, 2019.[39]

In addition, considering the SDF's increasing reliance on space for information gathering, communications, and positioning in its missions, the SDF is expanding the use of microsatellites and commercial satellites equipped with a variety of sensors in order to enhance its communications and information-gathering capabilities. Also, under consideration are measures to increase the resilience of satellites, as well as the building of capabilities in both space and electromagnetic domains to disrupt the command, control, and communications of opponents.

In the cyberspace domain, the information and communication network forms the foundation of the SDF's operations, and an attack on it would have a serious impact on the SDF's organizational activities. Therefore, the SDF is initiating organizational development and securing and training human resources to drastically increase its cyber defense capabilities.

Firstly, on the organizational development front, the SDF Cyber Defense Command (provisional name) will be established to substantially strengthen cyber defense capabilities.[40] Thus far, the SDF has formed the Cyber Defense Group under the SDF Command, Control, Communication and Computers Systems Command, a joint unit of GSDF, MSDF, and ASDF, in FY2013, and has been monitoring and protecting the Defense Information Infrastructure, a common network of the MOD/SDF. The Cyber Defense Group is to be further expanded by about 70 personnel to reach approximately 290 personnel in FY2020.[41] At present, the GSDF System Protection Unit, the MSDF Communication Security Group, and the ASDF Computer Security Evaluation Squadron have been monitoring and protecting information systems in their respective forces. Instead, the SDF Cyber Defense Command (provisional name) will be formed by abolishing the SDF Command, Control, Communication and Computers Systems Command and transferring personnel from the Cyber Defense Group and cyber-related units of the GSDF, MSDF, and ASDF. The newly formed unit aims to centralize cyber defense functions in order for the SDF to perform its missions more effectively and efficiently.

Furthermore, in terms of securing and developing human resources, the MOD is expanding the common cyber course at the GSDF Signal School and training cyber warfare command personnel in the United States. The MOD also plans to recruit highly skilled cyber talents and train personnel with advanced knowledge and expertise on cybersecurity by sending them to external educational institutions from FY2021.[42]

Lastly, the electromagnetic spectrum domain has been utilized thus far for command, control and communications as well as warning and surveillance, but its scope of use and applications are expanding. In the new way of warfare, it is expected that both sides try to maintain the electromagnetic spectrum's use and effectiveness on one's own side and disrupt the adversary's use, which necessitates use of frequencies previously thought unsuitable for military use.[43] Therefore, it has become urgent for the SDF to acquire and strengthen its capability to secure superiority in the electromagnetic spectrum domain.

On the organizational front, the GSDF currently deploys the 1st Electronic Warfare Unit in Hokkaido to constantly gather and analyze information on the electromagnetic spectrum. The Medium Term Defense Program (FY2019–FY2023) lays out a plan to establish new electronic warfare units under the Ground Component Command. The plan is to establish a new 80-member electronic warfare unit in Kumamoto Prefecture during FY2020, as well as additional electronic warfare units in six garrisons and camps in Japan in FY2021.[44]

As for capabilities, in addition to the development of stand-off electronic warfare aircraft and the acquisition of a network electronic warfare system, the MOD is conducting research to improve the capabilities of naval vessels' radio detection and jamming capabilities. In the electromagnetic spectrum domain, high-power microwaves and high-power laser weapons that can instantaneously disable large numbers of unmanned aerial vehicles (drones) and missiles at low cost and with a short reaction time are potential game-changing technologies, thus the MOD is emphasizing research and development of such technologies.[45]

(2) Challenges for the New Way of Warfare

Building capabilities in response to the new way of warfare outlined in the 2018 NDPG will be considered again in planning the next NDPG. Japan's NDPGs are formulated for a period of about 10 years, based on which the Medium Term Defense Program determines the amount of equipment and the total amount of defense spending for five years. About 20 years separate the first NDPG formulated in 1976 from the second NDPG approved by the Cabinet in 1995, while the third NDPG was reviewed after nine years. The subsequent NDPGs in 2010, 2013, and 2018 were reviewed after significantly less than 10 years.

The quickening pace of reviews demonstrates that the security environment surrounding Japan is rapidly changing and becoming more severe, requiring constant adjustment of the defense strategy. The changing international situation has increased the momentum for a review of the 2018 NDPG as well. At the same time, it is necessary to be cognizant of long-term challenges in conducting successive reviews, considering that it takes more than 10 years to develop a defense capability from conceptualization to equipment procurement and operationalization. This is exactly the reason why NDPGs are formulated as long-term strategic guidance in the first place.

One of the major long-term challenges in responding to the new way of warfare is to develop innovative technologies, particularly so-called "game changers." The 2018 NDPG articulates that the MOD will direct focused investments through selection and concentration in important technologies, including cutting-edge technologies that could be game changers, and suggests artificial intelligence (AI) as a potential candidate.

The need for game-changing technologies partly comes from the growing threat of ballistic and cruise missiles, especially those possessed by Japan's neighbors. In order to respond to the missile threat, Japan has been improving its missile defense system, mainly with the Patriot system and Aegis-equipped destroyers. However, in light of the significant improvements in the capabilities of various types of missiles as well as the current situation in which attackers have an edge in terms of cost-effectiveness, it will become difficult to respond to the growing missile threats in the future.

This concern seems to be behind former prime minister Abe's statement on September 11, 2020, urging consideration of a "new course for security policy regarding countering missiles."[46] On December 18, the Cabinet approved "Procurement of a New Missile Defense System, etc. and Strengthening Stand-off Defense Capability," stating the policy that the Japanese government "will continue its deliberation on the enhancement of deterrence." This policy should of course include consideration of means to deter missile launches other than interceptor capabilities. At the same time, it should not exclude the development of technologies that would transform the cost-effectiveness of missile strikes and defense as well. In this regard, such cutting-edge technologies as high-power microwaves and high-power laser weapons have the potential to handle a large number of missiles while reducing the cost of interception, and they are highly likely to be game changers in missile defense if they can be put to practical use. Therefore, the key challenge will be to identify promising technologies and commit to their long-term development.

The next important challenge is the long-term development of human resources. Human resource development was clearly addressed in the 2018 NDPG, which emphasizes the need to reinforce the human resource base. The NDPG also makes it clear that the MOD will devote more efforts to recruit and retain talented personnel and improve their capabilities and morale, based on the principle that "the core element of defense capability is SDF personnel." For example, efforts have been put forth to expand the applicant pool so as to recruit more college graduates and promote the appointment of women. The 2018 NDPG also lists such measures as extending SDF personnel's mandatory retirement ages, utilizing retired uniformed officers and SDF Reserve Personnel as well as improving the fulfillment rate of the SDF service members.

Also, cross-domain operations require more than upgrading the existing capabilities of the SDF. As in the case of the newly formed Space Operations Squadron, it is essential to secure and develop novel human resources who lead the way within the SDF to leverage the new domains of space, cyberspace, and the electromagnetic spectrum, which is addressed in the Medium Term Defense Program (FY2019–FY2023).

The SDF already established the necessary training courses and began to train experts in the new domains in cooperation with other countries, particularly the United States. With the advancement of military technology and the increasing sophistication of equipment, SDF service members are required to have a high level of expertise and knowledge. The SDF thus needs to send personnel to higher educational institutions in Japan and abroad, promote cooperation in human resource development, and implement personnel management to develop their expertise. At the same time, it is equally important to utilize the skills of retired officers in highly specialized fields together with raising the retirement age of uniformed officers and making use of reenrollment of retired officers.

Since the new domains require new areas of expertise within the SDF, it is also necessary to consider whether training of specialized personnel should be all carried out in-house, or whether outside experts should be more aggressively pursued. The basic human resource development model of the SDF is to enroll personnel at a young age and train them over a long period of time. However, there are quite a few hiring options for experts, including part-time and fixed-term employment systems. Therefore, systematic development of highly capable human resources is indispensable while leveraging top-notch expertise in the civilian sector by utilizing these flexible hiring options.

Furthermore, units in charge of the new domains, namely the Space Operations Squadron, the SDF Cyber Defense Command (provisional name), and the electronic warfare units, are to be expanded in the coming years. In doing so, the SDF will need to transfer some personnel to the new units by reorganizing existing units and organizations with decreasing relevance. However, transferring personnel with different expertise is not always easy and feasible, as it is often difficult for them to acquire the high level of expertise required in the new domains through in-house training alone.

It is also critical for the SDF to retain the highly skilled experts it has trained. Consideration is thus necessary for improving the working conditions of experts in the new domains including their benefits and promotion. How to replace resigned experts is another critical issue to be considered. More flexible personnel management will be required to this end while utilizing the above-mentioned employment systems including fixed term and part-time employment systems.

The MOD has already started recruiting civilian defense officials in a fixed term employment system and through mid-career recruitment, and it would be beneficial to hire experts in the new domains in the same manner. In 2020, the MOD recruited civilian staff in a fixed term system for positions related to space and maritime policy, AI, and cybersecurity, as well as recruited mid-career cybersecurity experts.[47] The MOD's new recruitment efforts are likely due to its recognition that recruiting outside experts with specialized knowledge and experience in the new domains is an urgent matter. The mid-career recruitment has already been introduced for commissioned and noncommissioned officers specialized in technology and engineering. However, in concert with the expansion of part-time and fixed-term employment systems, it is worthwhile to consider further expanding the areas of expertise applicable to the new recruitment methods while there remain some issues in terms of their career path.

In any event, the new domains that enable cross-domain operations bring new challenges as well as opportunities to the SDF. In particular, there is a clear trend that Japan's declining birthrate will make it increasingly difficult to recruit talented personnel in the future, which is expected to trigger a fundamental review of the development and redistribution of human resources in response to the new domains.

NOTES

1)   Euan Graham, "The Armed Forces and COVID-19," International Institute for Strategic Studies (IISS) (April 8, 2020).

2)   Ministry of Defense (MOD), "Shingata koronauirusu kansensho ni taisuru mizugiwa taisaku kyoka ni kakaru saigai haken no jisshi ni tsuite" [Implementation of disaster relief operations in relation to strengthening border enforcement measures against COVID-19] (March 28, 2020).

3)   MOD, "Shingata koronauirusu kansensho ni taisuru shichu kansen taio ni kakaru saigai hakento ni tsuite" [Disaster relief, etc. in relation to responding to community spread of COVID-19] (November 20, 2020).

4)   MOD, "Boei daijin kisha kaiken" [Press conference by the Minister of Defense] (September

1, 2020).

5) MOD, "Shingata koronauirusu kansensho ni taisuru shichu kansen taio ni kakaru saigai hakento ni tsuite."

6) Ibid.

7) MOD, "Shingata koronauirusu kansen kakudai wo uketa boeisho jieitai no torikumi" [Initiatives by the MOD/SDF in response to COVID-19] (October 30, 2020).

8) On this point, see, for example, Richard K. Betts, "The New Threat of Mass Destruction," *Foreign Affairs* 77, no. 1 (January/February 1998): 26–41.

9) Designated medical institutions for Category 1 infectious diseases are in charge of admitting patients with Category 1 infectious diseases (Ebola hemorrhagic fever, Crimean-Congo hemorrhagic fever, smallpox, South American hemorrhagic fever, plague, Marburg virus disease, Lassa fever), Category 2 infectious diseases (acute poliomyelitis, tuberculosis, diphtheria, severe acute respiratory syndrome (SARS), Middle East respiratory syndrome (MERS), avian influenza), or Novel Influenza Infections, etc., and are designated by the prefectural governor.

10) MOD, *Defense of Japan 2020*, English edition (2020), 454.

11) MOD, *Defense of Japan 2020*, 281.

12) Graham, "The Armed Forces and COVID-19."

13) Prime Minister's Office, "Reception to Commemorate the Sixtieth Anniversary of the Japan-U.S. Security Treaty" (January 19, 2020).

14) Sado Akihiro, *Sengo seiji to jieitai* [The Self-Defense Forces and postwar politics in Japan] (Tokyo: Yoshikawa Kobunkan, 2006), 29.

15) Kusunoki Ayako, "Nichibei domei no seiritsu kara okinawa henkan made" [From the establishment of the Japan-U.S. Alliance to the return of Okinawa], in *Nichibei domei ron: Rekishi, kino, shuhen shokoku no shiten* [The Japan-U.S. alliance: History, functions, and viewpoints of neighboring countries], ed. Takeuchi Toshitaka (Kyoto: Minerva Shobo, 2011), 85.

16) MOD, "Senryaku kokusai mondai kenkyujo (CSIS) ni okeru Kono boei daijin koen" [Speech by Defense Minister Kono at the Center for Strategic and International Studies (CSIS)] (January 14, 2020).

17) On the significance of the ACM as a framework for seamless coordination between Japan and the United States, see: Takahashi Sugio, "Japan: Upgrading of National Security Policy," in *East Asian Strategic Review 2016*, English edition, ed. National Institute for Defense Studies (NIDS) (Tokyo: NIDS, 2016), 312–314.

18) MOD, "Nichibei boei kaidan no gaiyo" [Outline of the Japan-U.S. defense ministers' meeting] (January 15, 2020).

19) MOD, "Joint Statement on the Sixtieth Anniversary of the Signing of the Treaty of Mutual Cooperation and Security between Japan and the United States of America" (January 17, 2020).

20) Prime Minister's Office, "Press Conference by the Prime Minister" (September 16, 2020).

21) Prime Minister's Office, "Press Conference by the Prime Minister (Telephone Talks with President-elect Biden)" (November 12, 2020).

22) On this point, see in particular, Dennis C. Blair and John T. Hanley, Jr., "From Wheels to Webs: Reconstructing Asia-Pacific Security Arrangements," *Washington Quarterly* 24, no. 1 (Winter 2001): 7–17. Blair was a former commander in chief of the U.S. Pacific Command (now Indo-Pacific Command).

23) MOD, "Guidelines for Japan-U.S. Defense Cooperation" (April 27, 2015).

24) Satake Tomohiko, "The Rise of China and Strengthening of Security Cooperation between Japan, the United States, and Australia: With a Focus on the 2000s," *NIDS Journal of Defense and Security* 20 (December 2019): 65.

25) MOD, *Defense of Japan 2020*, 347–348.

26) Public Relations Office, Ground Staff Office, "Reiwa gannendo goshu ni okeru beigun tono jitsudo kunren ni tsuite" [Field training exercises with the U.S. and Australian militaries in Australia in FY2019] (May 9, 2019).

27) Satake, "The Rise of China and Strengthening of Security Cooperation between Japan, the United States, and Australia," 49–50.

28) Cabinet Office, "Gaiko ni kansuru yoron chosa: Nihon to shogaikoku chiiki tono kankei" [Overview of the public opinion survey on diplomacy: Relations between Japan and other countries] (December 20, 2019).

29) MOD, "Boei jitsumusha kyogi (DTT) kekka gaiyo ni tsuite" [Summary of the results of the Defense Trilateral Talks (DTT)] (May 13, 2020).

30) MOD, *Defense of Japan 2020*, 359.

31) Ministry of Foreign Affairs, "Japan-U.S.-India Summit Meeting" (June 28, 2019).

32) MOD, *Defense of Japan 2020*, 349.

33) MOD, "Boei daijin rinji kisha kaiken" [Extraordinary press conference by the Minister of Defense] (October 7, 2020).

34) MOD, "Boei daijin kisha kaiken" [Press conference by the Minister of Defense] (October 20, 2020).

35) Satake Tomohiko, "Will Japan-U.S.-Australia-India Security Cooperation be Realized? Different Perceptions for Order and Implications for Japan," *Briefing Memo*, NIDS (July 2018).

36) CSIS, "Online Event: Mt. Fuji DC Event; The U.S.-Japan Alliance at 60" (September 9,

2020).

37) Air Self-Defense Force, "Uchu sakusentai no shinpen ni tsuite" [New formation of the Space Operations Squadron] (May 18, 2020).

38) MOD, "Defense Programs and Budget of Japan Overview of FY2021 Budget Request" (December 18, 2020), 8.

39) Prime Minister's Office, "Daigojusankai jieitai kokyu kanbu kaido Abe naikaku sori daijin kunji" [53rd Meeting of the Ministry of Defense and Self-Defense Force Senior Personnel: Address by Prime Minister Abe] (September 17, 2019).

40) MOD, "Defense Programs and Budget of Japan," 9.

41) MOD, *Defense of Japan 2020*, 272.

42) MOD, "Defense Programs and Budget of Japan," 9.

43) Bryan Clark and Mark Gunzinger, *Winning the Airwaves: Regaining America's Dominance in the Electromagnetic Spectrum* (Washington, DC: Center for Strategic and Budgetary Assessments, 2015), 30–32.

44) NHK, October 2, 2020.

45) MOD, "Defense Programs and Budget of Japan," 11.

46) Prime Minister's Office, "Statement by the Prime Minister" (September 11, 2020).

47) MOD, "Saiyo joho: Chuto saiyo (senko saiyo)" [Recruitment information: Mid-career recruitment (recruiting via competitive selection)], updated on December 28, 2020.

Contributors

Ishihara Yusuke   Senior Fellow, Policy Simulation Division   Chapter 1

Tanaka Ryosuke   Research Fellow, America, Europe & Russia   Chapter 1
Division, Regional Studies Department

Iida Masafumi   Head, America, Europe & Russia Division,   Chapter 2
Regional Studies Department

Watanabe Takeshi   Senior Fellow, Asia & Africa Division,   Chapter 3
Regional Studies Department

Matsuura Yoshihide   Head, Government & Law Division, Security   Chapter 4
Studies Department

Tomikawa Hideo   Senior Fellow, Security & Economy Division,   Chapter 4
Security Studies Department

Hasegawa Takeyuki   Research Fellow, America, Europe & Russia   Chapter 5
Division, Regional Studies Department

Sakaguchi Yoshiaki   Senior Fellow, America, Europe & Russia   Chapter 5
Division, Regional Studies Department

Kikuchi Shigeo   Head, China Division, Regional Studies   Chapter 6
Department

Tsukamoto Katsuya   Head, Security & Economy Division, Security   Chapter 7
Studies Department